The Conservative Agenda

Jack Donahue

Published by Defenestration Press, 2024.

While every precaution has been taken in the preparation of this book, the publisher assumes no responsibility for errors or omissions, or for damages resulting from the use of the information contained herein.

THE CONSERVATIVE AGENDA

First edition. February 9, 2024.

Copyright © 2024 Jack Donahue.

ISBN: 979-8224718498

Written by Jack Donahue.

Table of Contents

Introduction to Conservative Principles.............................1

Foundations of Conservative Thought 20

Limited Government and Individual Liberty..................... 43

Free Market Economics.. 62

National Security and Foreign Policy........................... 77

Traditional Values and Social Conservatism.................... 96

Individual Liberty and Personal Responsibility................ 115

Family and Community Values 141

Education Reform 162

Healthcare and Social Welfare................................ 180

Environmental Stewardship 204

Criminal Justice and Law Enforcement........................224

Immigration Policies 243

Cultural Challenges and Shifts 258

Media and Information 279

Technology and Innovation..................................296

Globalization and International Relations.......................321

The Role of Religion 344

Political Activism and Advocacy..............................364

Looking Forward: The Future of the Conservative Agenda..........385

Introduction

"To be conservative, then, is to prefer the familiar to the unknown, to prefer the tried to the untried, fact to mystery, the actual to the possible..." – Michael Oakeshott.

In the labyrinth of political philosophy, these words from Michael Oakeshott serve as a torch, illuminating a path walked by generations. They encapsulate an enduring allure for the tried and true, the structured over the chaotic, which has shaped nations and defined epochs. Yet, in the complex tapestry of the 21st century, the conservative agenda finds itself at a crucible, tasked with reconciling the immemorial with the inexorable march of progress. As we chart a course through the storied past and precarious present of conservative thought, we uncover not just a set of political principles, but a living, breathing worldview that grapples with the very essence of culture, governance, and human nature. The issues we face are not mere policy debates; they are the battle cries of an ideological crusade, echoing through classrooms, parliaments, and the silent digital halls of the Internet. And as dusk approaches on the horizon of tradition, a question lingers, pregnant with possibility. Will the conservative agenda rise to meet the dawn of tomorrow, or will it succumb to the relentless march of change?

The relevance of Oakeshott's words resonates deeply within the core of the conservative agenda. They embody a steadfast commitment to stability, continuity, and the preservation of time-honored values. This commitment, deeply ingrained in the conservative psyche, has profound implications for our understanding of governance, society, and individual freedom. The conservative ideology is not merely a collection of policies; it is a philosophical stance that shapes the very fabric of our social and political landscape. It stands as a bulwark against the tempests of radical change, a call to cherish the wisdom of the past while navigating the uncharted waters of the future.

However, in today's rapidly evolving world, the conservative agenda faces a myriad of complex dilemmas. As societies grapple with technological advancements, shifting cultural norms, and global interconnectedness, the traditional conservative stance on governance and social order is being tested. The very essence of conservatism is being challenged by the relentless march of progress. This presents a paradox for conservatives: how to uphold timeless values while adapting to the demands of a rapidly changing world.

Commonly held beliefs about conservatism often paint it as rigid, resistant to change, and out of touch with the modern world. Critics argue that conservatism is inherently regressive, clinging to outdated ideals in the face of progress. This pervasive misconception has led to a lack of understanding of the nuanced complexities that underpin conservative thought. It is time to challenge these preconceptions and unveil the true essence of conservative ideology.

The conservative agenda, as presented in this book, seeks to illuminate the path forward in this tumultuous landscape. It is not merely a defense of tradition, but a thoughtful and forward-looking approach to governance and societal progress. It acknowledges the need for adaptation while emphasizing the preservation of foundational principles that have stood the test of time. The conservative perspective offers a unique lens through which to view the intricacies of contemporary challenges, from economic reforms to social issues, from national security to environmental policies.

As we embark on this intellectual journey, it is imperative to forge an intellectual bond with the reader. This book is not a mere exposition of conservative principles; it is an invitation to engage in a profound exploration of ideas, to challenge preconceived notions, and to open the mind to a spectrum of perspectives. It is a call to delve into the depths of conservative thought and emerge with a comprehensive understanding of its relevance in today's world.

Imagine a world where the conservative agenda is not confined to the narrow corridors of political discourse but is embraced as a dynamic and adaptive force, shaping the trajectory of global governance and societal progress. Envision a society where the conservative principles of limited government, free-market economics, traditional values, and individual liberty are not viewed as relics of the past, but as guiding beacons for a prosperous future. This vision, though not without its challenges, holds the promise of a balanced and harmonious coexistence between tradition and progress, between stability and innovation.

As we delve deeper into the chapters of this book, you will be immersed in a comprehensive exploration of conservative perspectives. From the historical foundations that have shaped conservative thought to the contemporary challenges that demand innovative solutions, each chapter will unravel the intricate tapestry of conservative ideology. We will examine the role of conservatism in education, healthcare, and environmental policies, shedding light on the nuanced approaches that underpin conservative solutions to these critical domains. Moreover, we will delve into the cultural shifts, media influence, and technology's role, illuminating the conservative responses to these dynamic forces that shape our society.

The conservative agenda does not exist in isolation; it is deeply intertwined with global outlook, religious convictions, and political activism. These interconnected threads form the fabric of conservative thought, and it is through a holistic understanding of these elements that we can truly grasp the essence of the conservative agenda. As we journey through these pages, we will unravel the intricate web of conservative principles, shedding light on their interconnectedness and their relevance in a rapidly changing world.

Ultimately, this book will culminate in an exploration of the future trajectory of the conservative agenda. It will not only envision the path forward but also outline the strategies and approaches that can propel conservatism into the future. The conservative agenda is not a relic of the past; it is a living, evolving force that has the potential to shape the destiny of nations and the global community. It is a call to action, a call to engage in the intellectual discourse that will define the future of governance, society, and human progress.

It is with a sense of anticipation and intellectual curiosity that we embark on this journey through the conservative agenda. The path ahead is filled with challenges, paradoxes, and opportunities, but it is also illuminated by the unwavering spirit of conservative thought. As we venture forth, let us embrace the complexity of conservative ideology, challenge our assumptions, and open our minds to the transformative potential of the conservative agenda. This is not merely a book about conservatism; it is a call to engage in a profound exploration of ideas that can shape the course of history. Join me as we unravel the intricate tapestry of the conservative agenda and discover the enduring relevance of its principles in a rapidly changing world.

Introduction to Conservative Principles

What Is Conservatism?

Understanding conservatism requires a deep dive into the fundamental principles that underpin this ideological stance. By unraveling the key terms and concepts within conservatism, we can gain a comprehensive understanding of its relevance and implications in the complex landscape of governance, society, and human nature. It is through this exploration that we can appreciate the nuanced complexities of conservative ideology and its enduring impact on the world.

1. Tradition forms the bedrock of conservative thought, representing the collective wisdom and customs passed down through generations. It encompasses cultural practices, moral values, and societal norms that provide a sense of continuity and stability.

2. Stability is a core principle within conservatism, emphasizing the importance of maintaining a steady and reliable social order. It seeks to preserve the established structures and institutions that contribute to a sense of security and predictability in society.

3. Continuity reflects the conservative commitment to preserving enduring principles and traditions across time. It acknowledges the value of historical continuity in shaping societal identity and fostering a sense of belonging and rootedness.

4. Time-honored values encapsulate the ethical and moral beliefs that have withstood the test of time, serving as guiding principles for individual behavior and societal norms. These values often derive from religious, cultural, and philosophical traditions.

5. While conservatism cherishes tradition, it also recognizes the need for prudent adaptation to changing circumstances. This principle highlights the conservative approach to evolving societal challenges while upholding foundational values.

6. The concept of limited government advocates for a restrained role of the state in the lives of citizens, emphasizing individual autonomy, free markets, and minimal government intervention in private affairs.

7. Free-market economics aligns with conservative principles, promoting economic freedom, competition, and minimal regulation as drivers of prosperity and innovation within a society.

8. Individual liberty is a cornerstone of conservative ideology, emphasizing personal freedoms, property rights, and the protection of individual autonomy from excessive state control.

9. Cultural shifts refer to the dynamic changes in societal attitudes, behaviors, and norms over time. Conservatives navigate these shifts by balancing the preservation of cultural heritage with the need for societal progress.

10. A global outlook reflects the conservative perspective on international relations, emphasizing national sovereignty, strategic alliances, and a cautious approach to global engagement.

11. Religious convictions play a significant role in conservative thought, influencing moral values, societal ethics, and the preservation of religious freedoms within the fabric of governance.

12. Political activism within conservatism denotes the organized efforts to advocate for conservative policies, influence public opinion, and participate in the democratic process to uphold conservative principles.

The enduring values of individual liberty can be exemplified through historical struggles for civil rights, where individuals fought for the autonomy to shape their own destinies free from oppressive constraints. Additionally, the notion of adaptation can be observed in the realm of technological advancements, as conservative approaches seek to harness innovation while safeguarding ethical considerations and societal well-being.

Religious convictions, a pivotal aspect of conservative thought, find expression in the moral fabric of communities, where faith-based organizations provide essential services and uphold ethical standards. Moreover, the global outlook of conservatism can be illustrated through diplomatic negotiations that prioritize national sovereignty and strategic alliances, reflecting the conservative approach to international relations.

The Evolution of Conservative Thought

THE ORIGINS OF CONSERVATIVE thought can be traced back to ancient civilizations, where the preservation of tradition, stability, and continuity formed the basis of societal order. Early societies recognized the importance of upholding time-honored values and adapting to changing circumstances while maintaining a sense of rootedness in cultural heritage. The concept of limited governance can be observed in historical city-states, where the autonomy of individuals and the protection of property rights were foundational principles. As civilizations evolved, the influence of conservative ideals expanded, shaping the political, social, and economic landscapes.

1. The philosophical works of Plato and Aristotle laid the groundwork for conservative thought, emphasizing the importance of stability and the preservation of societal order. The Roman

Republic's emphasis on law and tradition reflects early conservative principles, influencing governance and societal norms.

2. Feudal societies in Europe upheld conservative values, prioritizing hierarchical structures, land ownership, and traditional customs. The stability provided by feudal systems and the preservation of cultural heritage were integral to societal continuity.

3. The Enlightenment era sparked debates on the role of tradition, reason, and progress. Conservative thinkers such as Edmund Burke articulated the significance of preserving established institutions and cautioned against radical societal transformations.

4. The rapid industrialization of the 19th century led to debates on the impact of progress on societal cohesion. Conservative responses emphasized the need to balance economic development with the preservation of traditional values and community structures.

5. The upheavals of two world wars and the ideological confrontations of the Cold War prompted reflections on the role of conservatism in shaping international relations and domestic policies. The rise of conservative movements and leaders across the globe underscored the enduring relevance of conservative thought in the modern era.

The evolution of conservative thought has exhibited diverse expressions across different cultures and regions. While the core principles of tradition, stability, and continuity remain fundamental, cultural variations have influenced the manifestations of conservatism. For example, the conservative traditions in East Asia emphasize Confucian values of filial piety, respect for authority, and harmony within society, shaping distinct approaches to governance and societal order. In contrast, the conservative movements in Western democracies have navigated the complexities of individual liberties, free-market economies, and the preservation of Judeo-Christian values.

In the contemporary landscape, conservative thought has undergone modern interpretations and adaptations in response to global challenges and societal transformations. The fusion of traditional conservative values with technological advancements, environmental concerns, and cultural diversity has led to nuanced expressions of conservatism. The emergence of digital platforms for political activism, the integration of conservative principles in environmental policies, and the advocacy for cultural preservation in a globalized world reflect the dynamic nature of modern conservative thought.

Challenges and controversies have punctuated the evolution of conservative thought, prompting introspection and adaptation. Debates on the balance between individual liberties and societal responsibilities, the role of government in addressing social inequalities, and the impact of globalization on traditional values have shaped the trajectory of conservatism. Turning points such as the emergence of new conservative movements, the redefinition of national identities, and the responses to technological disruptions have challenged traditional conservative paradigms, leading to critical reflections and recalibrations of ideological stances.

As we delve into the historical evolution of conservative thought, it becomes evident that the intricate tapestry of conservative ideology has been woven through centuries, incorporating diverse influences and responding to dynamic societal landscapes. The resilience and adaptability of conservative principles have shaped governance, societal norms, and global dynamics, offering enduring insights into the complexities of human nature and the pursuit of societal order.

The Role of Government

THE CONSERVATIVE BELIEF in limited government is a foundational principle that underpins the ideology's perspective on governance and individual liberty. Limited government, as advocated by conservative thinkers, represents a crucial safeguard against the potential encroachment of state power on the freedoms and rights of individuals within a society. This chapter aims to delve into the concept of limited government from a conservative standpoint, elucidating its significance in preserving individual liberty and fostering a thriving civil society.

At the core of conservative ideology lies the conviction that the government should have restricted authority, with its role primarily focused on maintaining public order, ensuring national security, and upholding the rule of law. This principle is rooted in the belief that excessive governmental intervention can undermine individual autonomy, stifle innovation, and erode the fabric of civil society. Limited government, therefore, seeks to establish a framework in which individuals are empowered to exercise their liberties without undue interference from the state.

The concept of limited government encompasses several key components. First and foremost, it emphasizes the necessity of clear and defined limitations on the powers of the government. These limitations serve as a safeguard against the potential abuse of authority and serve to maintain a balance between governmental responsibility and individual freedom. Additionally, limited government entails the promotion of decentralized decision-making, where power is dispersed across various levels of governance, thereby reducing the concentration of authority in a central body.

THE CONSERVATIVE AGENDA

Conservative proponents of limited government also underscore the importance of fiscal responsibility and prudence in public expenditure. By advocating for minimal government intervention in economic affairs, conservatives aim to mitigate the risks associated with excessive state control over market forces and individual enterprise. This approach aligns with the belief that economic prosperity and individual opportunity flourish in an environment characterized by minimal regulatory burdens and bureaucratic impediments.

Furthermore, the concept of limited government in conservative thought encompasses the protection of property rights and the preservation of individual liberties, including freedom of speech, religion, and association. By limiting the reach of government into the private lives of citizens, conservatives assert that the inherent dignity and autonomy of individuals can be upheld, fostering a society where personal responsibility and self-reliance are esteemed virtues.

To illustrate the practical implications of limited government, one can observe historical case studies and contemporary examples that highlight the impact of restrained state authority on individual liberty. For instance, the economic prosperity experienced in countries that have adopted free-market policies and minimized government intervention attests to the positive outcomes of limited governance. The resurgence of entrepreneurship, innovation, and job creation in such environments reflects the benefits of fostering an economic landscape unencumbered by excessive regulatory control.

Moreover, the protection of civil liberties and the preservation of individual rights in societies that uphold limited government principles serve as compelling illustrations of the concept in action. Countries where freedom of expression, private property rights, and the rule of law are respected within a restrained governmental framework provide tangible evidence of how limited government can promote a vibrant civil society and empower individuals to pursue their aspirations without undue impediments.

While the concept of limited government is integral to conservative ideology, it is important to acknowledge that differing viewpoints exist regarding the appropriate scope and role of government in society. From a liberal perspective, there is an emphasis on the positive role of government in addressing societal inequalities and providing essential services, such as healthcare, education, and social welfare. This contrasts with the conservative belief in limited government, which advocates for a more restrained approach to state involvement in these areas, with a greater reliance on personal responsibility, private enterprise, and local communities.

Additionally, libertarian perspectives share common ground with conservative principles of limited government, emphasizing individual freedoms and minimal state interference. However, libertarians may advocate for an even more minimal government presence, often questioning the necessity of certain regulatory frameworks and public institutions that conservatives may perceive as essential for maintaining societal order and stability.

Empirical evidence and factual data can provide valuable insights into the practical implications of limited government. Studies comparing economic performance, innovation indices, and measures of individual freedom across different governance models can offer compelling evidence in support of the conservative belief in limited government. Furthermore, historical analyses of societies that have experienced shifts in governmental scope and authority can elucidate the impact of such changes on individual liberties and economic dynamism.

Limited government, as a concept, may be characterized by various intricacies and nuances that require clarification for comprehensive understanding. It is essential to distinguish between limited government and the absence of government, emphasizing that conservative advocacy for limited government does not imply a complete absence of state authority. Instead, it underscores the necessity of circumscribing governmental powers within clearly defined boundaries to safeguard individual liberties and promote societal flourishing.

Furthermore, the distinction between limited government and authoritarian regimes is imperative to elucidate. While limited government seeks to uphold the rule of law and individual rights, authoritarian governance entails the concentration of unchecked power in the hands of a centralized authority, often resulting in the suppression of freedoms and the erosion of civil society.

The conservative belief in limited government stands as a cornerstone of the ideology's commitment to preserving individual liberty and fostering a thriving civil society. By advocating for clear limitations on governmental authority, decentralized decision-making, fiscal prudence, and the protection of individual rights and property, conservatives seek to establish a framework that empowers individuals to pursue their aspirations, innovate, and contribute to the betterment of society. Embracing the concept of limited government entails recognizing the intrinsic value of individual autonomy and the imperative of constraining state power to ensure the flourishing of free and vibrant communities.

The Value of Free Markets

THE VALUE OF FREE MARKETS is a central tenet of conservative economic philosophy, rooted in the belief that minimal government intervention in economic affairs fosters innovation, entrepreneurship, and prosperity. This chapter aims to delve into the conservative perspective on free market principles, exploring their impact on economic growth and individual opportunity.

Conservative advocates assert that free markets, unencumbered by excessive regulatory burdens and bureaucratic impediments, form the bedrock of vibrant and dynamic economies, providing an environment conducive to individual initiative, innovation, and wealth creation.

Historical evidence supports the conservative claim that free markets have facilitated unprecedented economic growth and societal advancement. For instance, the Industrial Revolution, characterized by limited government intervention in economic activities, led to remarkable technological progress, increased living standards, and the expansion of individual freedoms. Additionally, contemporary examples in countries that have embraced free market policies demonstrate the correlation between economic prosperity and minimal governmental intrusion in market forces.

The success of free markets in driving economic growth can be attributed to their ability to incentivize entrepreneurship and investment. By allowing individuals and businesses to operate in a competitive landscape, free markets encourage the pursuit of efficiency, innovation, and consumer satisfaction. This dynamic environment fosters the creation of new industries, the development of groundbreaking technologies, and the generation of employment opportunities, ultimately contributing to overall economic expansion.

Furthermore, the efficiency of free markets in allocating resources is exemplified through the price mechanism, where supply and demand dynamics determine the distribution of goods and services.

This decentralized decision-making process ensures that resources are allocated to their most valued uses, promoting optimal productivity and the satisfaction of consumer preferences without the need for centralized planning or control.

Critics of free markets often point to instances of market failures, income inequality, and environmental degradation as evidence against the conservative claim. They argue that unregulated markets can lead to monopolistic practices, exploitation of labor, and the neglect of social and environmental considerations in pursuit of profit maximization.

In response to these criticisms, conservative proponents emphasize that the potential drawbacks of free markets can be mitigated through targeted regulatory measures and the enforcement of antitrust laws to prevent monopolistic behavior. Additionally, advocates assert that free markets, when coupled with a strong legal framework, can incentivize businesses to operate responsibly, recognizing the importance of ethical conduct and sustainable practices in the long-term success of their enterprises.

Empirical studies have demonstrated that countries with a greater degree of economic freedom, characterized by free market principles, exhibit higher levels of income per capita, lower poverty rates, and increased access to goods and services. This evidence reinforces the conservative contention that free markets contribute to improved living standards and broader economic opportunities for individuals.

The conservative perspective on free markets emphasizes the pivotal role of minimal government intervention in fostering economic growth, innovation, and individual opportunity. By enabling entrepreneurship, incentivizing efficiency, and promoting resource allocation based on consumer preferences, free markets have historically and consistently proven to be catalysts for prosperity and societal advancement. Embracing the value of free markets entails recognizing their capacity to empower individuals, drive economic progress, and enrich the fabric of civil society.

Defending National Security

IN THE REALM OF NATIONAL security, conservative ideology holds a distinct perspective on defense, security, and foreign policy. This chapter aims to delve into the conservative viewpoint on these critical matters, comparing it to alternative perspectives and highlighting the nuances and broader implications of conservative national security policies.

National security is a multifaceted concept that encompasses the protection of a nation's sovereignty, territorial integrity, and the well-being of its citizens. It involves defense against external threats, the maintenance of internal stability, and the pursuit of diplomatic and military strategies to safeguard national interests. Conservative viewpoints on national security emphasize the role of a strong military, clear foreign policy objectives, and a commitment to protecting national sovereignty.

The purpose of comparing conservative perspectives on national security with alternative viewpoints is to provide insights into the underlying rationales and intended outcomes of differing approaches. This comparative analysis aims to shed light on the effectiveness, feasibility, and ethical considerations of conservative national security policies in contrast to other proposed strategies.

The benchmarks for comparison in this analysis encompass the effectiveness of defense strategies, the ethical considerations of military interventions, the prioritization of national interests, and the impact of foreign policy decisions on global stability.

THE CONSERVATIVE AGENDA

Conservative national security policies advocate for a robust military capability as a deterrent against potential adversaries. This emphasis on military strength is grounded in the belief that a strong defense is essential for deterring aggression, protecting national interests, and preserving global stability. Furthermore, conservative viewpoints stress the importance of maintaining a clear and assertive foreign policy that prioritizes national sovereignty and security.

In contrast, alternative perspectives may prioritize diplomatic initiatives, multilateral cooperation, and non-military approaches to conflict resolution. These approaches may emphasize dialogue, negotiation, and international cooperation as primary means of addressing security challenges.

The distinctions between conservative and alternative national security perspectives underscore the nuances of each approach. Conservative viewpoints often emphasize the necessity of a strong military as a deterrent and a means to protect national interests, while alternative perspectives may prioritize non-military solutions, conflict prevention, and peacebuilding efforts.

Delving into the comparisons reveals insights into the potential strengths and weaknesses of conservative national security policies. The emphasis on military strength and assertive foreign policy may provide a robust deterrent against potential adversaries, but it also raises concerns about the potential for escalation, the ethical considerations of military interventions, and the prioritization of diplomatic solutions.

Conversely, alternative perspectives that prioritize diplomacy and conflict prevention may offer avenues for de-escalation, international cooperation, and long-term stability, but they may also face challenges in deterring aggression and protecting national interests in a rapidly evolving global security landscape.

Connecting historical or theoretical comparisons to current realities enhances the relevance of this analysis. In the context of contemporary national security challenges, such as asymmetric warfare, cyber threats, and global terrorism, the effectiveness of conservative military strategies and alternative diplomatic approaches can be assessed in light of real-world security dynamics.

The evolving nature of global security threats, the rise of non-state actors, and the increasing interconnectedness of national security challenges underscore the importance of critically evaluating the effectiveness and ethical considerations of conservative national security policies in comparison to alternative approaches.

The conservative perspective on national security, characterized by an emphasis on military strength and assertive foreign policy, offers a distinct approach to safeguarding national interests and global stability. By comparing and contrasting conservative viewpoints with alternative national security perspectives, this analysis provides valuable insights into the complexities and implications of defense, security, and foreign policy from a conservative standpoint.

Preserving Traditional Values

IN EXAMINING THE EMPHASIS on traditional values within conservative circles, it is essential to unravel the significance and impact of these values on various aspects of society. This list aims to shed light on the fundamental traditional values upheld by conservatives and their role in shaping societal norms, institutions, and cultural identity.

Conservative ideology places a strong emphasis on the traditional family unit as the cornerstone of society. The nuclear family, comprising a married heterosexual couple and their children, is considered the ideal structure for raising children and fostering stability. This emphasis stems from the belief that traditional family values, including marital commitment, parental responsibility, and moral guidance, are essential for societal cohesion and the well-being of future generations. The conservative viewpoint emphasizes the importance of traditional gender roles within the family, with an emphasis on the complementary nature of the roles of husbands and wives in providing a stable and nurturing environment for children to thrive.

Central to conservative ideology is the preservation and promotion of religious and moral principles as guiding forces in individual and societal conduct. Traditional values rooted in religious teachings and moral absolutes serve as the bedrock for ethical decision-making, personal integrity, and social order. Conservatives advocate for the acknowledgment and protection of religious freedom, the display of religious symbols in public spaces, and the integration of moral teachings in educational curricula. The belief in the intrinsic value of human life, the sanctity of marriage, and the moral absolutes delineating right from wrong underpin conservative stances on social issues such as abortion, euthanasia, and same-sex marriage.

Conservative circles place a premium on preserving and celebrating the cultural heritage and national identity that have shaped a society's traditions and values. Traditional customs, historical narratives, and shared cultural experiences are regarded as essential elements that bind communities together and provide a sense of continuity across generations. Conservatives advocate for the preservation of traditional celebrations, historical commemorations, and cultural symbols that reinforce a collective identity and instill a sense of pride in one's heritage. The safeguarding of linguistic, artistic, and culinary traditions is seen as vital in maintaining cultural vibrancy and resilience in the face of globalization and homogenizing influences.

The conservative agenda prioritizes the transmission of traditional knowledge, historical narratives, and foundational principles to future generations through education. Conservatives emphasize the importance of instilling a sense of national pride, historical context, and moral virtues in the educational curriculum. Traditional values, critical thinking, and respect for authority are emphasized as essential components of a well-rounded education that equips students with a strong moral compass and a deep appreciation for their cultural inheritance. Furthermore, conservatives advocate for parental authority in shaping their children's education, including the option for homeschooling and the promotion of private and religious education as alternatives to public schooling.

Conservative principles underscore the significance of individual responsibility, self-reliance, and active civic engagement as foundational elements of a well-functioning society. Traditional values of hard work, personal accountability, and respect for authority are seen as crucial for the maintenance of social order and the preservation of community cohesion. Conservatives emphasize the importance of volunteerism, charitable giving, and community-based initiatives that foster a sense of communal responsibility and mutual support. The preservation of traditional community structures, such as neighborhood associations, religious congregations, and local civic organizations, is viewed as integral to sustaining social bonds and addressing societal challenges at the grassroots level.

The significance of traditional values within conservative circles is evident in various social and political movements that advocate for the preservation of traditional family structures, religious freedoms, cultural heritage, and educational autonomy. Testimonials from conservative leaders, scholars, and grassroots activists underscore the foundational role of traditional values in shaping individual character, societal norms, and the broader cultural landscape. Additionally, historical precedents and sociological studies provide empirical evidence of the enduring influence of traditional values on societal institutions and collective identities.

The practical implications of upholding traditional values are reflected in policies and initiatives aimed at safeguarding family integrity, promoting religious liberties, preserving cultural heritage, shaping educational curricula, and fostering community resilience. These practical applications manifest in legislative efforts to protect parental rights in education, initiatives to promote family-friendly policies, and advocacy for the preservation of historical landmarks and cultural traditions. Furthermore, community-based programs and grassroots movements actively promote the transmission of traditional values through mentorship, educational outreach, and cultural preservation efforts, thereby reinforcing the practical significance of traditional values in everyday life.

As we transition from the exploration of traditional values within conservative ideology to the broader implications of these values on societal dynamics, it becomes evident that the preservation of traditional values profoundly influences social cohesion, individual well-being, and the overall fabric of society. This seamless transition underscores the interconnectedness of traditional values with various facets of societal life and underscores their enduring relevance in an ever-changing world.

By delving into the multifaceted aspects of traditional values within conservative circles, we gain a comprehensive understanding of their foundational role in shaping societal norms, cultural identity, and the preservation of enduring principles that underpin the conservative agenda.

Championing Individual Liberty

HOW CAN WE SAFEGUARD and champion individual liberty in a rapidly changing and interconnected world, while also upholding the traditional values that have long been the bedrock of our society?

Let's contextualize this question by understanding the importance of individual liberty within the broader discourse of conservative ideology. Individual liberty forms the cornerstone of conservative thought, emphasizing personal responsibility, limited government intervention, and the preservation of individual rights. In today's dynamic and often tumultuous societal landscape, the concept of individual liberty faces multifaceted challenges, from technological advancements to shifting cultural norms. It is within this context that we delve into the complexities and nuances of championing individual liberty.

At the heart of our exploration lies the fundamental problem of balancing individual liberty with the common good. While individual liberty is cherished and safeguarded within conservative circles, it is imperative to recognize the potential tensions that arise when individual freedoms intersect with societal responsibilities. The challenge is to navigate the evolving terrain of rights and responsibilities, ensuring that individual liberty thrives without compromising the well-being of the community.

Often, the conventional approaches to addressing this challenge overlook the intricate balance required to uphold individual liberty while fostering a cohesive and harmonious society. Many take for granted the interplay between personal freedoms and communal welfare, assuming that these values are inherently at odds. However, as we will uncover, the real solution lies in embracing a nuanced understanding of individual liberty and its symbiotic relationship with the broader community.

Here's what most people do not realize: championing individual liberty does not entail an abandonment of communal responsibility. It requires a delicate equilibrium, where the preservation of individual rights harmonizes with a collective commitment to the common good. By unraveling this misconception, we pave the way for a fresh perspective that reconciles personal freedoms with societal well-being.

The real solution lies in cultivating a society where individual liberty is not only upheld but actively contributes to the betterment of the community. It involves fostering a culture of personal responsibility, mutual respect, and civic engagement, where individual liberties coexist with a sense of duty towards others. This nuanced understanding of individual liberty empowers individuals to thrive within a supportive community, amplifying the significance of personal freedoms while recognizing the interconnectedness of society.

Envision a society where the pursuit of individual liberty is not merely a legal concept but a lived experience, evoking a profound sense of fulfillment and empowerment. By championing individual liberty, we kindle the flames of hope, inspiration, and resilience within the hearts of individuals, fostering a society where personal freedoms are cherished and protected.

Foundations of Conservative Thought

Classical Liberalism and the Enlightenment

The Enlightenment was a period in 18th century Europe characterized by a focus on reason, scientific inquiry, and advancing ideas of liberty and progress. This intellectual movement laid the foundation for classical liberalism. As conservatives, we can appreciate several positive outcomes of this era, while also recognizing some problematic developments that still impact society today.

On the positive side, Enlightenment thinkers championed core conservative principles like limited government, individualism, and free market economics. They challenged the divine right of kings, standing up for fundamental liberties. Thinkers like John Locke developed theories of natural rights and a social contract between citizens and rulers, holding governments accountable to protect essential freedoms. These were foundational ideas that influenced the American revolutionaries.

However, the Enlightenment also promoted misguided notions of perfectionism and utopianism. There was an overconfidence in reason alone to solve social problems and remake society from first principles. This gave rise to radical revolutions aiming to abruptly destroy old traditions and institutions. Edmund Burke rightly criticized this dangerous perfectionist impulse of the French Revolution. As conservatives, we understand the limits of human reason and support gradual, prudent reforms over radical social experiments.

In economic thought, classical liberal Adam Smith developed persuasive theories about free trade, arguing it led to increasing wealth and prosperity. This supported conservatives' faith in markets and skepticism toward government intervention. However, the Enlightenment also gave rise to socialists like Jean-Jacques Rousseau who inspired Karl Marx. They laid foundations for communism's eventual hostility toward private property, religion, and family - institutions vital for conservatism.

While we credit Enlightenment thinkers for espousing liberty and opposing tyranny, conservatives must separate their valuable insights from their overreaching ambitions. We do not accept the view of human nature as entirely perfectible or malleable. We understand mankind's inherent constraints and the limits of activist government. Our duty is to thoughtfully conserve and reaffirm those timeless moral truths and traditions that sustain a good society.

Burkean Conservatism

EDMUND BURKE, AN INFLUENTIAL figure in the realm of conservative philosophy, significantly shaped the foundation of modern conservative thought through his writings and political endeavors. His ideas have left a lasting impact on the principles and values upheld by conservative thinkers and leaders. In this chapter, we will delve into the essence of Burkean conservatism, exploring its key tenets and elucidating its relevance in contemporary society.

At the core of Burkean conservatism lies the belief in the intrinsic value of tradition and established institutions. Burke emphasized the importance of preserving time-honored customs, societal norms, and institutional arrangements, viewing them as the accumulated wisdom of generations. This reverence for tradition serves as a stabilizing force, providing continuity and coherence in the fabric of society. Moreover, Burkean conservatism emphasizes the organic development of societal structures, eschewing radical reforms in favor of gradual, pragmatic change. Burke's concept of organic society posits that institutions and societal order evolve naturally over time, reflecting the collective wisdom and experience of the community.

To illustrate the significance of tradition in Burkean conservatism, consider the example of the British Monarchy. Burke ardently defended the monarchy as a vital institution that symbolized continuity and stability. He cautioned against abrupt upheavals or revolutionary changes, citing the importance of retaining established structures that had endured the test of time. Furthermore, the agricultural metaphor employed by Burke to describe society as a "partnership in all science, a partnership in all art, a partnership in every virtue and in all perfection" vividly portrays his belief in the organic unity of society.

It is essential to recognize that Burke's emphasis on tradition and gradual reform has garnered both admiration and criticism. While some laud his approach as a safeguard against radical disruptions and the erosion of societal cohesion, others contend that excessive veneration of tradition may hinder progress and perpetuate unjust practices. By examining diverse viewpoints on the role of tradition, we gain a more nuanced understanding of the complexities inherent in Burkean conservatism.

When examining the impact of Burkean conservatism, empirical evidence supports the assertion that stable, well-functioning institutions contribute to societal resilience and cohesion. Studies have shown that societies with strong institutional frameworks and respect for tradition tend to exhibit greater social stability and resilience in the face of external challenges.

Burkean conservatism often invokes the notion of "prescription," which refers to the accumulated wisdom embedded in traditional practices and customs. This concept underscores the idea that established norms and institutions embody valuable insights accrued over time, providing a guide for societal conduct and governance.

The philosophy of Burkean conservatism, as expounded by Edmund Burke, underscores the enduring significance of tradition, gradual reform, and the organic development of societal institutions. By embracing the wisdom of the past and advocating for incremental change, Burkean conservatism seeks to cultivate a stable and cohesive social order. The legacy of Edmund Burke continues to shape conservative thought, offering valuable insights into the preservation of societal values and institutions.

The Conservative Intellectual Tradition

THE CONSERVATIVE INTELLECTUAL tradition has been molded and enriched by the contributions of remarkable thinkers and visionaries. In this chapter, we will embark on a comprehensive exploration of the enduring impact of conservative intellectuals such as Russell Kirk, William F. Buckley Jr., and Friedrich Hayek. Their philosophical insights and societal endeavors have left an indelible mark on the landscape of conservative thought, inspiring generations and shaping the contours of political discourse.

Russell Kirk, an eminent figure in post-World War II conservative thought, emphasized the significance of tradition, virtue, and prudence in sustaining a healthy society. His seminal work, "The Conservative Mind," offered a compelling narrative of conservative intellectual history, highlighting the essential role of tradition and continuity in preserving societal order.

William F. Buckley Jr., founder of the National Review and host of the television program "Firing Line," wielded his eloquence and erudition to champion conservative principles and engage in spirited debates with ideological opponents. His articulate defense of traditional values and free-market principles resonated deeply with a broad audience, solidifying his status as a prominent conservative voice.

Friedrich Hayek, a Nobel laureate in economics, contributed significantly to the development of classical liberal thought and the critique of centralized planning. His groundbreaking work, "The Road to Serfdom," warned against the perils of collectivism and advocated for individual liberty, free markets, and the rule of law as indispensable pillars of a free society.

The conservative intellectual tradition confronted a formidable challenge in the face of prevailing statist ideologies and the allure of centralized planning. As the post-war era witnessed the ascendancy of collectivist visions and expansionist government policies, conservative intellectuals grappled with the task of articulating a compelling alternative rooted in individual autonomy, limited government, and robust civil society.

Russell Kirk, in response to the pervasive collectivist ethos, articulated a vision of conservatism centered on the preservation of moral and cultural norms, decentralized authority, and the importance of intermediary institutions. By elucidating the enduring value of tradition and the virtues of prudence, Kirk sought to counter the allure of utopian schemes and reaffirm the indispensability of moral order in societal governance.

William F. Buckley Jr., through the National Review and "Firing Line," harnessed the power of media and public discourse to advance conservative ideas and engage in substantive dialogues with proponents of statist ideologies. His erudition, wit, and unwavering commitment to conservative principles provided a compelling counterpoint to prevailing narratives, invigorating the conservative movement and broadening its intellectual appeal.

Friedrich Hayek, in "The Road to Serfdom" and subsequent works, meticulously dissected the fallacies of central planning and the pernicious consequences of unchecked government intervention. By elucidating the intricate dynamics of spontaneous order, the knowledge problem, and the dangers of coercive collectivism, Hayek fortified the intellectual arsenal of conservatives and libertarians, offering a robust defense of individual liberty and free markets.

The enduring impact of these conservative intellectuals reverberates across the realms of political philosophy, public policy, and societal discourse. Russell Kirk's emphasis on tradition and prudence has permeated conservative thought, nurturing a deeper appreciation for the cultural foundations of a flourishing society. William F. Buckley Jr.'s eloquence and spirited advocacy have emboldened generations of conservatives, fostering a vibrant intellectual tradition that continues to shape public discourse. Friedrich Hayek's incisive critiques of collectivism and his steadfast defense of individual liberty have fortified the intellectual edifice of classical liberal thought, inspiring successive generations to safeguard the principles of a free society.

The case study of conservative intellectuals Russell Kirk, William F. Buckley Jr., and Friedrich Hayek offers profound insights into the enduring vitality of conservative thought in the face of ideological challenges. Their intellectual contributions underscore the enduring resonance of conservative principles and the imperative of engaging in robust intellectual discourse to defend the foundations of a free and flourishing society. However, it is crucial to critically assess and refine conservative ideas to address contemporary challenges and foster a more inclusive and dynamic conservative intellectual tradition.

Graphical representations or images related to the case study could include historical photographs of Russell Kirk, William F. Buckley Jr., and Friedrich Hayek engaging in public discourse or delivering seminal speeches that encapsulate their intellectual contributions.

The case study of Russell Kirk, William F. Buckley Jr., and Friedrich Hayek serves as a testament to the enduring resilience and adaptability of conservative thought amidst shifting ideological currents. Their intellectual legacies continue to enrich the conservative intellectual tradition, offering timeless principles and insights that resonate with the larger narrative of preserving individual liberty, limited government, and the flourishing of civil society.

As we contemplate the intellectual contributions of Russell Kirk, William F. Buckley Jr., and Friedrich Hayek, we are compelled to explore the broader implications of conservative thought in navigating the complexities of contemporary society. How can the insights gleaned from their intellectual endeavors inform and invigorate the ongoing discourse on conservative principles and policies in the modern era? This question beckons us to embark on a deeper exploration of the evolving conservative intellectual tradition and its relevance in shaping the trajectory of societal progress and governance.

Modern Conservative Thought

TO UNDERSTAND THE EVOLUTION of conservative thought in the 20th and 21st centuries, it is imperative to transport ourselves back to the pivotal moments that set the stage for the contemporary landscape of conservative ideology. The aftermath of the two world wars, the rise of totalitarian regimes, and the challenges posed by rapid technological advancements and globalization have profoundly shaped the trajectory of conservative thought, necessitating a thoughtful exploration of its evolution.

The mid-20th century was marked by a seismic shift in global politics, with the aftermath of World War II witnessing the emergence of two superpowers, the United States and the Soviet Union, engaged in a protracted ideological and geopolitical struggle. The rise of communism and the spread of socialist ideologies presented a formidable challenge to traditional conservative values of individual liberty, limited government, and free markets.

The Cold War era, characterized by heightened tensions and the pervasive specter of nuclear conflict, underscored the ideological divide between the proponents of collectivist ideologies and those advocating for the preservation of democratic freedoms and free-market capitalism. This ideological struggle significantly influenced the course of conservative thought, prompting intellectuals and policymakers to articulate a compelling alternative to the encroachment of statist ideologies.

The latter half of the 20th century witnessed the ascendancy of the conservative movement in response to the perceived excesses of the welfare state, the erosion of traditional values, and the challenges posed by rapid social change. The resurgence of conservative thought was fueled by a renewed emphasis on individual responsibility, moral order, and the need to curtail the expansion of government intervention in the economy and society.

The legacy of historical milestones, such as the Cold War struggle against collectivism and the resurgence of conservative principles in response to societal changes, informs contemporary debates on the role of government, the preservation of individual liberties, and the cultivation of a virtuous society.

The contemporary challenges of global terrorism, economic globalization, and the impact of technological advancements on labor markets and social cohesion necessitate a nuanced understanding of conservative thought in addressing these complex issues. The enduring values of prudence, individual responsibility, and the importance of intermediary institutions are integral to navigating the complexities of modern governance and societal cohesion.

Conveying the importance of historical understanding in tackling modern-day issues or benefiting from present opportunities, it is imperative to recognize the relevance of historical context in informing contemporary policy debates and societal challenges. The lessons gleaned from the ideological struggle of the Cold War era and the resurgence of conservative thought in response to societal changes provide valuable insights into navigating the complexities of modern governance and fostering a resilient and principled society.

The understanding of historical milestones and their impact on the trajectory of conservative thought equips individuals and policymakers with the intellectual tools necessary to address contemporary challenges, fostering a more informed and nuanced approach to governance, public policy, and societal progress.

As we delve deeper into the multifaceted dimensions of modern conservative thought, it is essential to critically assess and refine conservative ideas to address the complexities of contemporary society and foster a more inclusive and dynamic conservative intellectual tradition.

Conservative Think Tanks and Organizations

THE LANDSCAPE OF CONSERVATIVE thought and policymaking is profoundly shaped by the presence and influence of conservative think tanks and organizations. These institutions play a pivotal role in formulating, promoting, and disseminating conservative policies and ideas, exerting a significant impact on public discourse, electoral politics, and policy implementation. This exploration delves into the diverse array of conservative think tanks and organizations, unpacking their roles, strategies, and contributions in shaping conservative agendas and influencing public policy.

Founded in 1973, The Heritage Foundation has been a vanguard of conservative thought and policy development, advocating for limited government, free enterprise, individual freedom, traditional values, and a strong national defense. Its research and analysis have exerted a profound influence on conservative policymaking, spanning issues such as tax reform, healthcare, immigration, and national security.

The Heritage Foundation's impact is not confined to theoretical discourse; it actively engages with lawmakers, policymakers, and the public to advance its policy recommendations. Its policy experts and scholars produce a wealth of research reports, policy papers, and publications that serve as intellectual ammunition for conservative lawmakers and advocates. Its influence is further amplified through media appearances and public events that disseminate conservative ideas to a broader audience.

The foundation's research and recommendations have been cited and endorsed by numerous policymakers and lawmakers, shaping legislative proposals and government actions. Its comprehensive policy prescriptions have garnered support from conservative leaders and have been instrumental in shaping public opinion on critical policy issues.

The Heritage Foundation's policy proposals have translated into concrete legislative and executive actions, exemplified by the Tax Cuts and Jobs Act of 2017, which drew heavily from Heritage's recommendations on tax reform. This practical application underscores the foundation's tangible impact on shaping conservative policies and legislative initiatives.

As we transition to the next pivotal organization in the conservative landscape, it is imperative to recognize the multifaceted influence of conservative think tanks and organizations in shaping the contours of conservative thought and policy implementation.

The American Enterprise Institute, established in 1943, stands as a bastion of free-market principles, individual liberty, and a strong national defense. Its research spans a wide array of policy areas, including economics, foreign policy, education, healthcare, and social welfare, reflecting a comprehensive approach to conservative policymaking.

AEI's scholars and experts conduct rigorous policy analysis and produce influential research publications that inform public policy debates and legislative initiatives. Its scholars are actively engaged in shaping the national dialogue on issues such as economic growth, healthcare reform, and free trade, offering conservative perspectives that resonate with policymakers and the public.

AEI's research and policy recommendations have been cited in legislative hearings, congressional debates, and media discussions, attesting to the institute's substantial influence on conservative policymaking. Its scholars' expertise and analysis have been sought after by policymakers and have contributed to the development of conservative policy solutions.

AEI's policy prescriptions have been instrumental in shaping legislative proposals, influencing regulatory reforms, and guiding public discourse on pressing policy issues. The institute's influence extends beyond the realm of theoretical debate, permeating the practical implementation of conservative policies in various domains of governance.

The multifaceted contributions of conservative think tanks and organizations underscore the profound impact of their research, analysis, and advocacy on the formulation and dissemination of conservative policies and ideas. As we traverse through the diverse landscape of conservative institutions, it becomes evident that their collective influence shapes the contours of contemporary conservative thought and policymaking.

The Cato Institute, founded in 1977, is renowned for its unwavering commitment to individual liberty, limited government, free markets, and peace. Its policy research and analysis span a wide spectrum of issues, including civil liberties, economic freedom, foreign policy, and constitutional principles, reflecting a principled and comprehensive approach to advancing conservative ideas.

Cato's scholars produce a wealth of policy studies, white papers, and commentaries that articulate a compelling case for libertarian and conservative principles, influencing public opinion and policy debates. Its research on issues such as criminal justice reform, fiscal responsibility, and regulatory restraint has informed legislative proposals and public policy initiatives.

The institute's research and policy recommendations have been referenced by lawmakers, policymakers, and media outlets, amplifying the impact of Cato's contributions to conservative policymaking. Its scholars' expertise and thought leadership have enriched the conservative intellectual tradition and have provided a principled framework for addressing contemporary policy challenges.

Cato's policy prescriptions have translated into tangible policy reforms, exemplified by its influence on criminal justice policies at the state and federal levels. The institute's commitment to advancing conservative principles has manifested in actionable policy solutions that resonate with policymakers and stakeholders across the ideological spectrum.

The influential role of conservative think tanks and organizations in shaping public discourse and policy implementation underscores the significance of their contributions to the evolution of conservative thought and governance. As we navigate through the diverse array of conservative institutions, it becomes evident that their collective impact reverberates across the landscape of contemporary conservative policymaking.

The Hoover Institution, established in 1919, has been a cornerstone of conservative thought, advocating for the principles of individual freedom, private enterprise, and limited government. Its research and scholarship encompass a wide range of policy domains, including national security, economic policy, governance, and international relations, reflecting a comprehensive and interdisciplinary approach to conservative policymaking.

The institution's scholars and fellows produce seminal works, policy briefs, and books that contribute to a deeper understanding of conservative principles and policy solutions. Its research on issues such as defense strategy, economic liberty, and foreign policy has informed public discourse and policymaking, offering conservative perspectives that resonate with policymakers and the public.

The Hoover Institution's research findings and policy recommendations have been cited in legislative debates, executive actions, and international policy forums, attesting to the institute's substantial influence on conservative policymaking. Its scholars' expertise and thought leadership have enriched the conservative intellectual tradition and have provided a principled framework for addressing contemporary national and global challenges.

The institution's policy prescriptions have translated into actionable policy reforms and strategic initiatives, exemplified by its influence on defense and foreign policy strategies. The Hoover Institution's commitment to advancing conservative principles has manifested in tangible policy solutions that have had a lasting impact on national and international governance.

The enduring influence of conservative think tanks and organizations in shaping public policy and governance underscores the significance of their contributions to the development and dissemination of conservative ideas. As we navigate through the tapestry of conservative institutions, it becomes clear that their collective impact resonates across the spectrum of contemporary conservative thought and policymaking.

The Federalist Society, established in 1982, has emerged as a preeminent force in promoting conservative and libertarian legal thought, advancing the principles of textualism, originalism, and limited judicial activism. Its engagement with legal scholars, practitioners, and policymakers has significantly influenced the development of conservative legal theories, shaping judicial appointments, legal education, and constitutional interpretation.

The society's chapters, events, and publications provide a platform for robust debates and discussions on constitutional law, legal philosophy, and the role of the judiciary in interpreting and upholding the rule of law. Its advocacy for conservative legal principles has permeated the legal profession and has garnered attention from policymakers, jurists, and legal scholars, fostering a vibrant conservative legal intellectual tradition.

The Federalist Society's impact on the legal landscape is evident in the appointment of judges and justices who embrace conservative legal principles, as well as in its influence on legal education and scholarship. Its advocacy for originalist and textualist interpretations of the Constitution has shaped judicial decisions and legal arguments, reflecting the enduring influence of conservative legal thought in contemporary jurisprudence.

The society's commitment to advancing conservative legal principles has translated into tangible outcomes, exemplified by the appointment of judges who adhere to constitutional originalism and textualist principles. The Federalist Society's influence on the legal profession and judiciary underscores the enduring impact of conservative legal thought on the interpretation and application of the law.

The profound influence of conservative think tanks and organizations on the development and dissemination of conservative ideas extends to the realm of legal

The Influence of Conservative Media

IN THE LANDSCAPE OF conservative thought and policymaking, the role of conservative media outlets and personalities cannot be understated. The profound influence of these entities extends far beyond the realm of traditional news reporting, shaping public opinion, influencing political discourse, and fostering a distinct conservative narrative on a wide array of issues. This exploration delves into the multifaceted impact of conservative media outlets and personalities, unpacking their roles, strategies, and contributions in shaping conservative discourse and influencing public opinion.

Conservative media encompasses a diverse array of platforms and personalities, spanning from traditional news outlets to digital media platforms, talk radio hosts, and opinion commentators. These entities play a pivotal role in advancing conservative perspectives, promoting traditional values, and providing an alternative voice in the media landscape. Their significance lies in their ability to shape public discourse, challenge mainstream narratives, and mobilize conservative audiences around key policy issues and cultural debates.

The comparison of conservative media outlets and personalities aims to elucidate the distinct strategies, narratives, and impact of these entities on shaping conservative discourse. By examining their approaches, messaging, and influence, this analysis seeks to provide insights into the ways in which conservative media outlets and personalities contribute to the broader conservative agenda, influence public opinion, and shape the contours of contemporary conservative thought.

The comparison of conservative media outlets and personalities will be guided by their influence and reach, encompassing factors such as audience size, engagement levels, ideological positioning, and impact on public opinion. Additionally, the analysis will consider the strategies employed by these entities to convey conservative narratives, the alignment of their messaging with conservative principles, and their role in shaping public discourse on key policy issues and cultural trends.

Conservative media outlets and personalities wield significant influence through their ability to capture and engage conservative audiences, disseminate conservative perspectives, and challenge mainstream narratives. While traditional news outlets such as Fox News and The Wall Street Journal command large viewership and readership, digital platforms and opinion commentators like The Daily Wire and Ben Shapiro have garnered substantial online followings, demonstrating the diverse reach of conservative media.

Despite their shared commitment to advancing conservative principles, conservative media outlets and personalities employ distinct strategies and messaging to convey their narratives. While some outlets prioritize investigative journalism and in-depth analysis, others focus on opinion-based commentary and cultural commentary. These divergent approaches reflect the nuanced landscape of conservative media, catering to varied audience preferences and consumption habits.

The comparison of conservative media outlets and personalities reveals the multifaceted nature of conservative discourse, characterized by diverse narratives, ideological alignments, and audience engagement. By analyzing the influence and reach of these entities, insights emerge into the ways in which conservative media shapes public opinion, mobilizes conservative audiences, and contributes to the framing of key policy debates and cultural discussions.

The influence of conservative media outlets and personalities extends to contemporary realities, where their narratives and messaging play a significant role in shaping public discourse and political dynamics. By examining their impact on current events, cultural trends, and policy debates, the comparison underscores the enduring relevance of conservative media in influencing public opinion and contributing to the broader conservative agenda.

As we navigate through the diverse landscape of conservative media outlets and personalities, it becomes evident that their collective influence shapes the contours of contemporary conservative thought and public discourse. The examination of their strategies, narratives, and impact provides valuable insights into the dynamic role of conservative media in shaping public opinion and fostering a distinct conservative narrative in the media landscape.

Fox News, established in 1996, has emerged as a dominant force in conservative media, offering a platform for news reporting, opinion-based commentary, and investigative journalism from a conservative perspective. Its programming spans a wide array of topics, including politics, culture, business, and international affairs, catering to a diverse conservative audience.

Fox News' lineup of hosts and commentators provides a comprehensive coverage of conservative viewpoints, offering in-depth analysis, live discussions, and diverse perspectives on key policy issues and current events. Its engagement with conservative audiences and its emphasis on balanced reporting have solidified its position as a leading conservative media outlet, influencing public opinion and shaping political discourse.

Fox News' influence is evident in its large viewership numbers, high levels of audience engagement, and its impact on public opinion on critical policy issues and electoral dynamics. Its coverage of events and its role in amplifying conservative voices have garnered support from conservative policymakers and audiences, reflecting its substantial influence on shaping conservative discourse.

The network's programming and content have translated into tangible impacts on public opinion and political dynamics, exemplified by its coverage of election campaigns, policy debates, and cultural trends. Fox News' commitment to providing a platform for conservative voices has contributed to the framing of public discourse and has mobilized conservative audiences around key policy and cultural issues.

The Daily Wire, founded by Ben Shapiro in 2015, has rapidly risen as a prominent digital media platform, offering conservative news, commentary, and cultural analysis to a diverse online audience. Its content spans a wide range of topics, including politics, entertainment, and societal trends, providing a fresh and dynamic perspective on conservative narratives.

The Daily Wire's approach to conservative commentary and analysis resonates with a younger conservative audience, leveraging digital platforms and social media to reach and engage with a broad segment of conservative viewers and readers. Its emphasis on thought-provoking content, interactive engagement, and diverse voices within the conservative movement has positioned it as a leading digital media outlet, influencing public opinion and shaping cultural discussions.

The Daily Wire's online reach, social media interactions, and content engagement metrics reflect its substantial impact on shaping conservative narratives and fostering a vibrant online conservative community. Its coverage of contemporary issues and its role in amplifying diverse conservative voices have garnered testimonials from conservative audiences and influencers, demonstrating its influence on public discourse.

The platform's digital content and interactive engagement have translated into tangible impacts on public opinion and cultural dynamics, exemplified by its coverage of hot-button issues, ideological debates, and societal developments. The Daily Wire's commitment to providing an alternative voice in the digital media sphere has contributed to the framing of public discourse and has mobilized conservative audiences around key policy and cultural discussions.

The Wall Street Journal, renowned for its comprehensive coverage of business, finance, and global affairs, stands as a leading conservative voice in print journalism and digital media. Its reporting and analysis span a wide spectrum of topics, including economic policy, international relations, and societal trends, catering to a diverse readership of conservative-minded individuals and businesses.

The Wall Street Journal's commitment to rigorous journalism and balanced reporting has solidified its position as a trusted source for conservative perspectives on economic and global issues. Its coverage of market trends, policy analysis, and geopolitical developments provides a nuanced and insightful conservative narrative, influencing public opinion and shaping business and policy discussions.

The Wall Street Journal's readership numbers, online engagement metrics, and its impact on business and policy circles reflect its substantial influence on shaping conservative perspectives and fostering informed public discourse. Its coverage of economic trends, policy debates, and global developments has garnered testimonials from conservative leaders and business communities, highlighting its role in shaping conservative narratives.

The publication's reporting and analysis have translated into tangible impacts on public opinion and policy discussions, exemplified by its coverage of economic indicators, policy proposals, and global affairs. The Wall Street Journal's commitment to providing credible and insightful conservative perspectives has contributed to the framing of public discourse and has influenced business and policy communities around key economic and international issues.

Ben Shapiro, a prominent conservative commentator, author, and media personality, has emerged as a leading voice in shaping conservative narratives and fostering ideological discussions. His commentary spans a wide array of topics, including politics, culture, and societal trends, providing a compelling and articulate conservative perspective to diverse audiences.

Shapiro's approach to conservative commentary and analysis resonates with a younger conservative audience, leveraging digital platforms, podcasts, and live events to reach and engage with a broad segment of conservative viewers and readers. His emphasis on intellectual discussions, logical reasoning, and respectful debate has positioned him as a leading conservative personality, influencing public opinion and shaping cultural and political discussions.

The Future of Conservative Thought

THE LANDSCAPE OF CONSERVATIVE thought and policymaking is rapidly evolving in the 21st century, presenting new challenges and opportunities for the conservative agenda. As we navigate through this dynamic terrain, it becomes imperative to analyze the emerging trends and potential consequences that may shape the future of conservative ideology. This chapter delves into the multifaceted issues, their potential ramifications, and proposes practical solutions to fortify and advance the conservative agenda.

One of the primary challenges facing conservative thought in the 21st century is the increasing polarization and divisiveness within political discourse. The rise of identity politics, radical ideologies, and the erosion of traditional values has created a volatile environment that threatens the foundational principles of conservatism. This widening ideological chasm not only hampers constructive dialogue but also impedes the formulation and implementation of effective conservative policies.

If the issue of polarization and divisiveness is not addressed, it could lead to a further breakdown of civil discourse, hinder bipartisan cooperation, and sow societal discord. The consequences may manifest in the form of legislative gridlock, social unrest, and a diminished capacity to tackle pressing national and global challenges. Moreover, the erosion of trust in institutions and the exacerbation of cultural rifts may undermine the cohesive fabric of society, curtailing the advancement of conservative values and policies.

To counter the challenge of polarization and divisiveness, a multifaceted approach is essential. It necessitates a renewed commitment to fostering inclusive dialogue, promoting mutual understanding, and reasserting the shared values that underpin conservative thought. Emphasizing the importance of respectful discourse, promoting common ground, and engaging in constructive debates can serve as pivotal strategies to bridge ideological divides and fortify the conservative agenda.

The implementation of this solution entails proactive engagement with diverse communities, educational initiatives to promote civic literacy, and the cultivation of platforms that facilitate constructive dialogue. By fostering partnerships with community organizations, educational institutions, and media outlets, conservatives can amplify their message and engage with a broader spectrum of individuals. Moreover, advocating for policies that promote unity, social cohesion, and the preservation of traditional values can serve as a tangible manifestation of this solution.

Historical precedents and predictive outcomes indicate that a concerted effort to bridge ideological divides and promote civil discourse can yield tangible results. Instances where political leaders have transcended partisan barriers to collaborate on critical issues have led to legislative breakthroughs and societal cohesion. By embracing inclusivity and respectful dialogue, conservative thought can resonate with a broader audience and foster a more cohesive and resilient society.

While the proposed solution emphasizes the restoration of civil discourse and unity, alternative approaches such as targeted policy advocacy, strategic coalition-building, and the utilization of digital platforms for grassroots engagement can also complement the overarching strategy. These alternatives, when integrated with the primary solution, have the potential to bolster the conservative agenda from multiple vantage points and enhance its relevance in the 21st-century landscape.

By championing civil discourse, promoting unity, and advocating for policies that resonate across ideological spectrums, conservatism can not only weather the currents of change but also emerge as a unifying force in shaping the future of governance and societal progress.

Limited Government and Individual Liberty

The Constitutional Basis for Limited Government

As the United States of America was founded on the principles of limited government, it is crucial to explore the constitutional basis for this fundamental concept. Limited government, a cornerstone of American democracy, is deeply rooted in the U.S. Constitution, and understanding its underpinnings is essential to grasp the essence of the nation's governance system.

Limited government refers to a political system in which the powers of the government are restricted by law, usually in a written constitution, to protect individual rights and prevent abuse of authority. This concept aims to preserve the sovereignty of the people and ensure that the government operates within specific boundaries, thereby preventing it from becoming too powerful or oppressive.

The key elements of limited government include the division of powers among different branches of government, such as the executive, legislative, and judicial branches, and the establishment of a system of checks and balances to prevent any one branch from gaining too much control. Additionally, the principle of federalism, which delegates certain powers to the federal government while reserving others for the states, is integral to the concept of limited government.

The concept of limited government has historical roots dating back to ancient civilizations, such as ancient Greece and Rome, where philosophers and political thinkers advocated for constraints on the power of rulers. In more recent history, the Magna Carta of 1215, often regarded as an early precursor to constitutional limitations on government power, laid the groundwork for the principle of limited government by establishing certain legal restraints on the authority of the English monarchy.

Limited government is situated within a broader framework of democratic governance, emphasizing the rule of law, protection of individual liberties, and the accountability of government officials to the people. By placing constraints on the government's authority, limited government seeks to safeguard the rights of citizens and prevent arbitrary or tyrannical rule.

The concept of limited government finds practical application in the U.S. Constitution, which explicitly delineates the powers and limitations of the federal government, allocates specific responsibilities to the states, and enshrines the rights of individuals in the Bill of Rights. The separation of powers, as embodied in the three branches of government, and the system of checks and balances exemplify how the principle of limited government operates in the American political system.

Furthermore, the Tenth Amendment, which reserves powers not delegated to the federal government to the states or the people, exemplifies the practical application of limited government principles at the state level. This allocation of powers ensures that decisions affecting local communities can be made by those who are most directly affected by them, thus reinforcing the idea of limited government and promoting individual autonomy.

A common misunderstanding of limited government is the belief that it implies a lack of government involvement in any aspect of society. In reality, limited government does not advocate for the absence of government, but rather advocates for a government that operates within defined parameters and respects the rights and freedoms of its citizens. This distinction is crucial in understanding that limited government does not oppose all government action but seeks to ensure that such action is conducted in a manner consistent with the principles of liberty and justice.

The constitutional basis for limited government is deeply embedded in the U.S. Constitution, shaping the framework of American governance and safeguarding individual liberties. By understanding the principles and historical context of limited government, we gain insight into the foundational values that underpin the nation's political system and the mechanisms put in place to prevent the abuse of power. As we continue to explore the implications of limited government on public policy and the role of government in society, it becomes evident that this foundational principle remains essential to the preservation of freedom and democracy in the United States.

The Separation of Powers

AS WE DELVE DEEPER into the conservative agenda, it becomes imperative to discuss the conservative belief in the separation of powers as a safeguard against government overreach. The principle of the separation of powers, deeply ingrained in conservative political philosophy, plays a pivotal role in shaping the governance system and ensuring the preservation of individual liberties and the rule of law. In this chapter, we will explore the concept of the separation of powers, its historical foundations, its practical implications in modern governance, and its significance in upholding limited government.

The separation of powers is a fundamental concept in conservative political thought, serving as a mechanism to prevent the concentration of power in the hands of any single entity within the government. This concept is based on the idea that the division of governmental authority among distinct branches—typically the executive, legislative, and judicial branches—serves as a check on the potential abuse of power and promotes accountability and transparency in governance. By examining the intricacies of this principle, we can gain a comprehensive understanding of its significance in safeguarding individual freedoms and maintaining the balance of power within a constitutional framework.

The concept of the separation of powers stems from the philosophical underpinnings of classical liberalism, which emphasizes the importance of limiting government authority to protect individual rights and prevent tyranny. At its core, the separation of powers involves the allocation of distinct functions and powers to different branches of government, each acting as a check on the others. The executive branch is responsible for implementing and enforcing laws, the legislative branch is tasked with making laws, and the judicial branch interprets and applies the laws.

This division of powers is not merely a matter of administrative convenience; it is a deliberate design to prevent the accumulation of unchecked authority in any one branch. By dispersing power across multiple branches, the separation of powers aims to create a system of shared responsibilities and mutual oversight, thereby reducing the risk of governmental overreach and abuse of authority. Moreover, this system fosters a healthy competition among the branches, encouraging them to act as counterweights to one another and ensuring that no single branch can dominate the others.

To illustrate the practical implications of the separation of powers, we can examine the role of each branch in the U.S. government. The executive branch, headed by the President, is responsible for executing and enforcing laws, conducting foreign policy, and overseeing the administration of government agencies. The legislative branch, consisting of the Congress, is responsible for making laws, appropriating funds, and providing oversight of the executive branch. The judicial branch, embodied in the federal courts, is responsible for interpreting the laws, adjudicating disputes, and ensuring that the actions of the other branches adhere to the Constitution.

For instance, when the executive branch proposes a policy or enforces a law, it must work within the confines of legislation passed by the legislative branch and is subject to review by the judicial branch to ensure compliance with constitutional principles. Similarly, the legislative branch can check the power of the executive through the power of the purse, controlling the allocation of funds necessary for the execution of policies. This system of checks and balances, derived from the separation of powers, serves as a bulwark against unilateral decision-making and fosters deliberation and compromise in the legislative process.

While the separation of powers is a fundamental tenet of conservative political thought, it is important to recognize that this concept has garnered support across the political spectrum. Advocates of this principle argue that it serves as a safeguard against the concentration of power and the potential for authoritarian rule. Moreover, proponents of limited government, regardless of political affiliation, recognize the importance of maintaining a system of divided powers to protect individual liberties and prevent the erosion of democratic norms.

Conversely, critics may argue that the separation of powers can lead to gridlock and inefficiency, particularly when branches of government are controlled by opposing parties. They may contend that the system of checks and balances, while intended to prevent abuse of power, can also impede the government's ability to address pressing issues in a timely manner. However, proponents of the separation of powers assert that the deliberate diffusion of authority is a small price to pay for the preservation of liberty and the prevention of government overreach.

Empirical evidence from constitutional democracies around the world demonstrates the practical benefits of the separation of powers in promoting accountable governance and protecting individual freedoms. Countries that adhere to a system of divided powers have been shown to exhibit lower levels of corruption, greater respect for the rule of law, and a more robust defense of civil liberties. For example, the World Justice Project's Rule of Law Index consistently identifies countries with strong separation of powers as having higher overall scores in adherence to the rule of law and constraints on government powers.

Additionally, historical case studies, such as the abuses of power in authoritarian regimes, serve as cautionary tales of what can occur in the absence of a robust separation of powers. Instances of unchecked executive authority, legislative rubber-stamping of executive actions, and judicial subservience to the ruling regime highlight the dangers of concentrated power and the erosion of democratic institutions. By contrast, nations that have successfully maintained a system of divided powers have been able to withstand political crises, preserve constitutional order, and protect the rights of their citizens.

In understanding the separation of powers, it is important to clarify the distinction between the concept of separation of powers and the related concept of checks and balances. While the separation of powers refers to the allocation of distinct functions to different branches of government, checks and balances denote the mechanisms by which each branch can restrain the actions of the others. This distinction is crucial in comprehending how the system of divided powers operates and how it prevents any one branch from exerting unchecked authority.

Moreover, the term "overreach" in the context of government refers to the excessive or unjustified exercise of authority beyond the limits prescribed by law or constitutional principles. The separation of powers serves as a bulwark against governmental overreach by imposing restraints on the exercise of power and establishing mechanisms for accountability and oversight. By delineating the powers of each branch and creating avenues for mutual scrutiny, the system of separation of powers acts as a safeguard against the abuse of governmental authority.

The conservative belief in the separation of powers as a safeguard against government overreach is rooted in the enduring commitment to limited government and the protection of individual liberties. By dispersing authority across multiple branches of government, the separation of powers serves as a vital mechanism for preventing the concentration of power and upholding the rule of law. Through a comprehensive understanding of this principle, we gain insight into the foundational values that underpin conservative governance and the enduring significance of the separation of powers in preserving freedom and democracy.

The Importance of Individual Rights

THE CONSERVATIVE AGENDA places a strong emphasis on protecting individual rights and freedoms. It is rooted in the belief that individuals should have the autonomy to make their own decisions and that government intervention should be limited. This chapter aims to explore the conservative perspective on the importance of individual rights and the mechanisms through which these rights are safeguarded within the framework of a limited government.

The conservative ideology places significant value on the protection of individual rights and freedoms as a cornerstone of a healthy society. It asserts that limited government, free markets, and personal responsibility are essential for the preservation of individual liberties.

The protection of individual rights is enshrined in the U.S. Constitution, specifically in the Bill of Rights. These rights include freedom of speech, religion, and assembly, the right to bear arms, and protection against unreasonable searches and seizures, among others. The Constitution's explicit recognition of these fundamental rights demonstrates the importance placed on individual liberties by the founding fathers of the United States.

The conservative philosophy argues that the protection of individual rights fosters a society where people are free to pursue their own goals and aspirations without undue interference from the government. This freedom is seen as essential for fostering innovation, creativity, and economic prosperity. Additionally, it is believed that the preservation of individual rights serves as a check on government overreach and prevents the concentration of power in the hands of the state, which historically has led to abuses of authority.

THE CONSERVATIVE AGENDA

Conservatives often highlight the role of free markets in upholding individual rights, contending that economic freedom allows individuals to engage in voluntary transactions, pursue entrepreneurship, and reap the rewards of their labor. The conservative viewpoint suggests that government intervention in the economy, such as excessive regulation and taxation, infringes upon the economic liberties of individuals and hinders the free exchange of goods and services.

Critics of the conservative emphasis on individual rights argue that an unchecked focus on individual liberties can lead to societal inequalities and injustices. They contend that without appropriate regulations and safeguards, certain individuals and groups may be marginalized or disadvantaged, undermining the overall well-being of society. Additionally, there are concerns that a strict adherence to individual rights may impede the implementation of necessary collective actions, such as environmental protection measures and social welfare programs.

Conservatives maintain that the protection of individual rights does not preclude the existence of regulations aimed at ensuring fairness and preventing exploitation. Rather, they argue that a balanced approach can be achieved by upholding individual liberties while also addressing societal concerns through voluntary associations, charitable efforts, and local community initiatives. Furthermore, they assert that free markets, when functioning within a framework of the rule of law, can promote equitable opportunities and prosperity for all members of society.

The historical examples of countries that have embraced individual rights and limited government, such as the United States and certain European nations, have demonstrated significant economic and social progress. These societies have fostered innovation, protected personal freedoms, and provided opportunities for upward mobility, further reinforcing the conservative position on the importance of individual rights. By upholding individual liberties and advocating for limited government intervention, conservatives assert that individuals can thrive, innovate, and contribute to the betterment of society while preserving the essential balance between personal freedom and collective responsibility.

The Role of the Judiciary

THE ROLE OF THE JUDICIARY is a key aspect of the conservative agenda, and it is essential to examine the conservative perspective on judicial activism and the importance of appointing conservative judges. This chapter will delve into the nuances of the judiciary's role within the framework of a limited government and the broader implications of conservative views on the judiciary.

The judiciary, as one of the three branches of government, plays a crucial role in interpreting and upholding the law. Judicial activism, on the other hand, refers to the practice of judges exceeding their constitutional authority by making laws from the bench rather than interpreting existing laws. The significance of these concepts lies in their impact on the balance of power within the government and the protection of individual rights.

The comparison between the judiciary's role and judicial activism aims to shed light on the conservative perspective regarding the proper function of the judiciary and the potential consequences of judicial overreach. By examining these subjects, we intend to gain insights into how the conservative agenda seeks to ensure the judiciary operates within its constitutional bounds and upholds the principles of limited government and individual liberties.

In evaluating the judiciary's role and judicial activism from a conservative standpoint, the benchmarks for comparison will include adherence to constitutional principles, respect for the separation of powers, and the preservation of individual rights. These criteria will provide a framework for analyzing the conservative view on the judiciary's function and the potential dangers of judicial activism.

The conservative perspective on the judiciary's role emphasizes the importance of judges interpreting the law as written and upholding the original intent of the Constitution. This approach seeks to maintain the balance of power among the three branches of government by preventing judicial overreach. Conversely, judicial activism involves judges expanding their authority beyond the scope defined by the Constitution, effectively legislating from the bench and infringing upon the responsibilities of the legislative branch.

In contrast to the judiciary's role as a neutral arbiter, judicial activism undermines the separation of powers by allowing judges to impose their own policy preferences, bypassing the democratic process and encroaching on the authority of the elected branches. The conservative perspective highlights the dangers of judicial activism, as it can lead to the erosion of individual rights and the subversion of democratic governance, contrary to the judiciary's intended role as a check on government power.

The comparison between the judiciary's role and judicial activism reveals the conservative commitment to preserving the original intent of the Constitution and the principles of limited government. By adhering to the rule of law and respecting the separation of powers, conservative judges are seen as guardians of individual rights and the constitutional order. In contrast, judicial activism poses a threat to these principles, potentially leading to the concentration of unchecked power in the judiciary and undermining the democratic process.

The contemporary relevance of this comparison is evident in recent debates surrounding judicial appointments and the impact of judicial decisions on issues such as religious liberties, property rights, and the scope of government authority. By examining these real-world implications, we can understand how the conservative perspective on the judiciary shapes the judicial nomination process and influences legal outcomes that impact the lives of citizens.

Conservatives argue that appointing judges who respect the Constitution and the rule of law is essential to upholding the principles of individual rights, limited government, and the separation of powers. By maintaining a judiciary that operates within its constitutional bounds, conservatives aim to safeguard the liberties of the people and prevent the intrusion of judicial activism, which could undermine the foundations of a free and democratic society.

The conservative perspective on the judiciary emphasizes the critical role of judges in interpreting the law and upholding the Constitution. By contrasting this with the dangers of judicial activism, conservatives seek to uphold the principles of limited government and individual rights, ensuring that the judiciary serves as a protector of the rule of law and the rights of the people. This conservative approach to the judiciary has significant implications for the preservation of a free and democratic society, reinforcing the broader conservative agenda of upholding individual liberties and the constitutional framework of the United States.

Defending Second Amendment Rights

THE SECOND AMENDMENT of the United States Constitution, which states, "A well regulated Militia, being necessary to the security of a free State, the right of the people to keep and bear Arms, shall not be infringed," has been a subject of heated debate and contention in the current political landscape. The conservative agenda seeks to defend the Second Amendment rights and uphold the individual's right to bear arms, which is deeply rooted in the principles of liberty and self-defense.

The primary issue at hand revolves around the constant threat of legislative measures aimed at restricting or undermining the Second Amendment rights of law-abiding citizens. These measures often arise in response to tragic incidents of gun violence, leading to calls for stricter gun control laws and regulations that could potentially infringe upon the fundamental rights guaranteed by the Second Amendment.

If the Second Amendment rights are not vigorously defended, there is a risk of eroding the liberties of law-abiding citizens while failing to address the root causes of gun violence. Stricter gun control measures may impede the ability of law-abiding citizens to protect themselves and their families, potentially leaving them vulnerable to harm. Moreover, such measures may also undermine the principles of individual freedom and self-reliance upon which the nation was founded.

The conservative approach to defending Second Amendment rights involves promoting responsible gun ownership, enhancing mental health resources, and strengthening law enforcement efforts to prevent unauthorized access to firearms. Emphasizing the importance of education and training in firearm handling and safety is also a crucial aspect of the proposed solution.

Implementing the solution involves fostering a culture of responsible gun ownership through community outreach programs, educational initiatives, and partnerships with law enforcement agencies.

Additionally, enhancing mental health resources and support networks can address the underlying factors contributing to gun violence, ensuring that individuals in distress receive the help they need.

Historical evidence suggests that areas with higher rates of responsible gun ownership and well-trained individuals have experienced lower rates of violent crime. By empowering law-abiding citizens to exercise their Second Amendment rights responsibly, the conservative approach aims to contribute to a safer and more secure society.

While some advocate for stricter gun control measures as a means to address gun violence, such approaches often overlook the deeper societal issues that contribute to such incidents. Additionally, alternative solutions may involve leveraging technology and innovation to enhance firearm safety and prevent unauthorized use without compromising the rights of law-abiding citizens.

The conservative agenda's commitment to defending Second Amendment rights aligns with the principles of individual liberties and self-preservation. By promoting responsible gun ownership, addressing underlying societal issues, and enhancing law enforcement efforts, the conservative approach seeks to uphold the fundamental rights enshrined in the Second Amendment while contributing to a safer and more secure society.

The conservative perspective on defending Second Amendment rights underscores the importance of preserving individual freedoms and ensuring the safety of law-abiding citizens. By addressing the root causes of gun violence and promoting responsible gun ownership, the conservative agenda endeavors to uphold the principles of liberty and self-defense while fostering a society where individuals can exercise their rights without compromising public safety. This conservative approach to defending Second Amendment rights has significant implications for safeguarding the constitutional liberties of the American people and reinforcing the broader conservative agenda of upholding individual rights and preserving the foundational principles of the United States.

Personal Responsibility and Self-Reliance

WHAT DOES IT TRULY mean to embrace personal responsibility and self-reliance in a society that often emphasizes dependency on external factors and institutions?

The significance of this question lies in its relevance to the broader discourse on individual freedom and the role of government in shaping our lives. In a world where the concept of personal responsibility can be overshadowed by societal expectations and entitlement mentalities, understanding the essence of self-reliance becomes imperative for preserving the fabric of individual liberty.

The central issue we face is the erosion of personal responsibility and self-reliance in favor of an increasingly dependent culture. From reliance on government assistance to seeking validation and direction from external sources, the fundamental values of accountability and self-sufficiency are at risk of being diluted in the modern societal landscape.

Many individuals have succumbed to the allure of seeking external solutions to their challenges, whether it be relying on government programs for support or looking for quick fixes to complex problems. The prevailing narrative often emphasizes external factors and systemic solutions, inadvertently overshadowing the potential of individual agency and self-determination.

The real solution lies in a paradigm shift towards embracing personal responsibility and self-reliance as foundational principles of individual liberty. It involves reclaiming the power of self-accountability and recognizing the inherent capacity within each individual to chart their own course and overcome obstacles through their efforts and determination.

Picture a world where individuals are empowered to take charge of their lives, where self-reliance is celebrated, and personal responsibility is the cornerstone of progress. Imagine the sense of fulfillment and pride that comes from overcoming challenges through your own efforts and determination, knowing that you have the power to shape your destiny.

The conservative belief in personal responsibility and self-reliance is not merely a philosophical stance; it is a call to action, a foundational ethos that empowers individuals to thrive in a society that champions freedom and autonomy. At its core, this belief holds the key to unlocking the true potential of each person, transcending barriers and shaping a future built on the bedrock of individual agency.

To understand the depth of this belief, we must first recognize the historical significance of personal responsibility and self-reliance in shaping the fabric of our society. From the pioneers who ventured into uncharted territories to build new lives to the entrepreneurs who forged their own paths through innovation and hard work, the spirit of self-reliance has been ingrained in the American ethos.

However, in our contemporary landscape, the allure of dependency and external solutions has subtly shifted the narrative, leading to a gradual dilution of these foundational values. The proliferation of entitlement mentalities and the normalization of seeking external validation have contributed to a culture that often overlooks the transformative power of personal responsibility and self-reliance.

The consequences of this shift are profound, manifesting in a society where individuals are increasingly disconnected from their innate capacity to overcome challenges and pursue their aspirations. The erosion of personal responsibility has given rise to a culture of blame-shifting and victim mentalities, where externalizing challenges becomes the norm rather than embracing them as opportunities for growth and self-improvement.

In this context, the conservative belief in personal responsibility and self-reliance emerges as a beacon of hope, offering a unique perspective that challenges the status quo and rekindles the spirit of individual agency. It champions the idea that each person possesses the inherent capacity to shape their destiny, guided by the principles of accountability, resilience, and determination.

At the heart of this belief is the recognition that true freedom and autonomy can only be realized through a steadfast commitment to personal responsibility. It calls upon individuals to take ownership of their choices, to acknowledge the consequences of their actions, and to embrace the power of self-accountability as a driving force for personal growth and societal progress.

The conservative agenda's emphasis on personal responsibility and self-reliance extends beyond rhetoric; it is a call for a cultural renaissance, a revival of the values that have historically propelled individuals to greatness. It advocates for a society where self-reliance is celebrated as a virtue, where individuals are empowered to pursue their dreams with unwavering determination, knowing that their efforts are the catalyst for their success.

To implement this vision, it is essential to foster a cultural shift that elevates personal responsibility and self-reliance as core tenets of individual liberty. This involves redefining the narrative surrounding challenges and adversity, reframing them as opportunities for personal growth and empowerment. It requires a recalibration of societal norms to celebrate resilience and determination, inspiring individuals to embrace their innate potential and chart their own paths.

Moreover, the conservative approach to personal responsibility and self-reliance underscores the importance of education and mentorship in nurturing these values within the fabric of society. By instilling a sense of accountability and self-determination in the next generation, we sow the seeds for a future where individuals are equipped to navigate the complexities of life with fortitude and grace.

In this endeavor, the real solution lies in empowering individuals to recognize their agency, to embrace personal responsibility, and to cultivate the spirit of self-reliance as a transformative force in their lives. It involves fostering a societal ethos that champions resilience, determination, and accountability, inspiring individuals to rise above challenges and shape their destinies with unwavering resolve.

This shift towards personal responsibility and self-reliance holds profound implications for each reader, transcending the pages of this discussion to resonate deeply with their personal and professional lives. It invites individuals to reevaluate their approach to challenges, to reclaim agency over their decisions, and to embrace the transformative power of self-accountability.

As we journey through this exploration of personal responsibility and self-reliance, I invite you to envision a world where individuals are empowered to overcome obstacles through their own efforts, where self-reliance is celebrated as a virtue, and where personal responsibility is the cornerstone of progress. Embrace the transformative power of these foundational values, and embark on a path that leads to true freedom and autonomy.

The conservative belief in personal responsibility and self-reliance serves as a guiding light in a world that often emphasizes dependency and external solutions. It offers a unique perspective that challenges the prevailing narrative, championing the transformative power of individual agency and accountability. By embracing personal responsibility and self-reliance, individuals reclaim the power to shape their destinies, transcending limitations and realizing their full potential in a society that champions freedom and autonomy.

This discussion is a call to action, a testament to the enduring spirit of self-reliance that has shaped the fabric of our society. It is a reminder that personal responsibility is not merely a philosophical concept; it is a transformative force that empowers individuals to thrive and flourish, transcending barriers and shaping a future built on the bedrock of individual agency. Embrace the essence of personal responsibility and self-reliance, and embark on a journey that leads to true freedom and autonomy.

Free Market Economics

The Benefits of Free Markets

Free market capitalism has proven over centuries and across nations to be the economic system most compatible with human freedom and prosperity. By allowing the voluntary exchange of goods and services with minimal government intervention, free markets harness human ingenuity and self-interest to meet the needs of society. There are manifold economic, political, and moral reasons why conservatives steadfastly defend economic liberty.

The most obvious benefit of free markets is their tendency to generate tremendous wealth and high standards of living for society. When individuals are free to start businesses, engage in commerce, develop new products, and pursue opportunities unimpeded by excessive regulation or taxation, economic growth flourishes. The efficiencies and innovations produced by exposing producers to competition leads to falling consumer prices, higher wages, increased technological progress, and rising availability of goods for people at all income levels over time.

Centuries of economic history prove this to be true, despite assertions to the contrary from socialists and other statists. The Industrial Revolution, beginning over 200 years ago, unleashed transformative economic growth, raising per capita income in market-based economies to levels unimaginable in prior eras. Where free market capitalism has spread over recent generations, such as Eastern Asia, living standards have markedly risen. Every historical instance of societies moving toward market-based systems shows material conditions for ordinary people meaningfully improving.

THE CONSERVATIVE AGENDA

As conservatives understand, however, the virtues of free markets extend beyond material prosperity. Free markets also promote efficient allocation of resources, accountability on producers to satisfy customers, meritocracy allowing anyone to get ahead through hard work, choice and personal responsibility for individuals, decentralization of power, and peaceable collaboration across borders. These virtues represent moral positives that conservatives cheer.

Additionally, free markets restrict state power since governments have less need to intervene in economic affairs. This accords with conservatives' skepticism of concentrated government authority. Free markets also promote a pluralism of interests, lifestyles, customs, and beliefs, consistent with conservatives' embrace of localism and civil society autonomy against coercive homogenization. Additionally, conservatives approve of how free markets reflect freedom of association and voluntary mutual exchange based on properly understood self-interest, rather than imposing systems against people's will.

There can be economically turbulent periods of business cycles in free market systems. However, by allowing dynamic adaptation through ever-changing signals of supply and demand, markets are self-correcting and economically resilient over the long run. Government interventions, by contrast, distort price signals and often exacerbate problems. It is ultimately the creativity, productivity, reasonableness, and good judgement of ordinary people, not central planners, that make markets work.

Conservatives will always defend free markets because history and logic prove them to best produce widespread prosperity while respecting moral virtues and individual liberty. Despite imperfections, true conservatism recognizes no alternative system coming remotely close to the benefits of free markets. Their sustained success redounds to greater social happiness, defenses of freedom, and cultivation of virtue. Any public policy actions conservatives support must uphold faith in free markets rather than undermine them through overregulation, frivolous litigation, or overly burdensome government. Our principles reflect deep wisdom in supporting economic freedom.

Limited Government Intervention

UNDERSTANDING THE CONCEPT of limited government intervention in the economy is crucial for grasping the fundamental principles of conservatism. It is essential to delve into the key words and concepts associated with this belief in order to gain a comprehensive understanding of its implications and benefits.

1. Limited government refers to the principle that the role of the government in the affairs of its citizens should be restricted to the bare essentials. This means that the government's powers and functions are limited to specific areas, such as maintaining law and order, protecting individual rights, and providing for national defense. The concept of limited government is deeply rooted in the belief that excessive government involvement can stifle personal freedom and hinder economic prosperity.

2. Intervention, in the context of limited government, refers to the active involvement of the government in the economy through regulations, subsidies, or other forms of interference. This can include measures such as price controls, trade restrictions, or government ownership of industries. The conservative ideology advocates for minimal intervention in the free market, allowing businesses and individuals to operate with minimal government interference.

3. The economy encompasses the production, distribution, and consumption of goods and services within a society. It is the.system through which resources are allocated and wealth is generated. A free-market economy, which aligns with the conservative agenda, operates based on voluntary exchange, private ownership, and minimal government intervention. This system is believed to foster innovation, competition, and economic growth.

4. Conservatism is a political ideology that emphasizes traditional values, limited government, free markets, and individual responsibility. It is grounded in the belief that society functions best when individuals are free to pursue their own interests, and when government interference is minimized. Conservatism advocates for a small, efficient government that allows for personal freedom and economic prosperity.

Consider a free-market economy as a bustling marketplace where individuals are free to exchange goods and services based on their own preferences and needs. In this scenario, limited government intervention acts as a facilitator, ensuring that the marketplace operates smoothly by enforcing property rights, contracts, and preventing fraud. This minimal oversight allows businesses to innovate, compete, and thrive, leading to economic growth and prosperity.

On the other hand, excessive government intervention can be likened to a heavy-handed moderator in the marketplace, imposing rigid rules, stifling competition, and distorting prices. This intervention can hinder the natural flow of supply and demand, leading to inefficiency, reduced innovation, and diminished consumer choice.

The concept of limited government intervention in the economy is integral to the conservative agenda. By understanding the key terms associated with this principle, and by relating them to real-world examples, we gain insight into the fundamental beliefs that underpin conservative economic philosophy. Through the lens of limited government intervention, we can appreciate the value of individual freedom, free markets, and the potential for economic prosperity.

Taxation and Fiscal Policy

AS THE CONSERVATIVE agenda emphasizes limited government intervention in the economy, the issue of taxation and fiscal policy plays a crucial role in shaping the economic landscape. In this chapter, we will delve into the conservative views on taxation, fiscal responsibility, and the role of government in managing the economy. By examining a specific instance and its broader implications, we aim to provide insights into the challenges, strategies, and outcomes associated with conservative fiscal policy.

The backdrop for this case study is a society facing economic challenges, where the role of taxation and fiscal policy is under intense scrutiny. The country's government is grappling with budget deficits, growing public debt, and increasing demands for social welfare programs. Amidst these challenges, conservative policymakers are advocating for a shift towards fiscal responsibility and a reevaluation of the government's role in economic management.

The central figures in this case study include policymakers, economists, and taxpayers. Policymakers are tasked with crafting and implementing fiscal policies that align with the conservative principles of limited government intervention and free-market economics. Economists provide insights and analysis on the potential impacts of fiscal policy changes, while taxpayers represent the individuals and businesses affected by taxation and government spending.

The core challenge at the heart of this case study is the need to address budget deficits and public debt while ensuring the efficient allocation of resources and promoting economic growth. The current taxation and fiscal policies are seen as burdensome, complex, and potentially inhibiting to economic dynamism. Conservative policymakers are aiming to tackle these challenges by reevaluating the existing tax system and advocating for fiscal restraint.

Conservative fiscal policy emphasizes the need for a simplified, transparent, and efficient tax system that promotes economic growth and individual prosperity. This approach involves lowering tax rates, broadening the tax base, and reducing the complexity of the tax code. Additionally, conservative policymakers advocate for responsible government spending, prioritizing essential functions such as national defense, infrastructure, and public safety while limiting the expansion of welfare programs and entitlements.

The outcomes of conservative fiscal policy are multifaceted. By lowering tax rates and simplifying the tax code, individuals and businesses experience reduced compliance costs and increased incentives for investment, innovation, and entrepreneurship. Lower taxes can stimulate economic activity, resulting in higher levels of employment, productivity, and overall prosperity. Moreover, responsible government spending and debt reduction efforts can instill confidence in the economy, leading to lower interest rates, increased private investment, and a more sustainable fiscal outlook.

The case study offers insights into the potential benefits and challenges associated with conservative fiscal policy. While lower tax rates and fiscal restraint can spur economic growth and individual prosperity, critics argue that such policies may exacerbate income inequality and lead to underinvestment in public goods and social safety nets. It is crucial to weigh these considerations and strive for a balance that promotes both economic dynamism and social welfare.

The specifics of this case study tie back to the overarching themes of limited government intervention and free-market economics. By advocating for a simplified tax system and responsible fiscal management, conservative fiscal policy aligns with the principles of individual freedom, economic liberty, and limited government intrusion in the economy.

As we reflect on the implications of conservative fiscal policy, one may ponder the following: How can conservative principles of taxation and fiscal responsibility be reconciled with the need for social welfare and equitable economic opportunities? This question encourages further engagement and exploration of the complexities surrounding fiscal policy within the conservative agenda.

Deregulation and Small Government

IN THE CONSERVATIVE push for deregulation and reducing the size and scope of government, there is a fundamental emphasis on fostering an environment that encourages free-market competition, individual initiative, and limited government intervention in business affairs. This chapter will delve into the intricacies of deregulation and small government, comparing and contrasting their impact on various sectors and offering insights into their broader implications for economic dynamism, public welfare, and regulatory governance.

Deregulation and small government are key components of the conservative agenda, reflecting the belief that excessive government regulations and interventions can stifle economic growth, innovation, and individual freedom. Deregulation pertains to the removal or reduction of government restrictions and mandates on businesses and industries, aiming to enhance market efficiency and flexibility. On the other hand, the concept of small government advocates for limited government involvement in economic and social affairs, promoting individual responsibility and autonomy.

The rationale behind comparing deregulation and small government lies in uncovering their synergies and distinctions, shedding light on their respective contributions to economic prosperity, consumer protection, and regulatory effectiveness. By dissecting their interplay, this comparison seeks to elucidate the underlying principles and intended outcomes of conservative regulatory and governance policies.

The benchmarks for comparison encompass the impact on market competition, consumer welfare, regulatory oversight, and administrative efficiency. These criteria will guide the analysis, providing a comprehensive assessment of the implications of deregulation and small government in diverse contexts.

When examining the similarities between deregulation and small government, it becomes evident that both prioritize reducing government interference in the marketplace. Deregulation aims to eliminate unnecessary regulatory burdens, streamlining processes and fostering innovation, while the concept of small government advocates for minimal government intrusion to allow market forces to allocate resources efficiently.

However, a nuanced distinction arises in their focus and scope. Deregulation primarily targets specific industries or sectors, aiming to address sector-specific challenges and promote competition, whereas small government pertains to the broader role of government in society, encompassing not only regulatory aspects but also social and public service functions.

Delving into the comparisons between deregulation and small government unveils their potential to foster economic innovation, efficiency, and consumer choice. However, it also highlights the need for effective regulatory frameworks to safeguard against market abuses, environmental degradation, and consumer exploitation. Striking a balance between deregulation and regulatory oversight within the context of a small government framework is crucial for promoting economic dynamism while ensuring public welfare and safety.

As we reflect on the implications of deregulation and small government, it is imperative to recognize that while these principles can foster economic growth and individual freedom, they must be implemented with a keen understanding of their potential impact on market dynamics, consumer protection, and public welfare. This chapter serves as a springboard for further exploration of the complexities surrounding conservative regulatory and governance policies, urging a balanced approach that upholds both economic liberty and social responsibility.

Conservative Economic Thinkers

CONSERVATIVE ECONOMIC thinkers have made significant contributions to the development and evolution of economic principles and policies. Their perspectives have shaped the discourse on economic governance, providing insights into the role of market forces, government intervention, and the impact of economic policies on societal well-being. In this chapter, we will delve into the contributions of prominent conservative economists, such as Milton Friedman and Friedrich Hayek, and explore how their ideas have influenced the conservative agenda in the realm of economics.

THE CONSERVATIVE AGENDA

The conservative approach to economics finds its earliest origins in the works of classical economists such as Adam Smith and David Ricardo. These scholars laid the groundwork for conservative economic thought by emphasizing the virtues of free markets, individual freedom, and limited government intervention in economic affairs. Their theories of comparative advantage, division of labor, and the invisible hand of the market provided the intellectual foundation for conservative economic principles that continue to influence policy debates today.

1. The 18th and 19th centuries marked a significant milestone in the development of conservative economic thought, with the emergence of classical liberal economists advocating for free trade, minimal government interference in the economy, and the protection of property rights as essential components of economic prosperity.

2. In the early 20th century, the Austrian School of Economics, led by Friedrich Hayek, emphasized the importance of individual knowledge, market competition, and the dangers of central planning. Hayek's seminal work, "The Road to Serfdom," warned against the perils of collectivism and government control, laying the groundwork for the conservative critique of socialist economic policies.

3. The mid-20th century witnessed the rise of monetarism, championed by Milton Friedman, as a conservative response to Keynesian economic policies. Friedman's advocacy for monetary stability, free markets, and limited government intervention reshaped the discourse on economic management, influencing conservative economic agendas around the world.

The evolution of conservative economic thought has exhibited variations across different cultural and regional contexts. In the United States, conservative economists have often emphasized the principles of individualism, free enterprise, and limited government intervention, reflecting the broader conservative ideology of personal freedom and self-reliance. In European contexts, conservative economic traditions have intersected with historical, political, and social factors, leading to nuanced approaches to economic governance and market regulation.

In contemporary times, conservative economic thinkers have adapted their principles to address pressing issues such as technological disruption, globalization, and income inequality. The application of conservative economic theories to these modern challenges has led to debates on the role of government in shaping economic outcomes, the impact of trade policies on domestic industries, and the need for innovative approaches to economic regulation in the digital age.

The conservative economic agenda has faced its share of challenges and controversies, particularly in the aftermath of financial crises and economic downturns. Debates surrounding the appropriate balance between market forces and regulatory oversight, the implications of income inequality, and the role of international trade agreements have prompted reevaluations of conservative economic principles, leading to ongoing discussions about the relevance and applicability of traditional conservative economic doctrines in a rapidly changing global economy.

As we explore the contributions of conservative economic thinkers, it becomes evident that their ideas have left a lasting imprint on economic policies and governance, shaping the contours of contemporary economic discourse and influencing policy decisions at local, national, and international levels. The evolution of conservative economic thought reflects a dynamic interplay of historical legacies, cultural contexts, and responses to modern challenges, underscoring the enduring relevance of conservative principles in the arena of economic governance.

The Future of Free Market Economics

THE GLOBAL ECONOMY is undergoing significant transformations, driven by technological advancements, geopolitical shifts, and societal changes. These dynamics have profound implications for conservative economic principles, which have long emphasized the virtues of free markets, individual liberty, and limited government intervention in economic affairs. As we navigate this evolving landscape, it is imperative to explore the emerging trends and challenges that confront free market economics and to consider their implications for the conservative economic agenda. By examining these developments, we can identify potential opportunities and formulate strategies to uphold and strengthen conservative principles in the economic realm.

One of the foremost challenges facing free market economics is the rapid pace of technological disruption. The advent of automation, artificial intelligence, and digital platforms has reshaped industries, altered labor markets, and redefined the nature of economic competition. While these advancements have brought about unprecedented efficiencies and innovations, they have also raised concerns about job displacement, income inequality, and the concentration of economic power in the hands of a few tech giants. This presents a clear challenge to the traditional understanding of free markets as engines of opportunity and meritocracy, as the benefits of technological progress are not uniformly distributed across society.

If the challenge of technological disruption is not effectively addressed, it could exacerbate existing disparities in the labor market, leading to heightened unemployment, underemployment, and wage stagnation for certain segments of the population. Moreover, the erosion of traditional employment models may strain social cohesion, as individuals and communities grapple with the social and economic dislocation caused by technological shifts. This could potentially fuel social unrest and political polarization, undermining the stability of free market economies and eroding public trust in the economic system.

To confront the challenge of technological disruption, a comprehensive approach is necessary. Conservative economic principles can be leveraged to champion innovation and entrepreneurship while safeguarding the interests of workers and communities affected by technological change. Embracing technological innovation involves fostering an environment conducive to entrepreneurship, research, and development, which aligns with the core tenets of free market economics. At the same time, it is essential to implement policies that ensure workers have the skills and support necessary to adapt to the evolving demands of the labor market.

The implementation of such a strategy requires a multifaceted policy framework that addresses the challenges posed by technological disruption. This includes investing in education and vocational training to equip individuals with the skills needed for emerging industries, fostering labor market flexibility through initiatives such as portable benefits that accompany workers throughout their careers, and promoting entrepreneurship and small business growth to diversify economic opportunities. Additionally, regulatory frameworks should be updated to facilitate the responsible deployment of new technologies while upholding standards for consumer protection and fair competition.

By pursuing these solutions, conservative economic principles can drive inclusive economic growth that harnesses the potential of technological innovation while ensuring that the benefits are widely shared. Past examples of successful adaptation to technological change, such as the Industrial Revolution, demonstrate that proactive measures can mitigate the disruptive effects of transformative technologies and ultimately lead to expanded opportunities and improved living standards for society at large. Furthermore, predicted outcomes indicate that embracing innovation while safeguarding workers can foster a dynamic economy that is both competitive and compassionate, responsive to the needs of individuals and communities in an era of rapid change.

While the proposed solutions align with conservative principles, alternative perspectives may emphasize the role of government intervention in managing technological disruption. Advocates of a more interventionist approach may argue for stronger regulations to control the impact of new technologies on employment and income distribution, or for international cooperation to address the global implications of technological change. Evaluating these alternative solutions provides a comprehensive understanding of the policy options available and the trade-offs associated with each approach.

The future of free market economics is intricately linked to the ability of conservative principles to adapt to the challenges posed by technological disruption. By embracing innovation, safeguarding workers, and fostering inclusive economic growth, conservative economic thinkers can steer the global economy towards a future that upholds the values of free markets, individual freedom, and prosperity for all. As we navigate this transformative period, it is imperative to recognize the potential of conservative economic principles to shape a future that is both dynamic and equitable, harnessing the forces of innovation to build a resilient and prosperous society.

National Security and Foreign Policy

American Exceptionalism

America is an extraordinary nation unlike any other in history. The concept of "American Exceptionalism" refers to the United States as uniquely embodying core conservative ideals like liberty, individualism, popular rule, and free market economics. Our nation has thrived by avoiding utopian schemes, remaining grounded in realism regarding human nature while aspiring to moral virtues and transcendent truths. We have forged prosperity and social cohesion by prudently balancing order with freedom in our political economy and culture. Though imperfect, the richness of the American experience vindicates profound truths within conservatism.

The Founding Fathers studied history and political philosophy to design our constitutional system of self-government. America upended assumptions that securing rights and checking power required hereditary aristocracy. Our Constitution elevated reason, civic participation and representation. The American people exercise self-rule while avoiding the extremes of direct democracy's destabilizing whims and tendencies towardconcentrated power unsafeguarding minority rights. The genius of federalism allows appropriate self-determination locally, regionally and nationally.

Our free market system produced astonishing affluence. It did so not through state regimentation but individuals freely pursuing dreams. America demonstrated capitalism's compatibility with social mobility. The majority of our people achieved middle-class standards of living even while we welcomed generations of immigrants. Fair opportunity and merit-based social ascent replaced older social hierarchies.

Critically, American conservatism resists the determinism underwriting radical ideologies of the Left and Right. We neither accept Marxism's rigid economic formulae nor reactionary racial nationalism. Human potential remains open-ended, multidimensional and unpredictable when liberty thrives. The American experience verifies this truth.

American exceptionalism is moreover ethical, upholding universal moral truths grounded in faith and reason. The Declaration of Independence evokes a higher standard of justice beyond capricious statutes or coercive rule by men. Conservatives see rights as God-given, government as limited, and people as imbued with worth and agency. Tyranny is illegitimate; human freedom inviolable. American conservatism fuses inherited wisdom with progress guided by ethical guardrails.

This exceptionalism empowers reform yet counsels prudence. Tempering passions, we affirm continuity in community, caution regarding human nature's egoistic aspects, and pragmatism judging policies by outcomes not intentions. Such skepticism toward centralized power distinguishes conservatism. America's balance endures where radical experiments like communism and fascism devolved into nightmarish dystopias.

With privilege comes great responsibility. Conservatives believe America should lead globally not by arrogant imposition of our specific regime, but by example – a mature beacon of opportunity, liberty and culture. Leadership means bolstering market economies and consensual governments respecting cultural pluralism.

American exceptionalism is proven not by nationalistic bluster but dynamic achievement. We who inherit this great tradition must carry it forward with moral seriousness and courage. This requires open patriotic hearts discerning and rejoicing in accomplishments while confronting shortcomings with candor. A renewed American conservatism must articulate transcendent yet pragmatic principles powering future greatness true to our legacy.

Military Strength and Preparedness

CONSERVATIVES UNDERSTAND that maintaining overwhelming military power is essential to national sovereignty, global stability, and peace through deterrence of aggression. The costs of properly funding a robust military are trivial compared to the existential perils of failing to sufficiently equip our armed forces. A dominant military enables protection of national interests while checking tyrannical regimes and violent non-state actors abroad. Diplomatic leadership also derives from commanding strength.

Our founders recognized that chief purposes of the Constitution were providing for the common defense and securing liberties. To avoid debt and foreign entanglements, there were calls for standing armies to be minimal in peacetime. However, proponents of vigilant readiness like Alexander Hamilton rightly prevailed. Great armies would only be maintained in times of crisis or necessity through Congressional oversight. But emergency preparation remains imperative.

Today we spend over 3% of GDP on defense annually, higher than most allies but below Cold War levels exceeding 5%. This represents excellent value securing public goods: our interests and principles worldwide. Further savings via cuts risk catastrophic recklessness. Threat environments demand modernization of capabilities.

The claims by some on the left and libertarian right for radical military reductions make flawed assumptions ofinherent global harmony, benevolent foreign powers, and overconfidence in soft power. But conditions in international affairs reflect a Hobbesian realm bereft of centralized authority where bad actors exploit weakness and misplaced trust. While we work cooperatively with allies in good faith, and promote justice where possible, we must accept hard truths about human nature and avoid naïve idealism.

Deterrence requires deploying cutting-edge platforms across air, land, sea, space and cyber domains guided by strategies maximizing flexibility for unknowns ahead. Modernization sustaining qualitative military superiority enables upholding international access, regional balances, counterterrorism efforts, and managing rogue regimes. It hedges against malicious counterbalancing coalitions. Communicating unquestionable strength temperstesting by rivals. Preserving credibility of security commitments to treaty allies also maintains stability while pursuing peace profitably.

Budgetary savings from military cuts are fiction given how diminished capability, strategic ambiguity and emboldened enemies historically result in future wars becoming more probable. Preventative intervention and peace-through-strength are far less costly in lives and treasure than avoidable conflicts permitted through hollow weakness. This lesson echoes across centuries of statecraft. True national security spending equates to insurance premiums against preventable cataclysms.

Conservatives maintain that so long as anarchy reigns internationally, military deterrence is freedom's guardian. George Washington stated "to be prepared for war is one of the most effectual means of preserving peace." Ronald Reagan proved wisdom in that quote. Responsible policy, moral values and long-term interests mandate the United States sustaining military supremacy for generations ahead.

Border Security and Immigration

AS WE DELVE INTO THE complex and multifaceted realm of border security and immigration, it is imperative to comprehend the underlying significance of these subjects and their profound impact on the fabric of society. This comparison seeks to elucidate the conservative perspective on immigration policies and the indispensable need for secure borders, shedding light on the nuances and broader implications of these crucial aspects of governance.

sovereignty, security, and the regulation of human movement across geographical boundaries. Border security encompasses the measures and policies implemented by a nation to safeguard its borders, prevent unauthorized entry, and combat illicit activities such as drug trafficking and human smuggling. On the other hand, immigration pertains to the movement of individuals from one country to another with the intention of establishing permanent or temporary residence, often driven by factors such as economic opportunities, family reunification, or seeking refuge from persecution.

The rationale behind comparing border security and immigration lies in unraveling the conservative perspective on these issues and the intended insights that stem from this juxtaposition. By juxtaposing these two subjects, we aim to elucidate the conservative stance on the need for stringent border security measures in light of immigration policies, thereby offering a comprehensive understanding of the underlying conservative agenda in this domain.

In order to effectively compare and contrast these subjects, it is imperative to establish the benchmarks and parameters for analysis. The criteria for comparison will revolve around the fundamental principles of national security, sovereignty, rule of law, and the preservation of cultural and economic interests. These benchmarks will serve as the guiding framework for a balanced and nuanced view of border security and immigration from a conservative standpoint.

From a conservative perspective, both border security and immigration are intrinsically linked to the preservation of national sovereignty and security. The emphasis is placed on the need for robust border security measures to regulate the flow of immigration, prevent illegal entry, and uphold the rule of law. Conservative ideology advocates for a structured and merit-based immigration system that prioritizes national interests, economic viability, and the assimilation of immigrants into the social fabric of the host nation. This approach underscores the significance of maintaining secure borders as a foundational element of a nation's sovereignty and self-determination.

While border security and immigration are interconnected, it is essential to highlight the distinctions between these subjects to underscore the nuances of each. Border security primarily focuses on the enforcement of laws and policies to protect the territorial integrity of a nation, combat transnational crime, and prevent unauthorized entry. In contrast, immigration policies encompass a broader spectrum of regulations and frameworks governing the admission, integration, and management of foreign nationals within a country. The conservative perspective underscores the need for a balanced approach that upholds the rule of law, national interests, and the assimilation of immigrants, while also acknowledging the humanitarian aspects of immigration.

Delving into the comparisons between border security and immigration reveals profound insights into the conservative perspective on these critical issues. The emphasis on the rule of law, national sovereignty, and the preservation of cultural identity forms the cornerstone of conservative ideology in shaping immigration policies and border security measures. The conservative agenda advocates for a comprehensive and pragmatic approach that balances national security imperatives with the recognition of the contributions and aspirations of lawful immigrants, thereby fostering a cohesive and resilient society.

Connecting historical or theoretical comparisons to current realities enhances the relevance of the conservative agenda on border security and immigration. In today's global context, the challenges of managing immigration flows, combating transnational threats, and upholding national sovereignty have intensified. The conservative perspective on border security and immigration resonates with contemporary debates surrounding immigration reform, border enforcement, and the need for a coherent and sustainable immigration system that aligns with national interests and security imperatives.

As we navigate through the intricate terrain of border security and immigration, it becomes evident that the conservative perspective offers a compelling framework for addressing these critical issues. By dissecting the similarities and differences, exploring the underlying principles, and unraveling the broader implications, we gain a comprehensive understanding of the conservative agenda in shaping immigration policies and advocating for secure borders. This comparison serves as a pertinent lens through which to comprehend the conservative stance on border security and immigration, offering invaluable insights into the nuances and complexities of these vital subjects.

JACK DONAHUE

International Alliances and Diplomacy

THE CONSERVATIVE AGENDA on international alliances and diplomacy is multifaceted, encompassing strategic alliances, diplomatic engagement, and the promotion of national interests in the global arena. This chapter will commence by delineating the foundational principles that guide conservative foreign policy, followed by an exploration of the strategic considerations that shape the formation and maintenance of international alliances. Subsequently, it will delve into the diplomatic strategies employed by conservative administrations to advance national interests and foster cooperation with allied nations. Furthermore, the chapter will analyze the conservative approach to multilateral institutions and international agreements, shedding light on the principles that underpin their engagement.

The conservative approach to international alliances and diplomacy is underpinned by a set of foundational principles that emphasize national sovereignty, strategic interests, and a pragmatic assessment of global dynamics. Conservatism advocates for a realistic and cautious approach to international relations, prioritizing stability, security, and the preservation of national identity. This entails a judicious assessment of the risks and benefits associated with alliances and diplomatic engagements, ensuring that they align with the long-term interests of the nation.

Conservative foreign policy emphasizes the strategic considerations that inform the formation of alliances, with a focus on mutual defense, shared values, and geopolitical alignment. The conservative approach underscores the significance of robust and reliable alliances that serve as bulwarks against common adversaries, promote regional stability, and safeguard the national security interests of the allied nations. The strategic calculus of alliance formation entails an assessment of the credibility and commitment of potential partners, the distribution of burdens and responsibilities, and the alignment of interests in addressing global challenges.

Diplomacy occupies a central role in conservative foreign policy, serving as a primary instrument for advancing national interests, resolving disputes, and fostering cooperation with international partners. The conservative approach to diplomacy emphasizes the importance of direct and principled engagement, leveraging diplomatic channels to negotiate treaties, resolve conflicts, and promote economic and security cooperation. Furthermore, conservative diplomacy prioritizes the projection of strength, clarity, and unwavering commitment to national interests while engaging in diplomatic negotiations and dialogues.

Conservative foreign policy approaches multilateral institutions and agreements with a measured and pragmatic stance, prioritizing national sovereignty, and the protection of vital interests. While recognizing the potential benefits of multilateral cooperation, conservatives advocate for a cautious approach to international agreements, ensuring that they uphold national sovereignty, do not undermine domestic laws, and are consistent with the long-term strategic interests of the nation. The conservative approach to multilateral engagement involves a judicious assessment of the costs and benefits of participation, scrutinizing the impact of international agreements on domestic policies and sovereignty.

Countering Terrorism and Extremism

IN RECENT YEARS, THE global landscape has been marred by the rising threat of terrorism and extremism. From the heinous attacks on innocent civilians to the propagation of radical ideologies, these phenomena have posed significant challenges to the stability and security of nations worldwide. It is imperative for conservative policymakers to address this pressing issue with strategic and nuanced approaches that not only combat terrorism and extremism but also uphold fundamental democratic values and principles.

The primary issue at hand is the proliferation of terrorism and extremism, which undermines the social fabric, destabilizes governance structures, and poses a direct threat to the safety and security of citizens. Extremist groups and individuals exploit vulnerabilities within societies, disseminating messages of hatred and violence, and perpetrating acts of terror that instill fear and discord. Furthermore, the transnational nature of terrorism necessitates a coordinated and comprehensive response to mitigate its impact on global peace and security.

Failing to address the menace of terrorism and extremism can have dire consequences. It not only leads to loss of life and destruction of infrastructure but also fuels fear, discrimination, and polarization within societies. Additionally, the spread of extremist ideologies can erode the values of tolerance and pluralism, undermining the foundation of democratic societies and creating fertile ground for further radicalization and violence.

The conservative agenda for countering terrorism and extremism involves a multifaceted and proactive approach that integrates robust security measures with comprehensive strategies to address the root causes of radicalization. Emphasizing the protection of individual liberties and democratic values, conservative policymakers advocate for a balanced and pragmatic response that upholds the rule of law and safeguards civil liberties while effectively combating terrorism and extremism.

Implementing the conservative approach to countering terrorism and extremism necessitates a combination of security measures, intelligence cooperation, and targeted interventions to address the underlying factors that contribute to radicalization. This includes enhancing border security, strengthening law enforcement capabilities, and investing in counter-radicalization programs that offer alternative pathways to individuals vulnerable to extremist ideologies.

The conservative approach to countering terrorism and extremism has demonstrated its efficacy in various contexts. By prioritizing intelligence sharing, disrupting financial networks that fund extremist activities, and engaging in strategic military operations against terrorist organizations, conservative-led initiatives have contributed to the dismantling of extremist networks and the prevention of terrorist attacks. Moreover, investment in community-based programs aimed at addressing the grievances that fuel radicalization has shown promising results in diverting individuals from the path of violent extremism, thereby contributing to long-term societal resilience.

While the conservative approach offers a comprehensive framework for countering terrorism and extremism, it is essential to acknowledge alternative solutions that have been proposed. These may include a more interventionist approach that focuses on aggressive military interventions, or a purely diplomatic approach that seeks to address the root causes of extremism through dialogue and engagement with affected communities. However, conservative policymakers argue that a balanced approach that integrates security measures with targeted interventions is necessary to effectively combat terrorism and extremism while preserving democratic values and liberties.

The conservative agenda for countering terrorism and extremism provides a comprehensive and principled framework for addressing these critical challenges. By integrating security measures with initiatives aimed at addressing the underlying factors that fuel radicalization, conservative policymakers strive to safeguard the safety and freedoms of citizens while combating the spread of terrorism and extremism. As the global community grapples with these pressing issues, it is imperative to adopt strategies that not only mitigate immediate threats but also foster resilient and inclusive societies, guided by the principles of democracy, human rights, and the rule of law.

Cybersecurity and Emerging Threats

IN TODAY'S INTERCONNECTED world, cybersecurity has emerged as a critical concern for governments, businesses, and individuals. The conservative perspective on cybersecurity emphasizes the protection of digital infrastructure and the mitigation of emerging threats that pose significant risks to national security and economic stability. By examining conservative views on cybersecurity and the challenges posed by emerging threats in the digital age, this discussion aims to provide a comprehensive understanding of the conservative agenda in safeguarding digital assets and combating cyber threats.

The conservative approach to cybersecurity prioritizes proactive measures to defend against cyber threats and advocates for policies that promote resilience and deterrence in the digital domain. This includes strengthening cybersecurity capabilities, fostering public-private partnerships, and enhancing international cooperation to address the evolving nature of cyber threats.

One of the key pillars of the conservative agenda on cybersecurity is the recognition of cyberspace as a domain of warfare and the acknowledgment of the growing sophistication of cyber threats. The conservative viewpoint underscores the need for robust defense mechanisms to protect critical infrastructure, sensitive data, and national security assets from cyber attacks. This is evident in the allocation of resources towards developing advanced cybersecurity technologies and enhancing the capabilities of cyber defense organizations.

Conservative policymakers emphasize the importance of a comprehensive cybersecurity strategy that encompasses not only defensive measures but also offensive capabilities to deter and respond to cyber aggression. This involves investing in cyber intelligence, conducting cyber warfare exercises, and establishing clear protocols for attributing cyber attacks to hold malicious actors accountable. By delving deeper into this evidence, it becomes evident that the conservative approach to cybersecurity is rooted in a proactive and forward-looking mindset that anticipates and prepares for emerging cyber threats.

Critics of the conservative approach to cybersecurity may argue that an overly aggressive stance in cyberspace could escalate tensions and lead to a cyber arms race, resulting in increased vulnerability to cyber attacks. They may also contend that a focus on offensive cyber capabilities detracts from the need to strengthen defensive measures and prioritize resilience against cyber threats.

In response to these counterarguments, conservative proponents of cybersecurity assert that while offensive capabilities are essential for deterrence, the primary focus remains on bolstering defensive measures and resilience in cyberspace. The goal is to create a cyber ecosystem that is less susceptible to attacks and can effectively mitigate the impact of any breaches or intrusions. Additionally, conservative policymakers emphasize the importance of international norms and cooperation to prevent an escalation of cyber conflicts.

Further supporting the conservative stance on cybersecurity, recent cyber incidents and attacks have highlighted the significance of robust cyber defenses and the need for proactive measures to address emerging threats. Cyber attacks targeting critical infrastructure, intellectual property, and government networks have underscored the urgency of strengthening cybersecurity capabilities and fostering collaboration between public and private sectors.

The conservative agenda on cybersecurity emphasizes the proactive defense of digital assets and the deterrence of cyber threats through a comprehensive strategy that integrates defensive measures, offensive capabilities for deterrence, and international cooperation. By prioritizing cybersecurity and addressing emerging threats in the digital age, conservative policymakers aim to safeguard national interests, protect critical infrastructure, and promote a secure and resilient cyberspace for individuals and businesses.

The Future of National Security

AS THE WORLD CONTINUES to evolve, so do the threats and challenges to national security. The landscape of global security is constantly shifting, presenting new and complex risks that demand a fresh perspective and innovative solutions. Amidst this backdrop, it is imperative for conservative foreign policy to adapt and effectively address emerging threats and trends in global security. In this exploration, we will delve into the intricacies of these challenges and their implications for conservative foreign policy, aiming to provide a comprehensive understanding of the conservative agenda in safeguarding national security interests.

How can conservative foreign policy effectively navigate the ever-changing landscape of global security to safeguard national interests and promote stability?

The question of navigating global security is not merely theoretical; it is a pressing concern with real-world implications. As the world becomes increasingly interconnected, traditional notions of security are being redefined, requiring a nuanced and forward-thinking approach to address both conventional and emerging threats effectively.

The central issue at hand is the dynamic nature of global security, characterized by a multitude of interconnected challenges such as terrorism, cyber threats, geopolitical tensions, and the proliferation of weapons of mass destruction. These challenges are not isolated; they often intersect and compound, creating complex and multifaceted security risks that demand a comprehensive and adaptable approach.

Conventional approaches often prioritize short-term solutions or rely on outdated strategies that may not effectively address the evolving nature of global security. There is a tendency to focus on singular threats without fully considering their interconnectedness, leading to fragmented and ineffective responses.

The conservative approach to these challenges lies in a comprehensive and proactive strategy that encompasses not only traditional security concerns but also emerging threats. This approach emphasizes the importance of alliances, diplomacy, military strength, and technological innovation in addressing security challenges while adapting to the ever-changing global landscape.

Imagine a world where national security is not just a concern for policymakers and military strategists but a shared responsibility for all citizens. The conservative approach to global security seeks to create a world where individuals can live free from the fear of conflict, terrorism, and instability, fostering a sense of security for future generations.

The evolving nature of global security has brought forth a myriad of threats that challenge the traditional paradigms of national security. From the rise of non-state actors to the growing influence of cyber warfare, the landscape of global security is increasingly complex and interconnected. In this environment, conservative foreign policy must adapt and innovate to effectively safeguard national interests and promote stability.

How can conservative foreign policy balance the imperatives of national security with the complexities of global interdependence in the 21st century?

The question of balancing national security with global interdependence is not a simple dichotomy but a nuanced and multifaceted challenge. In an interconnected world, the actions and decisions of one nation can have far-reaching implications, necessitating a delicate balance between protecting national interests and engaging with the global community.

The central issue lies in navigating the tension between safeguarding national sovereignty and participating in the interconnected global arena. This tension is further exacerbated by emerging threats such as transnational terrorism, cyber attacks, and the proliferation of weapons of mass destruction, which transcend traditional boundaries and demand a collaborative and forward-thinking approach.

Many approaches tend to oversimplify the complexities of global interdependence, either advocating for complete isolationism or unconditional engagement without fully accounting for the security implications. These polarized perspectives often fail to provide a comprehensive and pragmatic solution to the challenges posed by global interdependence.

The conservative approach to this intricate challenge lies in a balanced and pragmatic strategy that takes into account the imperatives of national security while recognizing the benefits of constructive engagement with the global community. This approach emphasizes the importance of alliances, diplomacy, economic strength, and a robust national defense in navigating the complexities of global interdependence.

The implications of global interdependence are not abstract concepts but tangible realities that shape the everyday lives of individuals and communities. By understanding the conservative approach to balancing national security with global interdependence, readers can gain insights that may inform their perspectives on foreign policy and global engagement.

Envision a world where nations collaborate and engage with one another without compromising their fundamental security interests, fostering a sense of mutual respect, stability, and prosperity. The conservative approach to global interdependence seeks to create a world where nations can coexist peacefully and thrive in an interconnected global community, preserving both security and prosperity for future generations.

The evolving nature of global security presents a compelling challenge for conservative foreign policy: how to navigate the complexities of global interdependence while safeguarding national security interests. In an era of interconnectedness, the conservative agenda must address this challenge with a forward-thinking and pragmatic approach that balances the imperatives of national security with the benefits of constructive engagement with the global community.

How can conservative foreign policy effectively mitigate the risks posed by emerging security threats while seizing the opportunities presented by global interdependence?

The question of mitigating risks and seizing opportunities in the context of global security is not merely theoretical; it is a practical imperative with significant implications for national interests and global stability. As the world becomes increasingly interconnected, the ability to navigate emerging threats and harness the benefits of global interdependence is crucial for conservative foreign policy.

The central issue at hand is the dynamic nature of emerging security threats, which demand a proactive and adaptable approach to mitigate risks effectively. From asymmetric warfare to cyber attacks, the landscape of security challenges is evolving rapidly, necessitating a comprehensive strategy that addresses both traditional and emerging threats.

Conventional approaches often focus on singular aspects of security threats or rely on outdated strategies that may not effectively address the complexities of emerging challenges. There is a tendency to overlook the interconnectedness of security risks, leading to fragmented and inadequate responses to the evolving landscape of global security.

The conservative approach to these challenges lies in a comprehensive and forward-thinking strategy that encompasses not only traditional security concerns but also emerging threats. This approach emphasizes the importance of leveraging alliances, technology, intelligence, and diplomacy to mitigate risks and seize opportunities in the context of global interdependence.

Envision a world where nations effectively navigate emerging security threats and harness the benefits of global interdependence, fostering a sense of security, stability, and prosperity for all. The conservative approach to global security seeks to create a world where emerging threats are effectively mitigated, and opportunities for collaboration and progress are seized, ensuring a better future for all.

The evolving landscape of global security presents a multifaceted challenge for conservative foreign policy, requiring a comprehensive and forward-thinking approach to safeguard national interests and promote stability amidst emerging threats and global interdependence. By embracing a pragmatic and balanced strategy, conservative foreign policy can navigate the complexities of global security, effectively mitigate risks, and seize opportunities to foster a secure, prosperous, and interconnected world.

Traditional Values and Social Conservatism

Defining Traditional Values

Healthy families are the bedrock of civilized, flourishing societies. As conservatives, we define and defend timeless family values rooted in biblical wisdom and human experience that offer the best chance for stability and human thriving.

The nuclear family model – centered around a loving marital partnership between a man and woman raising their biological or adopted children – represents an anthropological standard protecting dignity and nurturing virtue. This family structure mirrors nature's order, safeguards the sacred context for intimacy that produces children, and provides every child the biological mother and father figures needed for models of character development.

Strong families model commitment, unconditional love, patience and sacrificial service seasoned by affectionate discipline. The family is the first school of morality, the value and fragility of life, and shouldering duties towards vulnerable dependents while contributing within communities. As citizens, we must promote public policies that respect families' autonomy and social groups supporting healthy domestic life.

Conservatives firmly reject denigration of the nuclear family model by radical progressives seeking to broadly redefine family structures largely severed from traditional roles and relationships between men, women, biological parents and offspring. We oppose using law and public policy to arbitrarily validate any social grouping individuals may temporarily form or impose subjective identities confusing children's formative development.

Healthy families require members upholding ethical norms of sexual responsibility, prudent parenthood, fidelity and sanctity of life. Public role models should reinforce – not undermine through scandal – commitment, chastity and marital longevity. Stable families model faith, nurture conscience formation, and cement intergenerational continuity preserving community memory.

Conservatives support economic policies allowing families meeting material needs. We also stand against coercive population engineering through abortion or pressures against womanhood's singular gift in childbearing. Ever-experimenting welfare bureaucracies often exhibit hostility toward family integrity and moral ecology.

Conservatives celebrate the family's privileges and duties – centered around conjugal love and parental stewardship – that shape life's most important work. No institution undergirds flourishing communities as families living out timeless values.

Marriage and Family

MARRIAGE AND FAMILY have long been fundamental aspects of human society, serving as the cornerstone of stability, support, and growth. In conservative ideology, the institution of marriage and the traditional family unit are held in high regard, playing essential roles in shaping individuals and society as a whole. This chapter aims to explore conservative views on marriage, family, and the significance of traditional family structures in today's world.

Marriage, as viewed through a conservative lens, is often seen as a sacred and binding union between a man and a woman. It is revered as a foundational institution that provides stability, security, and a nurturing environment for raising children. Furthermore, the conservative perspective emphasizes the complementary nature of men and women within the marital relationship, with each gender bringing unique strengths and qualities to the partnership. This emphasis on complementarity is rooted in the belief that traditional gender roles contribute to the overall harmony and well-being of the family.

In addition to the marital relationship, the conservative view of family extends to the broader concept of the nuclear family, which typically includes a mother, a father, and their biological or adopted children. This traditional family structure is seen as the ideal environment for child-rearing, providing a stable and nurturing foundation for the physical, emotional, and psychological development of children. Conservative principles often stress the importance of parental involvement, guidance, and discipline in shaping the character and values of the next generation.

Furthermore, the role of marriage and family in providing a nurturing environment for children is exemplified in the timeless institution of the American family farm. For generations, family farms have served as the epitome of traditional family structures, with parents working alongside their children to cultivate the land and instill values of hard work, responsibility, and intergenerational cooperation. This enduring model of family-based agricultural enterprise not only sustains rural communities but also embodies the conservative ideal of familial unity and shared purpose.

While conservative views on marriage and family emphasize the traditional nuclear family as the ideal model, it is important to consider diverse family arrangements and their impact on individuals and society. From a conservative standpoint, recognizing and respecting alternative family structures does not diminish the value of traditional families but rather acknowledges the complexities of modern social dynamics. Single-parent households, blended families, and same-sex parenting arrangements are part of the contemporary social landscape, and while they may differ from the traditional model, they can still provide nurturing environments for children and contribute positively to society.

Supporting the conservative perspective on marriage and family are empirical data and research findings that underscore the benefits of traditional family structures. The U.S. Department of Health and Human Services reports that children in married, two-parent households are less likely to live in poverty and are more likely to have access to essential resources such as health care and education. Furthermore, longitudinal studies have demonstrated that children raised in intact, married families exhibit greater emotional resilience and are more likely to form stable, healthy relationships in adulthood.

In discussing conservative views on marriage and family, it is important to clarify the term "traditional family structure." This concept refers to the societal norm of a nuclear family consisting of a married heterosexual couple and their biological or adopted children. Traditional family structures are characterized by stability, mutual support, and a division of labor that often aligns with traditional gender roles. While this model may not encompass all modern family arrangements, it serves as a foundational reference point within conservative discourse on family values and societal well-being.

Conservative perspectives on marriage and family underscore the foundational roles of these institutions in shaping individuals and society. The traditional family unit, based on the marital bond between a man and a woman, is regarded as a fundamental building block of social stability and generational continuity. By recognizing the unique contributions of both parents and the value of stable, nurturing family environments, conservative ideology seeks to uphold the enduring significance of marriage and family in fostering a healthy and flourishing society. As we navigate the complexities of modern life, understanding and appreciating the conservative view on marriage and family can provide valuable insights into the enduring strengths of traditional family structures.

Religious Freedom and Faith

RELIGIOUS FREEDOM AND the role of faith in public life are pivotal elements of conservative ideology, emphasizing the preservation of individual liberties and the enduring influence of religious values in shaping societal norms. This chapter aims to delve into the conservative emphasis on protecting religious freedom and the significance of faith in public life, exploring their nuanced interplay and broader implications in contemporary society.

Religious freedom, enshrined in the First Amendment of the United States Constitution, holds profound significance within conservative discourse. It is viewed as a fundamental right that safeguards individuals and religious institutions from undue interference by the government, ensuring the autonomy to practice and express their faith without fear of persecution or censorship. This emphasis on religious liberty aligns with the conservative belief in limited government intervention, advocating for the protection of individual freedoms, including the freedom of conscience and religious expression.

Additionally, faith plays a central role in public life within conservative perspectives, influencing moral and ethical considerations that shape public policy and social discourse. The conservative emphasis on the Judeo-Christian heritage and traditional values underscores the enduring impact of faith-based principles on governance, law, and societal norms. The interplay between religious faith and public life is regarded as essential for upholding the moral fabric of society and preserving the cultural foundations that have historically guided Western civilization.

In examining the conservative stance on religious freedom and faith in public life, it is essential to establish the criteria for comparison, setting the parameters for analysis. This includes evaluating the legal protections and accommodations for religious practices, the impact of faith-based values on public policy, and the role of religious institutions in shaping societal values and community welfare.

Moreover, the criteria encompass the historical context of religious freedom and faith in public life, tracing their evolution and contemporary relevance amidst shifting social dynamics and cultural diversity. By considering these benchmarks, the following discussion will provide a comprehensive analysis of the conservative perspective on religious freedom and faith within the public sphere.

The conservative emphasis on religious freedom parallels its advocacy for individual liberties, emphasizing the protection of religious beliefs and practices from government intrusion. This commitment to religious freedom is underscored by efforts to safeguard the rights of individuals and religious organizations to exercise their faith in various domains, including education, healthcare, and the public square.

Furthermore, faith in public life is a cornerstone of conservative ideology, influencing policy debates and civic engagement. The infusion of religious values into public discourse is evident in conservative advocacy for policies aligned with traditional moral principles, such as the sanctity of life, the protection of religious conscience, and the promotion of family-centered initiatives. This direct comparison highlights the interconnectedness of religious freedom and faith in shaping the cultural and moral landscape of society.

While conservative ideology champions robust protections for religious freedom, contrasting perspectives often advocate for a more secular approach to public life, seeking to minimize the influence of religious values in governance and policy-making. This divergence underscores the nuanced tensions between accommodating diverse religious practices and beliefs while balancing the secular governance of public institutions. Additionally, contrasting perspectives may emphasize the separation of church and state as a means to uphold pluralism and prevent the imposition of specific religious doctrines within the public sphere.

In contrast, the conservative stance upholds the interplay between faith and public life, asserting that religious values contribute to the moral foundation of society and inform ethical considerations in public policy. This distinction underscores the conservative commitment to preserving the influence of faith-based principles in shaping societal norms and fostering a culture that upholds traditional values and moral standards.

The comparison and contrast of religious freedom and faith in public life offer profound insights into the broader implications of conservative ideology. The emphasis on religious freedom underscores the enduring commitment to safeguarding individual liberties and protecting the autonomy of religious institutions, reflecting a dedication to upholding the constitutional rights of all citizens, regardless of their faith traditions.

Furthermore, the interplay between faith and public life reveals the enduring influence of religious values in shaping societal norms, ethical considerations, and policy debates. Conservative perspectives highlight the integral role of faith-based principles in promoting social cohesion, moral integrity, and community welfare, underpinning the enduring significance of religious faith in public discourse.

In contemporary society, the conservative emphasis on religious freedom and faith holds significant relevance, especially amid debates surrounding religious accommodations, conscientious objection, and the role of faith-based organizations in providing essential social services. The intersection of religious freedom and public life continues to shape legal precedents, policy decisions, and cultural attitudes, underscoring the enduring impact of conservative principles on the protection of religious liberties and the preservation of faith-based values within the public sphere.

Moreover, the real-world relevance of religious freedom and faith in public life extends to global discussions on religious persecution, the protection of religious minorities, and the promotion of religious pluralism. Conservative perspectives advocate for the universal recognition of religious freedom as a fundamental human right, fostering dialogue and cooperation to uphold the diverse expressions of faith within the global community.

The conservative emphasis on religious freedom and faith in public life reflects a commitment to protecting individual liberties and upholding the enduring influence of religious values in shaping societal norms. By examining the nuances and broader implications of religious freedom and faith within the public sphere, conservative ideology provides valuable insights into the preservation of religious liberties and the enduring significance of faith-based principles in contemporary society. As we navigate the complexities of modern governance and cultural diversity, understanding and appreciating the conservative perspective on religious freedom and faith can enrich discussions on individual freedoms, moral foundations, and the enduring influence of faith in public life.

Pro-Life Movement

THE CONSERVATIVE AGENDA places significant emphasis on the pro-life movement and its stance on abortion, viewing the protection of innocent life as a fundamental moral imperative. This chapter aims to examine the conservative perspectives on abortion and the pro-life movement, delving into the nuanced considerations and broader implications that underpin this pivotal issue within conservative ideology.

The conservative perspective on the pro-life movement is rooted in the fundamental belief in the sanctity of human life from conception to natural death. This core principle underscores the intrinsic value and dignity of every human being, irrespective of age, development, or circumstances. The conservative ideology advocates for the protection of the unborn, considering abortion as a direct infringement upon the rights and worth of the most vulnerable members of society.

Conservative perspectives scrutinize the legal and ethical dimensions of abortion, engaging in rigorous discourse on the rights of the unborn, the implications of abortion on women's health and well-being, and the broader ethical considerations surrounding the termination of a developing human life. This multifaceted examination seeks to illuminate the complexities inherent in the abortion debate, navigating the intersection of individual autonomy, medical ethics, and societal responsibility.

Numerous studies and testimonies contribute to the conservative perspective on abortion, offering empirical evidence and personal narratives that underscore the profound impact of abortion on individuals, families, and society at large. Research on the psychological and emotional aftermath of abortion, as well as the development of the unborn child, provides substantial evidence that informs conservative viewpoints on the sanctity of human life and the ethical considerations surrounding abortion.

The conservative emphasis on the sanctity of human life translates into practical applications through advocacy for alternatives to abortion, such as adoption services, crisis pregnancy centers, and comprehensive support for expectant mothers facing challenging circumstances. This proactive approach aims to provide tangible resources and assistance to women and families, reinforcing the commitment to preserving life and offering compassionate alternatives to abortion.

As we transition to the next pivotal point within the conservative perspective on the pro-life movement, it is essential to maintain a comprehensive understanding of the multifaceted considerations that inform conservative ideology's approach to abortion and the protection of innocent life.

Conservative perspectives on the pro-life movement extend to the role of government and policy in safeguarding the rights of the unborn and promoting a culture that respects and protects all human life. This encompasses advocacy for legislative measures that align with the sanctity of human life, such as restrictions on late-term abortions, parental consent laws, and the allocation of public funds away from abortion providers. The conservative stance emphasizes the responsibility of government to enact policies that reflect the moral and ethical values of the society it represents.

The expansive discourse on the role of government and policy delves into the legislative, judicial, and executive branches' influence on shaping the legal landscape surrounding abortion. The conservative perspective underscores the importance of appointing judges and officials who uphold the principles of the sanctity of human life and prioritize policies that protect the unborn and support expectant mothers.

Legal precedents, constitutional interpretations, and testimonies from individuals impacted by abortion policies contribute to the evidentiary foundation of conservative perspectives on the role of government and policy in the pro-life movement. Court cases, legislative debates, and firsthand accounts of individuals affected by abortion regulations provide critical insights into the practical implications and ethical considerations of government involvement in the protection of human life.

The translation of conservative principles into practical applications involves grassroots activism, public education campaigns, and strategic initiatives aimed at fostering a culture that upholds the sanctity of human life. These practical applications seek to engage citizens, communities, and policymakers in dialogue and action that aligns with the conservative commitment to protecting the unborn and promoting policies that reflect the inherent worth of every human life.

As we navigate through the multifaceted landscape of conservative perspectives on the pro-life movement, the interconnected nature of these pivotal points underscores the comprehensive depth of conservative ideology's approach to abortion and the protection of innocent life.

Education and Moral Values

LET US JOURNEY BACK in time to the early development of education and the prominent role of moral values in shaping its foundations. Throughout history, education has been deeply intertwined with the transmission of moral and ethical principles, providing a framework for societal norms and values.

The ancient civilizations of Greece and Rome laid the groundwork for formal education, where moral virtues and civic duty were central to the curriculum. Philosophers such as Plato and Aristotle emphasized the importance of ethical education in shaping virtuous citizens capable of contributing to the well-being of the community. This historical context underscores the enduring link between education and moral values, a connection that has persisted through the centuries.

The Renaissance period marked a significant shift in educational philosophy, as humanist ideals and the revival of classical learning brought renewed attention to the moral and ethical dimensions of education. The emphasis on individual development and the pursuit of knowledge was accompanied by a renewed focus on character formation and the cultivation of moral virtues.

During the Enlightenment, the Age of Reason ushered in a period of intellectual and philosophical transformation. This era saw the emergence of educational reformers such as John Locke and Jean-Jacques Rousseau, who advocated for the integration of moral education into the curriculum to foster the development of rational and virtuous individuals capable of contributing to a just and enlightened society.

The Industrial Revolution and the subsequent rise of mass education systems brought about a shift in educational priorities. While the focus on practical skills and workforce readiness became paramount, the moral and ethical dimensions of education continued to be upheld as essential for the holistic development of individuals and the preservation of societal values.

Drawing clear lines from the historical context to current challenges, it is evident that the role of moral values in education has become increasingly complex in the modern era. The rapid advancement of technology, the globalization of information, and the evolving social landscape have presented new challenges in integrating moral education into contemporary curricula.

The proliferation of digital media and the internet has created unprecedented access to diverse perspectives and information, necessitating a critical examination of how moral values are conveyed and reinforced in the digital age. Furthermore, the increasingly multicultural and interconnected nature of society calls for a nuanced approach to moral education that is inclusive and reflective of diverse cultural and ethical perspectives.

Understanding the historical evolution of education and its intrinsic connection to moral values is essential in addressing modern-day challenges. The lessons gleaned from the past serve as a foundation for navigating the complexities of integrating moral education into the contemporary educational landscape.

By examining historical shifts in educational philosophy and the enduring emphasis on moral values, educators and policymakers can gain insight into effective strategies for promoting moral development and ethical reasoning among students. Furthermore, historical perspectives provide valuable context for engaging in meaningful dialogue about the role of moral education in addressing societal issues and nurturing responsible global citizens.

With a profound understanding of the historical interplay between education and moral values, we embark on a contemporary exploration of conservative approaches to education and the vital role of moral values in shaping curriculum and policies. This journey will unravel the multifaceted considerations and practical applications of conservative ideology in fostering moral education and upholding the timeless virtues that form the bedrock of a flourishing society.

Conservative Women's Movement

THE BACKDROP OF THE conservative women's movement is characterized by a landscape of evolving social and political dynamics. Against the backdrop of changing gender roles, shifting cultural norms, and ongoing debates on social issues, conservative women have emerged as influential voices advocating for traditional values and social conservatism. This movement has unfolded in various spheres, encompassing activism, policy advocacy, and grassroots mobilization to uphold principles that resonate with their vision of a well-ordered society.

The central figures in the conservative women's movement encompass a diverse array of leaders, activists, and supporters who have contributed to its growth and impact. Notable figures include political leaders, community organizers, scholars, and advocates who have championed causes related to family, faith, individual liberty, and limited government. These women come from different backgrounds, representing a spectrum of experiences and perspectives that inform their commitment to conservative principles.

The conservative women's movement has grappled with various challenges, including navigating societal expectations, overcoming stereotypes, and countering misconceptions about their advocacy. They have encountered resistance from those who question the compatibility of their perspectives with feminist ideals, and have had to address skepticism about the diversity of their movement and its relevance to broader gender equality issues.

In response to these challenges, conservative women have employed a multi-faceted approach to advance their goals. This has involved engaging in public discourse to articulate their viewpoints, fostering networks of support and mentorship, and actively participating in political and policy arenas to shape legislation and public initiatives that align with their values. Additionally, they have utilized digital platforms and media to amplify their voices and connect with like-minded individuals.

The outcomes of the conservative women's movement are reflected in its influence on public opinion, policy decisions, and cultural narratives. Through their efforts, conservative women have contributed to shaping public discourse on issues such as family values, religious freedom, and individual rights. They have also made significant strides in political representation, with a growing number of conservative women holding elected office and assuming leadership roles in various spheres of influence.

The conservative women's movement offers insights into the diverse expressions of feminism and the complexities of women's engagement in socio-political movements. Their experiences prompt reflection on the intersections of gender, ideology, and activism, challenging conventional narratives about the alignment of women's empowerment with specific political perspectives. It also invites scrutiny of the ways in which differing viewpoints on gender and societal roles are received and debated within broader feminist discourse.

The conservative women's movement intersects with broader themes of women's agency, ideological diversity, and the evolving landscape of gender politics. It underscores the significance of recognizing and engaging with diverse perspectives within feminist discourse, challenging monolithic portrayals of women's activism and advocacy. Furthermore, it prompts consideration of the impact of women's involvement in shaping societal values and policies across ideological spectrums.

As we contemplate the multifaceted nature of the conservative women's movement, it is imperative to recognize the depth and complexity of women's engagement in sociopolitical movements. How can inclusive dialogues and collaborations be fostered to embrace the diversity of women's perspectives and experiences in advancing shared goals for societal well-being and progress?

In exploring the conservative women's movement, we gain valuable insights into the diverse expressions of women's advocacy and the integral role of conservative women in shaping narratives, policies, and societal values. This case study serves as a testament to the breadth and depth of women's engagement in sociopolitical movements, challenging assumptions and prompting reflection on the intersections of gender, ideology, and activism. As we navigate the complexities of contemporary discourse, the voices and experiences of conservative women offer compelling contributions to the broader dialogue on women's agency and societal progress.

The Future of Traditional Values

IN THE WAKE OF SOCIETAL evolution, the promotion of traditional values has encountered both challenges and opportunities, necessitating a comprehensive examination of the strategies and solutions required to uphold these principles in a changing world. This exploration delves into the complexities of advocating for traditional values within contemporary society, outlining the potential consequences of neglecting these values and proposing practical solutions supported by evidence and projected outcomes.

The current landscape of societal dynamics is marked by a confluence of cultural shifts, technological advancements, and evolving perspectives on societal norms. In the midst of these changes, the preservation and promotion of traditional values have become increasingly pertinent, as they embody the foundational principles that have historically underpinned societal cohesion and well-being. Against the backdrop of rapid societal transformation, the necessity of upholding traditional values has emerged as a critical concern, warranting a deliberate and strategic approach to ensure their continuity and relevance.

The primary challenge lies in the potential erosion of traditional values amidst the currents of societal change. The increasing prevalence of individualism, relativism, and moral ambiguity has posed a significant threat to the preservation of traditional values, leading to their marginalization in public discourse and policymaking. This marginalization has the potential to diminish the moral fabric of society, engendering a culture of moral relativism that may erode the foundations of community, family, and ethical conduct.

If the erosion of traditional values is left unchecked, the consequences could manifest in multifaceted ways, impacting the fabric of society at individual, communal, and institutional levels. At an individual level, the absence of clear moral guidelines and ethical standards may lead to a sense of disorientation and moral crisis, diminishing the sense of purpose and cohesion within communities.

Furthermore, the breakdown of traditional values may contribute to the erosion of social capital and the fraying of communal bonds, diminishing trust and cooperation within society. Institutionally, the absence of traditional values may result in the formulation of policies and laws that lack a foundational moral compass, potentially leading to societal fragmentation and ethical ambiguity.

To address these challenges, a multifaceted approach is essential, encompassing educational initiatives, community engagement, and policy advocacy. Emphasizing the importance of ethical education and moral formation is crucial in cultivating an understanding and appreciation of traditional values, ensuring their continuity across generations. Additionally, fostering community-based initiatives that celebrate and uphold traditional values can contribute to the preservation of these principles within the fabric of society. Furthermore, proactive engagement in policy advocacy to integrate traditional values into public discourse and policymaking is imperative to ensure their recognition and influence in shaping the societal landscape.

The implementation of these solutions necessitates a concerted effort across various sectors of society, including educational institutions, community organizations, and policy advocacy groups. Educational initiatives should prioritize the integration of ethical education and character formation within curricula, fostering an understanding of the historical and societal significance of traditional values. Community engagement efforts should focus on celebrating and promoting traditional values through cultural events, intergenerational dialogue, and collaborative endeavors that reinforce the importance of these principles. Simultaneously, policy advocacy should strive to incorporate traditional values into legislative discussions and societal narratives, ensuring their representation in the formulation of laws and public policies.

Historical precedents and projected outcomes demonstrate the efficacy of initiatives aimed at preserving traditional values. Throughout history, societies that have prioritized the promotion of traditional values have exhibited greater societal cohesion, ethical resilience, and communal well-being. Furthermore, projections indicate that proactive measures to uphold traditional values can contribute to the cultivation of a more cohesive and morally grounded society, fostering a sense of purpose, belonging, and ethical responsibility among individuals and communities.

Alternative solutions to addressing the erosion of traditional values may encompass the utilization of media and digital platforms to disseminate narratives that underscore the significance and relevance of traditional values. Additionally, fostering interfaith and intercultural dialogues that emphasize the commonality of traditional values across diverse cultural and religious contexts can contribute to a broader societal appreciation of these principles.

The promotion of traditional values in an evolving society necessitates a concerted and strategic approach that encompasses educational, communal, and policy-oriented initiatives. By recognizing the potential consequences of neglecting these values and advocating for practical solutions grounded in evidence and projected outcomes, society can endeavor to safeguard the moral fabric that underpins communal well-being and societal coherence.

Individual Liberty and Personal Responsibility

The Importance of Individual Freedom

Among conservatism's most sacred principles is championing individual freedom. America's founding built upon the self-evident truth that liberty is every human's natural right within a justly ordered society. While balancing community solidarity, conservatives foremost celebrate sanctity of conscience, economic freedom, legal equality, and autonomy of civic institutions as bulwarks against tyranny.

Conscience rights prove paramount. The First Amendment codifies freedom of thought, religious exercise, speech and assembly. Without these, coercion and conformity supplant organically evolving social persuasion. Rigid ideological constraints also stifle creativity and productivity essential to prosperity. America guarantees citizens can freely choose religious affiliation or ethical beliefs informed by transcendent truths rather than temporally fashionable ideologies. This empowers our rich civil society and moral ecology.

Economic liberty is likewise indispensable, enabling individuals charting their family's course through enterprising initiative. Free markets efficiently match supply with demand while triggering innovations improving standards of living for all. Progress results from entrepreneurs taking risks after judiciously assessing local contexts, not central planners arrogantly imposing grand designs. Restraining bureaucracy preserves autonomy and just social relations between private property owners, laborers, consumers and communities.

Equal protection principles requiring impartial rule of law – not the whims of powerful men or mob passion – establish procedural justice and predictable order in which persons can exercise rights. Equality before the law enables reputations, families and livelihoods safe from arbitrary attacks. Such formal equity rejects transitory group hierarchies.

For communities to remain free, a vibrant civil society of autonomous churches, civic groups, schools, charities, cultural institutions and commerce must flourish between citizens and the state. Families in particular must retain sovereignty over childrearing. This diversity shields minorities while fostering participation, solidarity and experimentation with solutions to meet local needs.

A core conservative insight is recognizing how expanding state power inherently threatens freedom. Government properly protects natural rights and administers prudential regulation of markets for social well-being. But activism eroding personal responsibility, disestablishing community mediating structures, undermining markets' efficiency and dynamism, or zbureaucratizing cultural institutions kills freedom by a thousand paper cuts. America's unprecedented liberty required centuries of struggle against such incremental tyranny.

Conservatism cherishes the creativity source from free men and women. We advocate limited constitutional governance because human potential reaches its zenith when rights are grounded in moral truth and safeguarded for all. After tyranny is imposed, regaining such freedom proves immensely difficult. Our imperative is upholding guardrails so liberty long endures.

The Role of Government in Society

THE ROLE OF GOVERNMENT in society has long been a subject of debate and contention. From the conservative perspective, the primary function of government is to preserve individual liberty, ensuring that citizens have the freedom to pursue their goals and aspirations without undue interference. In this chapter, we will delve into the conservative viewpoint on the role of government, examining the principles and values that underpin this perspective.

Conservatives believe that the role of government should be limited, with a focus on protecting the natural rights of individuals. This entails upholding the rule of law, safeguarding property rights, and maintaining a system of justice that ensures all citizens are treated fairly and equally. The conservative philosophy emphasizes the importance of personal responsibility and self-reliance, advocating for minimal government intervention in the lives of its citizens. By limiting the reach of government, individuals are empowered to make their own choices and pursue their own paths, free from excessive regulation and control.

To illustrate the concept of limited government, consider the case of a small business owner. A conservative approach to governance would entail reducing bureaucratic red tape and onerous regulations that hinder the entrepreneur's ability to operate and expand their business. By allowing the free market to operate with minimal interference, the business owner can innovate, create jobs, and contribute to economic growth. This example underscores the conservative belief in individual initiative and the power of free enterprise when unencumbered by excessive government intrusion.

While the conservative viewpoint emphasizes limited government, it is important to recognize that other political ideologies may espouse different roles for government in society. For example, liberal perspectives often advocate for a more active government role in addressing social and economic inequalities, providing a safety net for those in need, and regulating industries to protect consumers and the environment. Understanding these contrasting viewpoints fosters a well-rounded understanding of the complexities surrounding the role of government in society.

Empirical evidence supports the conservative position on limited government. Studies have shown that countries with less government intervention in their economies tend to experience higher levels of economic growth and prosperity. Furthermore, historical examples, such as the collapse of centrally planned economies in the 20th century, demonstrate the failures of excessive government control and the benefits of free-market principles. These data and facts provide compelling support for the conservative approach to the role of government.

In discussing the role of government, it is important to clarify the term "limited government." This concept refers to a government that is constrained by a constitution or legal framework, with defined powers and limitations on its authority. Limited government does not imply an absence of governance, but rather a deliberate restraint on the scope and reach of governmental powers, particularly in relation to individual liberties and economic activities.

The conservative perspective on the role of government centers on the preservation of individual liberty through limited government intervention. By upholding the principles of personal responsibility, free markets, and the rule of law, conservatives believe that individuals can thrive and prosper in a society that values freedom and opportunity. Understanding the conservative viewpoint on the role of government provides valuable insight into the diverse perspectives that shape our political discourse and governance.

The Foundational Principles of Limited Government

BUILDING UPON THE CONSERVATIVE perspective on the role of government, it is essential to explore the foundational principles that underpin the concept of limited government. By examining these principles in depth, we can gain a deeper understanding of the philosophical framework that guides conservative thought on governance and individual freedom.

At the core of limited government are the principles of natural rights and the social contract. Conservatives assert that individuals possess inherent rights, such as life, liberty, and property, which are not granted by the government but are intrinsic to human existence. The social contract theory posits that individuals consent to be governed in exchange for the protection of their natural rights, thereby establishing the legitimate authority of the government. However, this authority is not absolute and must be circumscribed to prevent encroachment on individual liberties.

To illustrate the principles of natural rights and the social contract, consider the analogy of property ownership. In a society governed by the principles of limited government, individuals have the right to acquire and possess property without unwarranted government seizure or interference. This right is fundamental to the preservation of individual liberty and is grounded in the natural rights of self-determination and autonomy. By respecting property rights, the government upholds its end of the social contract, thereby fulfilling its legitimate role in preserving individual freedoms.

While the principles of natural rights and the social contract form the bedrock of limited government, alternative perspectives may challenge these foundational concepts. Some political ideologies prioritize collective rights over individual rights, advocating for expansive government powers to address societal inequities. Understanding these divergent viewpoints enriches the discourse on governance and encourages critical analysis of the underlying principles that shape public policy and legal frameworks.

Historical evidence supports the enduring relevance of the principles of limited government. The American founding fathers, deeply influenced by the ideas of John Locke and other Enlightenment thinkers, enshrined the protection of natural rights and limited government in the United States Constitution. The success of the American experiment in self-governance and the preservation of individual liberties stands as a testament to the enduring value of these principles in fostering a free and prosperous society.

In delving into the foundational principles of limited government, it is important to clarify the concept of natural rights. Natural rights are rights that are considered inherent to human beings, independent of government or societal recognition. These rights are often articulated as encompassing the rights to life, liberty, and property, forming the basis for the protection of individual freedoms from governmental overreach.

The foundational principles of limited government, rooted in the concepts of natural rights and the social contract, provide a principled framework for understanding the conservative approach to governance. By upholding these principles, conservatives seek to ensure that the role of government is circumscribed, thereby preserving individual liberty and fostering a society built on the values of freedom, responsibility, and self-determination.

The Rule of Law and Individual Liberty

CENTRAL TO THE CONSERVATIVE perspective on the role of government is the principle of the rule of law as a safeguard for individual liberty. This chapter explores the significance of the rule of law in preserving the rights and freedoms of citizens, emphasizing its critical role in limiting government power and ensuring justice and fairness for all.

Conservatives assert that the rule of law serves as a bulwark against arbitrary governmental actions and encroachments on individual liberties. By establishing clear legal frameworks and impartial judicial processes, the rule of law constrains the exercise of governmental authority, preventing the abuse of power and protecting citizens from unjust treatment. Under the rule of law, all individuals, including government officials, are subject to the same legal standards, thereby upholding the principle of equality before the law.

To illustrate the importance of the rule of law, consider the scenario of property rights protection. In a society governed by the rule of law, individuals have recourse to legal remedies if their property rights are infringed upon by the government or other entities. This legal protection provides a safeguard against arbitrary confiscation or seizure of property, reinforcing the fundamental principle of individual liberty and private ownership. The rule of law ensures that citizens can seek redress through established legal channels, thereby holding the government accountable for any overreach or violation of rights.

While the conservative perspective emphasizes the rule of law as a check on government power, alternative viewpoints may question the efficacy of legal constraints in addressing societal injustices. Some critics argue that the rule of law, if improperly applied, may perpetuate systemic inequalities or fail to address the needs of marginalized communities. Understanding these divergent perspectives encourages a nuanced examination of the complexities surrounding the rule of law and its implications for individual liberty.

Empirical evidence demonstrates the correlation between the rule of law and societal well-being. Countries that uphold the rule of law consistently exhibit higher levels of economic development, political stability, and respect for individual rights. Moreover, legal systems that prioritize the rule of law provide a foundation for transparent and accountable governance, fostering public trust in institutions and promoting a conducive environment for economic growth and innovation.

The rule of law stands as a cornerstone of the conservative vision for limited government, serving as a means to protect individual liberty and constrain governmental overreach. By upholding the rule of law, conservatives seek to ensure that the rights and freedoms of citizens are safeguarded, fostering a society where justice, fairness, and equal treatment under the law are foundational principles of governance.

Individual Responsibility and the Limits of Government Intervention

A FUNDAMENTAL TENET of conservative thought on the role of government is the emphasis on individual responsibility and the corollary limits of government intervention in the lives of citizens. This chapter delves into the concept of individual responsibility as a guiding principle for limited government, highlighting the rationale behind minimizing governmental intrusion in personal affairs.

Conservatives contend that individuals bear a primary responsibility for their own well-being and success, promoting self-reliance and autonomy as essential virtues. By embracing personal responsibility, individuals are empowered to make choices, take risks, and reap the rewards of

The Limits of Government

TO EMBARK ON THIS EXPLORATION, readers are encouraged to have an open mind and a willingness to critically analyze the role of government in society. Familiarity with the basic tenets of conservative philosophy and an interest in political theory and governance will further enrich the understanding of the material presented.

The conservative viewpoint on limited government is rooted in the conviction that governmental powers should be circumscribed to preserve individual liberty and autonomy. By examining the principles of limited government, we aim to elucidate the underlying values and philosophical foundations that inform conservative perspectives on governance and individual freedom.

The concept of limited government, as espoused by conservatives, centers on the idea that governmental authority should be restrained to prevent encroachment on the rights and liberties of individuals. This principle is underpinned by a belief in the inherent rights of individuals and the necessity of a social contract that delineates the legitimate role of government in protecting these rights. The conservative approach to governance emphasizes personal responsibility, self-reliance, and free market principles to foster a society where individuals have the freedom to pursue their goals and aspirations without undue interference.

Conservatives assert that limited government is essential for creating an environment where individuals can exercise their autonomy and make choices free from excessive regulation and control. By reducing bureaucratic red tape and onerous regulations, conservatives advocate for empowering individuals to innovate, create wealth, and contribute to economic growth. This approach is grounded in the belief that free enterprise, when unencumbered by excessive government intrusion, leads to greater prosperity and opportunity for all members of society.

As we navigate the discussion on limited government, it is important to approach the material with a critical and inquisitive mindset. While exploring the conservative perspective, it is valuable to consider alternative viewpoints and engage in thoughtful analysis of the complexities surrounding the role of government in society. Additionally, acknowledging the diversity of political ideologies and the multifaceted nature of governance can enrich the understanding of the subject matter.

As we delve into the conservative belief in limited government, it is imperative to scrutinize the underlying principles and values that shape this perspective. By examining the implications of limited government on personal freedom and societal well-being, we aim to foster a nuanced understanding of the conservative agenda and its impact on the governance of modern societies.

Personal Responsibility and Self-Reliance

AS WE CONTINUE OUR exploration of the conservative agenda, we now turn our attention to the fundamental principles of personal responsibility and self-reliance. These principles are deeply ingrained in conservative ideology, shaping the approach to governance, individual empowerment, and societal progress. In this chapter, we will delve into the compelling question of personal responsibility and self-reliance, providing context and a unique solution to forge a deep, emotional connection with the reader.

To fully comprehend the conservative emphasis on personal responsibility and self-reliance, it is essential to frame the question within the broader discourse of governance and individual empowerment. The significance of these principles extends beyond mere rhetoric; they form the bedrock of conservative philosophy and inform the approach to addressing societal challenges and fostering individual growth.

The central issue that underpins the discussion of personal responsibility and self-reliance lies in the contemporary societal shift towards dependency on external entities, particularly the government, to address individual needs and challenges. This shift has led to a diminishing sense of personal agency and accountability, eroding the fabric of self-sufficiency and resilience that is vital for societal progress.

In contemporary society, there is a pervasive trend towards placing the onus of individual well-being and progress on external factors, be it governmental programs, social initiatives, or institutional support. This conventional approach often overlooks the transformative power of personal responsibility and self-reliance, relegating these principles to the periphery of societal discourse.

The conservative perspective offers a unique solution to the challenges posed by the erosion of personal responsibility and self-reliance. It advocates for a paradigm shift towards fostering a culture of accountability, resilience, and self-sufficiency, empowering individuals to take charge of their lives and contribute meaningfully to the betterment of society.

Now, let us journey into the heart of personal responsibility and self-reliance, exploring the profound impact of these principles on individual empowerment, societal resilience, and the preservation of freedom and opportunity.

The conservative belief in personal responsibility and self-reliance stems from a profound understanding of human nature and the dynamics of societal progress. At its core, this belief emphasizes the inherent capacity of individuals to navigate the complexities of life, overcome challenges, and pursue their aspirations with determination and resilience. It rejects the notion of perpetual dependence on external support systems, advocating instead for the cultivation of a robust sense of personal agency and accountability.

Central to the conservative ethos is the recognition that individuals are not merely passive recipients of societal provisions or entitlements, but active agents capable of shaping their destinies through conscientious decision-making and industrious effort. This ethos aligns with the foundational principles of limited government, as it seeks to minimize the intrusion of external entities in the lives of individuals, allowing for the organic development of personal responsibility and self-reliance.

In contemporary discourse, the erosion of personal responsibility and self-reliance is often attributed to a myriad of factors, including the expansion of welfare state programs, the normalization of entitlement mentalities, and the perpetuation of victimhood narratives. While these factors undoubtedly play a role in shaping societal attitudes, the conservative perspective offers a compelling counter-narrative, emphasizing the transformative power of instilling and fostering personal responsibility and self-reliance at both the individual and societal levels.

To fully appreciate the implications of personal responsibility and self-reliance, we must first acknowledge the multifaceted nature of these principles and their far-reaching impact on various dimensions of human existence.

At the individual level, personal responsibility entails the conscientious acknowledgment of one's obligations, duties, and choices, coupled with the willingness to be accountable for the outcomes of those choices. It encompasses a proactive mindset that transcends mere reaction to external circumstances, empowering individuals to take ownership of their lives and actively shape their trajectories. This mindset catalyzes personal growth, resilience, and adaptability, enabling individuals to navigate life's challenges with fortitude and determination.

Similarly, self-reliance embodies the ethos of self-sufficiency and autonomy, encouraging individuals to cultivate the skills, resources, and competencies necessary to thrive in a dynamic and unpredictable world. It fosters a spirit of independence and industriousness, enabling individuals to harness their innate potential and contribute meaningfully to their communities and societies. Self-reliance is not a call for isolation or forsaking communal support; rather, it is a testament to the empowerment that arises from the adept utilization of one's capabilities and resources.

When these principles are embraced at the societal level, they engender a culture of resilience, innovation, and community cohesion. A society built on the foundations of personal responsibility and self-reliance is characterized by individuals who are driven to excel, collaborate, and uplift one another, fostering a dynamic environment where innovation and progress flourish. This societal ethos mitigates the tendency towards dependence on centralized authorities, engendering a spirit of civic engagement and mutual support that transcends the limitations of top-down governance.

The conservative emphasis on personal responsibility and self-reliance is not merely a theoretical construct; it finds practical application in numerous facets of societal organization and governance. From economic policies that prioritize entrepreneurship and individual initiative to social initiatives that encourage volunteerism and community involvement, the conservative agenda actively promotes the cultivation of personal responsibility and self-reliance as cornerstones of societal well-being and progress.

In the realm of education, the conservative perspective advocates for the inculcation of personal responsibility and self-reliance as foundational principles of character development and academic achievement. By instilling a sense of agency and accountability in students, educational institutions can foster a culture of ambition, resilience, and ethical decision-making, equipping the next generation with the tools necessary to thrive in an ever-evolving world.

Furthermore, the conservative approach to social welfare programs emphasizes the importance of empowering individuals to transcend cycles of dependency and embrace self-sufficiency. Rather than perpetuating a culture of entitlement and perpetual reliance on governmental assistance, conservative policies seek to provide a springboard for individuals to regain control of their lives, pursue meaningful employment, and contribute to the prosperity of their communities.

In the realm of public discourse and civic engagement, the conservative emphasis on personal responsibility and self-reliance serves as a rallying cry for active citizenship and community involvement. By fostering a culture that celebrates individual agency and initiative, conservative ideology encourages citizens to take an active role in shaping the trajectory of their communities, promoting grassroots solutions to local challenges, and fostering a sense of collective responsibility for the common good.

The conservative agenda for personal responsibility and self-reliance is not without its challenges and criticisms. Critics often contend that the emphasis on these principles neglects the systemic barriers and inequalities that impede individuals from exercising agency and achieving self-sufficiency. They argue that the conservative approach places undue burden on marginalized communities and overlooks the structural impediments that hinder equitable access to opportunity and resources.

To address these concerns, it is imperative to underscore that the conservative agenda for personal responsibility and self-reliance does not operate in isolation from the broader societal context. Rather, it necessitates a holistic approach that acknowledges the systemic challenges faced by certain segments of the population and endeavors to address them through targeted policies and initiatives. The promotion of personal responsibility and self-reliance should be accompanied by efforts to dismantle institutional barriers, expand access to educational and economic opportunities, and foster inclusive environments where all individuals can thrive.

Moreover, the conservative viewpoint on personal responsibility and self-reliance does not preclude the existence of a safety net or support systems for those facing dire circumstances or temporary setbacks. Rather, it advocates for a balanced approach that upholds the dignity of individuals while providing a hand up, not merely a handout, to facilitate their transition towards self-sufficiency and empowerment.

The conservative emphasis on personal responsibility and self-reliance represents a profound call to action for individuals and societies to reclaim agency, resilience, and purpose. It challenges the prevailing narrative of dependency and entitlement, offering a compelling vision of empowerment and progress rooted in the transformative power of individual initiative and accountability.

As we navigate the complexities of societal governance and individual liberty, the principles of personal responsibility and self-reliance stand as beacons of hope and resilience, guiding us towards a future where each individual is empowered to pursue their aspirations, contribute to the common good, and live a life of dignity and fulfillment. Let us embrace the transformative potential of these principles and forge a society where personal responsibility and self-reliance are not mere ideals, but lived realities that enrich the human experience and propel us towards a brighter tomorrow.

The Welfare State and Dependency

THE CONSERVATIVE AGENDA is deeply rooted in the principles of personal responsibility and self-reliance, shaping the ideological landscape of governance, individual empowerment, and societal progress. As we delve into the heart of this agenda, our focus now turns to the welfare state and the potential dangers of dependency. In this chapter, we will explore the contrasting ideologies of conservative views on the welfare state and the perils of dependency, offering insights into their nuances and broader implications.

The welfare state and dependency are significant concepts that have garnered significant attention in societal discourse. The welfare state refers to a system where the government plays a key role in providing social assistance and support to its citizens, particularly in areas such as healthcare, education, and social security. Dependency, on the other hand, denotes the reliance of individuals or communities on external aid or support, often leading to a diminished sense of personal agency and self-sufficiency.

The rationale behind comparing the welfare state and dependency is to shed light on the potential impact of expansive social welfare programs on individual and societal resilience. By examining the conservative perspective on these subjects, we aim to offer insights into the balance between societal support and personal accountability, as well as the implications of prolonged dependence on external provisions.

In analyzing the welfare state and dependency, we will set benchmarks that consider the balance between social welfare provisions and the cultivation of personal responsibility. The parameters for comparison will encompass the impact on individual agency, the role of government in societal well-being, and the long-term implications of dependency on societal progress.

The welfare state, as conceived in many modern societies, is designed to provide a safety net for individuals facing hardships, ensuring access to essential services and support. Similarly, the concept of dependency often arises from a reliance on these safety nets, leading to a diminished sense of personal responsibility and self-reliance. Both phenomena intersect at the juncture of societal support and individual accountability.

While the welfare state aims to address societal needs and mitigate disparities, dependency can lead to a culture of entitlement and reduced incentive for personal growth and achievement. The contrast between the two lies in the balance between societal assistance and the preservation of individual agency, underscoring the nuanced interplay between support systems and self-sufficiency.

Delving into the comparison and contrast of the welfare state and dependency reveals the delicate balance between societal welfare provisions and the preservation of individual agency. It offers insights into the potential ramifications of prolonged dependency on societal resilience and the cultivation of a culture of self-reliance.

The welfare state, a hallmark of many modern societies, embodies the commitment to providing essential social services and support to citizens, particularly those facing economic hardship, health challenges, or other adversities. Its inception was rooted in the acknowledgment of societal inequalities and the imperative to ensure equitable access to fundamental resources and opportunities. However, the conservative critique of the welfare state centers on the potential unintended consequences of extensive government intervention in societal welfare.

From the conservative viewpoint, the welfare state, when excessively expansive, has the potential to foster a culture of dependency, wherein individuals become reliant on governmental provisions and support, leading to a diminished sense of personal agency and self-sufficiency. This critique posits that while the intention of the welfare state is to offer a safety net for those in need, the proliferation of support programs can inadvertently disincentivize individual initiative and responsibility, perpetuating a cycle of reliance on external assistance.

The dangers of dependency, as illuminated by conservative analysis, are multifaceted. Prolonged reliance on governmental support can erode the intrinsic motivation and drive for self-improvement, as individuals may become accustomed to external provisions and lose the impetus to actively pursue their aspirations and self-sufficiency. Moreover, the perpetuation of dependency can lead to a societal mindset that places the onus of progress and well-being solely on governmental interventions, diminishing the role of individual and communal agency in addressing societal challenges.

In contrast to the welfare state's emphasis on societal support, the conservative emphasis on personal responsibility and self-reliance underscores the transformative power of individual agency and accountability. By fostering a culture that celebrates self-sufficiency and resilience, the conservative ideology seeks to mitigate the potential pitfalls of dependency and cultivate an environment where individuals are empowered to actively shape their destinies and contribute meaningfully to societal progress.

The nuanced interplay between the welfare state and dependency becomes particularly salient when considering the real-world implications of extensive social welfare programs. While these programs undoubtedly serve as lifelines for individuals facing adversities, the conservative analysis prompts critical reflection on the potential long-term impact of dependency on individual motivation, societal cohesion, and economic dynamism.

In contemporary society, the prevalence of government assistance programs and entitlement mentalities has perpetuated a culture of dependency that poses challenges to the preservation of individual agency and societal resilience. The conservative critique serves as a call to reevaluate the balance between societal support and individual accountability, emphasizing the need to foster a culture that encourages self-reliance and self-improvement while providing essential safety nets for those in need.

The conservative analysis of the welfare state and dependency serves as a holistic framework for evaluating the broader implications of societal support systems and the cultivation of individual agency. By delving into the intricate nuances of these subjects, we gain a deeper appreciation for the delicate equilibrium between societal welfare provisions and the preservation of personal responsibility, offering insights that transcend theoretical discourse and resonate with the realities of contemporary governance and societal dynamics.

The conservative critique of the welfare state and dependency underscores the imperative of striking a balance between societal support and the preservation of individual agency. It challenges the prevailing narrative of entitlement and prolonged reliance on external provisions, offering a compelling vision of empowerment and progress rooted in the transformative power of personal responsibility and self-reliance. As we navigate the complexities of societal governance and individual liberty, the conservative perspective serves as a thought-provoking lens through which to examine the interplay between societal welfare provisions and the cultivation of a culture of resilience and self-sufficiency.

The juxtaposition of the welfare state and dependency illuminates the multifaceted nature of societal support systems and their potential impact on individual motivation and societal progress. By critically evaluating the conservative critique, we gain valuable insights into the delicate equilibrium between societal welfare provisions and the preservation of personal responsibility, guiding us towards a future where individuals are empowered to pursue their aspirations, contribute to the common good, and live a life of dignity and fulfillment. Let us embrace the transformative potential of personal responsibility and self-reliance, forging a society where the balance between societal support and individual agency is not merely an aspiration, but a lived reality that enriches the human experience and propels us towards a brighter tomorrow.

The conservative agenda, as exemplified through the analysis of the welfare state and dependency, offers a compelling framework for navigating the complexities of governance and societal progress, rooted in the principles of personal responsibility and self-reliance. As we continue our exploration of conservative ideology, we will further examine the intersection of these principles with contemporary societal challenges, offering a nuanced perspective on governance, individual empowerment, and the preservation of freedom and opportunity.

Criminal Justice and Individual Rights

THE CONSERVATIVE APPROACH to criminal justice and the balance between individual rights and public safety is a complex and nuanced subject that lies at the intersection of law, ethics, and societal well-being. This chapter seeks to delve into the multifaceted landscape of conservative perspectives on criminal justice, examining the principles that underpin the preservation of individual rights while ensuring the maintenance of law and order for the greater good of society.

The conservative stance on criminal justice asserts that a robust legal framework must exist to protect individual rights while simultaneously upholding public safety and societal order. This claim emphasizes the importance of a balanced approach that respects the rights of the accused, promotes rehabilitation, and prioritizes the safety and security of law-abiding citizens.

The foundational evidence supporting this claim lies in the conservative emphasis on the rule of law, the presumption of innocence, and the recognition of individual agency and accountability. Conservative principles advocate for fair and impartial legal proceedings that safeguard the rights of the accused and ensure that justice is administered equitably.

The conservative perspective on criminal justice underscores the significance of due process, the right to a fair trial, and the avoidance of undue government intrusion into the lives of individuals. It emphasizes the necessity of evidence-based decision-making and the avoidance of arbitrary or discriminatory practices in law enforcement and judicial proceedings.

Critics of the conservative approach to criminal justice may argue that an unwavering focus on individual rights could potentially undermine efforts to maintain public safety and address the needs of crime victims. They may contend that stringent protection of individual rights might inadvertently create loopholes for the perpetrators of crime and hinder law enforcement efforts.

In response to these counterarguments, the conservative perspective emphasizes that the balanced preservation of individual rights and the pursuit of public safety are not mutually exclusive. It asserts that a well-functioning legal system is capable of upholding both objectives concurrently, ensuring justice for all while safeguarding the welfare of law-abiding citizens.

Further substantiation of the conservative claim can be found in the emphasis on criminal justice reform and rehabilitation programs that aim to address the root causes of criminal behavior, thus promoting societal reintegration and reducing recidivism rates.

The conservative approach to criminal justice underscores the imperative of upholding individual rights within the framework of a legal system that prioritizes public safety and societal order. It advocates for a balanced approach that respects the rights of the accused, promotes rehabilitation, and ensures the safety and security of law-abiding citizens, thereby fostering a harmonious coexistence of individual rights and collective well-being within the domain of criminal justice.

The Future of Individual Liberty

IN THE RAPIDLY EVOLVING landscape of technology and social interconnectedness, the future of individual liberty faces unprecedented challenges. The digital age has ushered in a wealth of opportunities for personal expression and empowerment, yet it has also given rise to concerns regarding privacy, surveillance, and the potential erosion of fundamental rights. As society grapples with the implications of artificial intelligence, biometric data collection, and the increasing integration of technology into everyday life, the preservation of individual liberty has become a pressing issue demanding careful consideration and proactive solutions.

The primary issue at hand revolves around the balance between harnessing the benefits of technological advancement and safeguarding the individual's right to privacy, autonomy, and freedom from undue intrusion. The proliferation of surveillance technologies, data mining, and algorithmic decision-making poses a significant threat to individual liberty, potentially undermining the very essence of personal agency and self-determination.

Failure to address these challenges could lead to a society where individual autonomy is compromised, where personal choices are influenced by external forces beyond one's awareness or control. The erosion of individual liberty in the digital age may result in a loss of privacy, limited freedom of expression, and the potential manipulation of personal data for commercial or political gain. Furthermore, unchecked technological encroachment on individual rights may lead to a decline in trust, social cohesion, and democratic principles, posing a threat to the very fabric of civil society.

To mitigate these challenges and safeguard individual liberty in the digital age, a multi-faceted approach is necessary. This approach should encompass legal and regulatory frameworks, technological design principles, and societal awareness initiatives that collectively work to uphold and protect individual rights within the digital landscape.

First, legal and regulatory measures must be enacted to establish clear boundaries for the collection, use, and sharing of personal data. These measures should include robust privacy laws, stringent data protection regulations, and mechanisms for holding accountable those who infringe upon individual privacy rights. Additionally, the implementation of transparency requirements for data processing, and the provision of meaningful consent for data collection and usage, are essential steps in empowering individuals to retain control over their personal information.

Second, the design and deployment of technology should prioritize privacy and user autonomy. This necessitates the integration of privacy-enhancing technologies, such as end-to-end encryption and data minimization practices, to limit the exposure of personal data to unwarranted access or misuse. Moreover, the promotion of user-centric design methodologies, where individuals have agency over their digital interactions and are empowered to make informed choices, is crucial in upholding individual liberty in the digital sphere.

Third, societal awareness initiatives and digital literacy programs should be established to educate individuals about their rights in the digital realm and to foster a culture of responsible data stewardship. By enhancing public understanding of the implications of digital technologies on individual liberty, individuals can become more discerning and assertive in safeguarding their own privacy and autonomy.

Examples from jurisdictions that have enacted comprehensive data protection laws and empowered regulatory bodies to enforce privacy regulations demonstrate the efficacy of legal and regulatory measures in preserving individual liberty in the digital age. These measures have resulted in increased accountability for data handling practices, greater transparency in data processing activities, and heightened awareness among individuals regarding their rights and options for data protection.

Furthermore, technological innovations that prioritize privacy and user autonomy, such as decentralized identity management systems and privacy-preserving data analytics, have showcased the potential for technological solutions to bolster individual liberty in the digital sphere. These innovations have enabled individuals to retain control over their personal data and digital interactions, thereby enhancing their agency in the digital domain.

Societal awareness initiatives and digital literacy programs have also yielded positive outcomes, empowering individuals to make informed decisions about their digital footprint and fostering a culture of digital responsibility and privacy advocacy. By equipping individuals with the knowledge and tools to protect their privacy rights, these initiatives have contributed to a more privacy-conscious and assertive populace in the face of digital challenges.

While the proposed approach emphasizes the interplay of legal, technological, and societal measures, alternative solutions may include the development of international standards for data protection and privacy, fostering global cooperation in addressing the cross-border implications of digital rights. Additionally, the establishment of independent oversight bodies tasked with auditing and monitoring the ethical use of emerging technologies, such as artificial intelligence and biometric systems, could serve as a complementary measure to reinforce individual liberty in the digital age.

The future of individual liberty hinges on proactive measures that address the challenges posed by technological advancements, data proliferation, and digital interconnectedness. By enacting comprehensive legal and regulatory frameworks, prioritizing privacy-enhancing technological designs, and fostering societal awareness and digital literacy, a harmonious coexistence of technological progress and individual liberty can be achieved, ensuring that the digital age remains a realm of empowerment, autonomy, and respect for fundamental rights.

Family and Community Values

The Importance of Strong Families

The conservative belief in the importance of strong families is deeply rooted in the foundation of society and the well-being of individuals. Understanding the key words related to this belief is essential for engaging with the content and appreciating the profound impact that strong families have on the fabric of our communities.

1. Family: The conservative belief in the importance of strong families rests on the understanding that the family unit is the cornerstone of society. It serves as the primary source of emotional support, guidance, and socialization for individuals. The family provides a nurturing environment for the development of children, instilling values, discipline, and a sense of identity. Furthermore, strong families contribute to the stability and cohesion of communities, fostering social harmony and collective well-being.

2. Stability: Within the context of strong families, stability refers to the consistent and secure environment that supports the physical, emotional, and psychological needs of its members. This stability is essential for fostering trust, confidence, and a sense of belonging within the family. It provides a strong foundation for personal growth and resilience, enabling individuals to navigate life's challenges with a sense of security and certainty.

3. Values: Conservative ideology places great emphasis on the transmission of traditional values within the family unit. These values encompass principles such as respect, integrity, hard work,

and self-discipline, which are considered essential for the moral and ethical development of individuals. Strong families serve as the primary source for imparting these values, instilling a sense of responsibility, empathy, and self-reliance in their members.

4. Responsibility: The conservative view of strong families emphasizes the importance of individual and collective responsibility. Family members are expected to fulfill their roles and obligations, contributing to the well-being and functioning of the household. This sense of responsibility extends beyond the immediate family, as strong families are also seen as active participants in the broader community, promoting social cohesion and civic engagement.

5. Resilience: Strong families are characterized by their ability to adapt and thrive in the face of adversity. Conservative ideology emphasizes the importance of resilience as a key trait instilled within the family unit. By nurturing resilience, families equip their members with the strength and determination to overcome challenges, setbacks, and hardships. This resilience fosters a sense of unity and mutual support within the family, reinforcing bonds and promoting emotional well-being.

6. Support: The provision of support within strong families is integral to their functioning and cohesiveness. This support encompasses emotional nurturing, practical assistance, and financial stability. Strong families prioritize mutual care and solidarity, creating a nurturing environment where individuals feel valued, understood, and empowered to face life's trials with confidence and endurance.

The significance of strong families in conservative ideology resonates with real-world experiences and familiar concepts, as it reflects the universal human need for connection, security, and belonging. The family serves as a microcosm of society, embodying values, responsibilities, and resilience that are essential for the well-being of individuals and communities. The timeless principles of love, sacrifice, and mutual support that characterize strong families are echoed in countless cultural narratives, literature, and personal experiences, underscoring their enduring relevance and impact on human existence.

The conservative belief in the importance of strong families is rooted in a profound understanding of the essential elements that contribute to their strength and resilience. By embracing the key terms of family, stability, values, responsibility, resilience, and support, individuals can appreciate the profound impact that strong families have on shaping character, fostering well-being, and sustaining communities. This understanding provides a framework for engaging with the conservative agenda's commitment to upholding and preserving the fundamental institution of the family, recognizing its pivotal role in nurturing individuals and safeguarding the fabric of society.

Traditional Gender Roles

TRADITIONAL GENDER roles have long been a defining aspect of conservative ideology, shaping societal expectations and family dynamics. In this chapter, we will delve into the concept of traditional gender roles, exploring their historical significance, their impact on family structures, and the varying perspectives surrounding these roles within conservative thought. By examining the underlying principles, practical examples, and societal implications, we aim to provide a comprehensive understanding of traditional gender roles and their enduring influence on family dynamics.

Traditional gender roles refer to the prescribed social and behavioral norms that dictate the expected roles, responsibilities, and behaviors of individuals based on their gender. In a traditional framework, men are often expected to assume the role of the primary breadwinner, protector, and decision-maker within the family, while women are typically assigned the responsibilities of caregiving, nurturing, and maintaining the household. These roles are deeply rooted in historical and cultural contexts, reflecting traditional notions of masculinity and femininity that have persisted across generations.

The concept of traditional gender roles encompasses a complex interplay of societal expectations, cultural norms, and historical traditions. It shapes the division of labor, decision-making processes, and power dynamics within the family unit, influencing the distribution of responsibilities and the allocation of resources. Moreover, traditional gender roles have historically reinforced distinct expectations for men and women, perpetuating stereotypes and limiting individual autonomy based on gender identity.

To illustrate the impact of traditional gender roles on family dynamics, consider the following scenario: In a traditional household, the husband is expected to work outside the home, providing financial support for the family, while the wife is responsible for managing domestic duties, caring for children, and supporting her husband's endeavors. This division of labor reflects the traditional gender roles that have historically shaped family structures, perpetuating distinct spheres of influence and reinforcing societal expectations regarding gender-specific roles.

Similarly, traditional gender roles may manifest in cultural practices and rituals that reinforce gendered expectations. For instance, certain religious or cultural traditions may dictate specific roles for men and women within the family, prescribing distinct behaviors and responsibilities based on gender. These examples highlight the practical implications of traditional gender roles within the context of family dynamics, underscoring their influence on individual experiences and familial relationships.

When examining traditional gender roles from a conservative perspective, it is essential to acknowledge the diverse viewpoints that exist within conservative thought. While some conservatives uphold traditional gender roles as essential for preserving family values, others may advocate for a more flexible approach that allows individuals to embrace roles based on personal choice rather than societal expectations. The spectrum of conservative viewpoints on traditional gender roles reflects the complexity of this topic within the conservative agenda, encompassing traditionalists, moderates, and progressive voices.

Furthermore, traditional gender roles are often scrutinized and debated within broader societal discourse, with feminists and gender equality advocates challenging the entrenched norms that perpetuate gender-based expectations. Their perspectives intersect with conservative ideologies, prompting discussions on individual autonomy, gender equality, and the evolving dynamics of family structures in contemporary society. By exploring these differing perspectives, we gain a comprehensive understanding of the multidimensional nature of traditional gender roles and their impact on family dynamics.

Incorporating relevant data and statistics provides empirical support for understanding the impact of traditional gender roles on family dynamics. Studies have indicated that adherence to traditional gender roles can influence marital satisfaction, division of labor, and economic outcomes within families. For example, research has shown that households adhering to traditional gender roles may exhibit distinct patterns of decision-making, resource allocation, and career opportunities based on gender, contributing to disparities in income and household dynamics.

Moreover, data on gender-based expectations and social norms shed light on the prevalence of traditional gender roles within diverse cultural and societal contexts. By examining these empirical findings, we can discern the tangible implications of traditional gender roles on family structures, individual well-being, and social dynamics, enriching our understanding of the multifaceted impact of these roles within conservative ideology.

Within the discourse surrounding traditional gender roles, it is essential to demystify complex terms and jargon to ensure clarity and accessibility. Concepts such as gender essentialism, gender identity, and gender expression are integral to understanding the nuanced nature of traditional gender roles within the conservative agenda. Gender essentialism refers to the belief that inherent, immutable differences exist between men and women, shaping their behaviors and roles within society. Understanding this concept illuminates the foundational principles that underpin traditional gender roles, informing discussions on the preservation of distinct gendered expectations within conservative thought.

Likewise, acknowledging the complexities of gender identity and expression provides a broader framework for exploring traditional gender roles, recognizing the diversity of experiences and perspectives that intersect with gendered expectations. By clarifying these complex terms, we foster a more inclusive and informed dialogue on traditional gender roles and their implications for family dynamics within conservative ideology.

Traditional gender roles are deeply entrenched in conservative thought, influencing family dynamics and societal expectations regarding gendered behaviors and responsibilities. By examining the historical significance, practical examples, diverse perspectives, empirical data, and complex terms related to traditional gender roles, we gain a comprehensive understanding of their enduring impact on family structures. This exploration provides key takeaways regarding the complexities of traditional gender roles within conservative ideology, emphasizing the need for nuanced discussions that encompass diverse viewpoints and empirical evidence. Understanding traditional gender roles is essential for engaging with the conservative agenda's emphasis on family values and societal dynamics, recognizing the intricate interplay of tradition, culture, and individual autonomy within family structures.

Community Engagement and Volunteering

THERE ARE NO SPECIFIC materials or prerequisites needed to engage in community service or volunteering efforts. However, a willingness to contribute to the betterment of one's community and a spirit of generosity are invaluable qualities for effective engagement.

Community engagement and volunteering are integral components of the conservative agenda, reflecting a commitment to civic responsibility, social cohesion, and the empowerment of local communities. The process of community engagement involves actively participating in initiatives, events, or projects that aim to improve the welfare of the community, while volunteering encompasses offering one's time and skills for the betterment of others without expecting monetary compensation.

Community engagement serves as a means to foster a sense of shared responsibility and solidarity within local communities. Whether through organized events, charitable initiatives, or collaborative projects, community engagement reflects the conservative principle of self-reliance and mutual support. It provides individuals with the opportunity to contribute to the betterment of their surroundings and actively participate in shaping a positive social environment.

Volunteering encompasses a diverse range of activities, including but not limited to, serving at local shelters, participating in environmental cleanup efforts, mentoring youth, or assisting in community development projects. By identifying areas for volunteering that align with one's interests and skills, individuals can make meaningful contributions to their communities while gaining personal fulfillment and a sense of purpose.

Effective community engagement often involves building partnerships and collaborations with local organizations, non-profits, and community groups. By forging alliances with like-minded entities, individuals and conservative groups can amplify their impact and leverage resources to address community needs more comprehensively.

Mobilizing resources, whether financial, material, or human, is a crucial aspect of community engagement and volunteering. Conservative principles emphasize the importance of decentralized, community-driven solutions, advocating for the active involvement of individuals and local entities in addressing societal challenges.

Community engagement provides an avenue for promoting civic education and empowerment, instilling a sense of ownership and accountability within communities. Through volunteering and active participation, individuals can educate and empower fellow community members, fostering a culture of self-reliance and collective responsibility.

- Prioritize Long-Term Impact: When engaging in community initiatives and volunteering efforts, consider the long-term impact of the activities. Seek sustainable solutions and initiatives that address root causes rather than temporary fixes.

- Align with Community Needs: It is essential to align volunteering efforts with the genuine needs of the community. Conduct thorough research and engage in dialogue with community members to ensure that initiatives are responsive to actual needs and concerns.

- Avoid Patronizing Approaches: Volunteering should be approached with humility and respect for local knowledge and expertise. Avoid imposing external solutions or adopting a patronizing attitude towards the community.

Successful community engagement and volunteering efforts can be validated through tangible outcomes such as improved community infrastructure, enhanced social cohesion, and the empowerment of marginalized groups within the community. Additionally, feedback from community members and stakeholders serves as a valuable validation of the impact of such initiatives.

In the event of challenges or setbacks in community engagement and volunteering efforts, it is important to reassess the alignment of initiatives with community needs, seek feedback from stakeholders, and adjust strategies to better address the genuine concerns of the community.

Community engagement and volunteering embody the conservative commitment to civic responsibility, social solidarity, and the empowerment of local communities. By actively participating in initiatives and projects that aim to improve the welfare of the community, individuals and conservative groups contribute to the preservation of community values and the advancement of societal well-being. Through sustained engagement and volunteering, conservatives uphold the principles of self-reliance, mutual support, and grassroots empowerment, fostering resilient and vibrant communities.

Faith-Based Organizations

FAITH-BASED ORGANIZATIONS have long been integral to the social fabric of communities, providing a vital foundation for promoting family and community values. In this case study, we delve into the role of a local faith-based organization in a suburban community, exploring the challenges they faced, the strategies they employed, and the impactful results they achieved in fostering strong family and community values.

The central figure in this case study is the Grace Community Church, a prominent faith-based organization deeply rooted in the suburban community of Oakridge. Established over three decades ago, the church has played an instrumental role in providing spiritual guidance and support to its members while also actively engaging in various community outreach programs. Reverend Michael Johnson, the charismatic and compassionate leader of the church, has been a driving force behind the organization's efforts to strengthen family and community values in Oakridge.

The Oakridge community, much like many suburban areas, faced a growing sense of disconnection and isolation among its residents. Families were struggling to find meaningful connections and support systems, and the prevalence of social issues such as substance abuse and mental health challenges was on the rise. The Grace Community Church recognized the pressing need to address these issues and sought to revitalize a sense of unity, purpose, and support within the community.

To tackle the challenge at hand, the church adopted a multifaceted approach that encompassed both spiritual and practical initiatives. Reverend Johnson and the church's leadership recognized the importance of providing holistic support to families and individuals in need. They initiated a series of targeted programs designed to strengthen family bonds, offer support for mental and emotional well-being, and create avenues for meaningful community engagement.

One of the key initiatives was the establishment of a comprehensive family support center within the church premises. This center provided counseling services, parenting workshops, and support groups for individuals dealing with various personal and family-related challenges. Additionally, the church organized regular community gatherings, picnics, and events that aimed to foster a sense of belonging and connectedness among residents.

The impact of the church's efforts was profound and far-reaching. Families who had previously felt isolated and unsupported found a welcoming and nurturing environment within the church community. The family support center became a beacon of hope, offering much-needed guidance and assistance to those grappling with personal and familial difficulties. The community gatherings and events facilitated by the church became vibrant occasions for residents to come together, share experiences, and form lasting bonds.

Empowered by the support and resources provided by the church, individuals and families began to experience positive transformations in their lives. The prevalence of substance abuse and mental health struggles within the community notably decreased as a result of the proactive interventions and support offered by the Grace Community Church.

This case study underscores the indispensable role that faith-based organizations can play in promoting family and community values. The success of the Grace Community Church in addressing the pressing needs of the Oakridge community serves as a testament to the potential impact of such organizations. However, it also raises important reflections on the broader societal recognition of the vital role that faith-based organizations can play in fostering resilient and cohesive communities.

Critically, the case study prompts a consideration of the potential limitations and challenges that faith-based organizations may encounter in their efforts to promote family and community values. It invites a nuanced reflection on the intersection of religious principles, societal inclusivity, and the diverse needs of communities.

The success of the Grace Community Church in nurturing family and community values serves as a microcosm of the broader narrative of the conservative agenda. It exemplifies the fundamental conservative principle of community empowerment and the value of localized, grassroots initiatives in addressing societal challenges. By recognizing and supporting the pivotal role of faith-based organizations, the conservative agenda embraces the mobilization of community resources and values in fostering social cohesion and resilience.

As we conclude this case study, we are prompted to consider the potential for further engagement and collaboration between faith-based organizations and broader community initiatives. How can the lessons learned from the Grace Community Church be extrapolated to inspire similar endeavors in diverse communities, and how can the support for such organizations be integrated into the fabric of societal governance and policy-making?

In exploring the role of faith-based organizations in promoting family and community values, we not only recognize their profound impact but also emphasize the imperative of embracing diverse sources of community empowerment and support within the conservative agenda.

Strengthening Marriage and Relationships

COMMUNICATION SERVES as the bedrock of any healthy relationship. Conservative strategies emphasize the importance of fostering open, honest, and empathetic communication between partners. By prioritizing communication, couples can navigate challenges, express their needs, and build a deeper understanding of each other's perspectives.

Effective communication entails active listening, empathy, and the willingness to engage in constructive dialogue. Conservative principles underscore the value of respectful discourse and the avoidance of divisive language or behaviors that may erode the foundation of a relationship.

Research studies have consistently highlighted the positive correlation between strong communication skills and relationship satisfaction. Testimonials from couples who have benefitted from improved communication underscore the transformative impact it has had on their marriages.

Conservative strategies advocate for the incorporation of communication skills workshops and resources within community and faith-based organizations. By equipping couples with the tools for effective communication, the broader community can witness the strengthening of marital bonds and the promotion of healthy relationship dynamics.

Transitioning from the focus on communication, we shift our attention to the significance of embracing traditional values and role models in nurturing enduring marriages and relationships.

Conservative approaches emphasize the appreciation of traditional values and role models that exemplify enduring and principled relationships. By celebrating and promoting these values, communities can provide a strong foundation for the formation and sustenance of healthy marriages and relationships.

Traditional values such as commitment, integrity, and mutual respect serve as guiding principles for couples navigating the complexities of modern relationships. By embracing these values, individuals are empowered to uphold the sanctity of their commitments and honor the significance of their relationships.

Historical and contemporary examples of couples who have embodied these traditional values and role models stand as testaments to the enduring strength and resilience of relationships rooted in conservative principles.

Community initiatives and educational programs that espouse the celebration of traditional values and role models can cultivate a cultural environment that values and upholds the sanctity of marriage and relationships. By infusing these values into the fabric of society, communities can nurture an ethos that prioritizes enduring and principled relationships.

The Role of Government in Supporting Families

FAMILIES FORM THE BEDROCK of society, providing a nurturing environment for individuals to grow, learn, and thrive. Conservative strategies regarding the role of government in supporting families are deeply rooted in the belief that strong families are essential for the flourishing of communities. In this chapter, we will explore key conservative principles and approaches aimed at bolstering the familial structure and fostering resilience within families.

At the core of conservative ideologies is the emphasis on parental responsibility and empowerment. Conservative approaches prioritize the role of parents as the primary influencers in their children's lives, recognizing the profound impact of parental involvement on the well-being and development of the next generation.

Parental responsibility encompasses not only the provision of physical necessities but also the cultivation of a nurturing and supportive environment for children to thrive. Conservative principles underscore the importance of instilling moral and ethical values within the family unit, fostering discipline, and nurturing resilience in children.

Studies have consistently demonstrated the positive outcomes associated with parental involvement in children's lives, including higher academic achievement, improved social skills, and enhanced emotional well-being. Testimonials from families who have embraced conservative principles of parental responsibility and empowerment further emphasize the transformative impact on their children's development.Conservative strategies advocate for the implementation of parenting workshops and resources within communities, equipping parents with the knowledge and skills necessary to fulfill their role effectively. By empowering parents, the broader community can witness the positive ripple effects on familial stability and the well-being of children.

Transitioning from the focus on parental responsibility, we shift our attention to the significance of advocating for family-focused policies and programs that uphold the sanctity of the familial unit.

Conservative principles underscore the importance of tailored policies and programs that prioritize the needs and well-being of families. By advocating for family-focused initiatives, governments can play a pivotal role in creating an environment conducive to familial stability and flourishing.

Family-focused policies encompass a wide array of measures, including tax incentives for families, accessible childcare options, and support for parental leave. These initiatives aim to alleviate financial burdens on families, promote work-life balance, and strengthen the familial bond.

Historical and contemporary examples of successful family-focused policies and programs highlight their positive impact on family well-being and community cohesion. Testimonials from families benefiting from such initiatives serve as compelling evidence of the tangible improvements in their quality of life.

Conservative strategies advocate for the implementation of targeted policies that recognize and support the diverse needs of families, including single-parent households, military families, and families with children with special needs. By tailoring support to specific familial circumstances, governments can demonstrate their commitment to upholding family values and promoting stability.

Now, let us delve into the essence of conservative approaches to government involvement in supporting families and the delicate balance between personal responsibility and social safety nets.

The purpose of this analysis is to illuminate the nuanced interplay between government support for families and the preservation of individual agency and accountability. By examining the intersection of conservative principles and the role of government, we seek to unravel the complexities inherent in addressing familial needs while upholding the fundamental tenets of personal responsibility and self-reliance.

The benchmarks for comparison lie in evaluating the efficacy of government support in maintaining familial stability and well-being, while concurrently safeguarding the autonomy and self-sufficiency of individuals and families. We will assess the balance between targeted interventions and the preservation of individual agency within the framework of conservative ideologies.

Conservative principles advocate for a limited but strategic role for government in supporting families, emphasizing the importance of empowering individuals to take personal responsibility for their familial obligations. By promoting self-reliance and minimizing government intrusion, conservatives aim to foster a culture of independence and self-sufficiency within families.

Simultaneously, governments are urged to provide targeted support for vulnerable families facing significant challenges, including economic hardship, healthcare needs, and access to quality education. This duality reflects the conservative commitment to preserving individual agency while recognizing the necessity of social safety nets for those facing genuine hardships.

In contrast, progressive approaches often advocate for more expansive government involvement in family support, advocating for comprehensive social welfare programs and extensive regulatory frameworks. While prioritizing the alleviation of societal inequities and systemic barriers, progressive ideologies may risk undermining the principles of personal responsibility and self-reliance, potentially fostering dependency on government assistance.

Graphical representations can effectively delineate the varying degrees of government involvement in family support across conservative and progressive paradigms, visually depicting the balance between targeted interventions and individual agency within each approach.

The comparison sheds light on the delicate equilibrium that conservative ideologies seek to maintain, balancing the imperative of familial self-sufficiency with the recognition of genuine need for government assistance. By preserving individual agency and responsibility, conservative approaches aim to cultivate a culture of resilience and independence within families, while concurrently acknowledging the necessity of targeted support for those facing adversity.

The contemporary landscape bears testimony to the relevance of this comparison, as governments grapple with the challenge of addressing familial needs while upholding conservative principles of self-reliance. The ongoing discourse surrounding welfare reform, childcare provisions, and healthcare accessibility underscores the enduring relevance of evaluating the role of government in supporting families through a conservative lens.

The conservative approach to government support for families reflects a nuanced balance between personal responsibility and social safety nets, rooted in the preservation of individual agency and familial self-sufficiency. This analysis illuminates the intricacies of governmental involvement in family support within the framework of conservative ideologies, providing insights into the enduring principles that underpin familial resilience and societal cohesion.

The Future of Family and Community Values

AS WE EMBARK ON THIS journey to explore the future of family and community values, it is imperative to recognize the pivotal role that strong families and resilient communities play in the fabric of society. The shifting dynamics of the modern world have presented both challenges and opportunities in promoting the core values that form the foundation of familial and communal well-being. In this chapter, we will delve into the multifaceted landscape of contemporary society, outlining the challenges faced by families and communities and proposing practical solutions that align with conservative principles.

The contemporary societal landscape is marked by rapid changes, characterized by technological advancements, evolving family structures, and shifting cultural norms. These transformations have given rise to a myriad of challenges that impact the stability and flourishing of families and communities. It is within this complex milieu that we must navigate the intricate interplay between tradition and progress, seeking to preserve the timeless values that underpin strong families and resilient communities while adapting to the demands of the modern era.

One of the primary challenges facing families and communities in the 21st century is the erosion of traditional values and the weakening of familial and communal bonds. The pervasive influence of digital connectivity, coupled with the fast-paced nature of contemporary life, has led to a gradual dilution of interpersonal connections and a decline in the prioritization of familial and communal well-being. This trend has contributed to a sense of disconnection and alienation, posing a threat to the cohesive fabric of society.

The potential consequences of neglecting the preservation and promotion of family and community values are far-reaching. In the absence of robust familial and communal support systems, individuals may experience heightened levels of isolation and mental health challenges. Moreover, the breakdown of familial and communal ties can exacerbate social fragmentation, leading to a diminished sense of belonging and collective purpose. Left unaddressed, these repercussions can permeate various aspects of society, contributing to an overall decline in societal well-being and resilience.

To address the challenges posed to family and community values, it is imperative to embrace a multifaceted approach that aligns with conservative principles. Central to this approach is the emphasis on the preservation of traditional values and the nurturing of strong familial and communal bonds. By prioritizing the cultivation of resilience, empathy, and mutual support within families and communities, conservative strategies aim to fortify the foundational pillars of society.

The implementation of solutions to bolster family and community values necessitates a concerted effort across various domains. Educational institutions, community organizations, and governmental bodies play pivotal roles in fostering an environment that upholds and promotes the importance of family and community values. Initiatives aimed at strengthening family relationships, fostering intergenerational connections, and cultivating community cohesion through shared activities and support networks are essential components of the implementation process.

Historical evidence and projections underscore the efficacy of conservative strategies in revitalizing family and community values.

Societies that have prioritized the preservation of traditional values and the promotion of familial and communal well-being have witnessed tangible improvements in social cohesion, mental well-being, and intergenerational continuity. By showcasing these outcomes, we gain valuable insights into the transformative power of aligning with conservative principles in safeguarding the future of family and community values.

While conservative strategies offer a robust framework for addressing the challenges facing family and community values, it is essential to acknowledge the existence of alternative solutions. Diverse perspectives and approaches enrich the discourse surrounding familial and communal well-being, presenting opportunities for collaborative efforts that harness the strengths of various ideologies to achieve a shared goal of nurturing strong families and resilient communities.

Education Reform

The Role of Education in Society

Education is a fundamental pillar of conservative ideology, emphasizing the importance of individual responsibility and self-improvement. It is viewed as the cornerstone of personal success and societal progress, providing individuals with the knowledge and skills necessary to contribute meaningfully to their communities and the wider society. Throughout history, conservative thinkers have emphasized the role of education in shaping a well-functioning and prosperous society. This chapter delves into the conservative belief in the significance of education, exploring its multifaceted impact on both the individual and the broader societal framework.

Education, as understood within the conservative framework, encompasses the process of acquiring knowledge, skills, and values through formal instruction, informal learning, and life experiences. It is a lifelong pursuit that nurtures intellectual growth, critical thinking, and civic engagement.

In the conservative context, education is defined as the systematic and purposeful transmission of knowledge and values that equips individuals with the tools needed to navigate the complexities of modern life and contribute positively to their communities.

The key elements of education within conservative ideology include the cultivation of critical thinking, moral and ethical development, and the acquisition of practical skills that prepare individuals for the workforce. This approach emphasizes the importance of character formation and the transmission of cultural heritage to future generations.

The concept of education has deep roots in human history, with its origins dating back to ancient civilizations. The word "education" itself is derived from the Latin word "educare," meaning to "bring up" or "rear." Throughout history, education has been recognized as a means of transmitting knowledge, preserving cultural traditions, and preparing individuals for their roles within society.

Conservative ideology situates education within the broader framework of societal development and progress. It is seen as an essential component for fostering a well-informed and responsible citizenry, promoting social cohesion, and ensuring the continuity of cultural values and traditions.

The conservative emphasis on education is exemplified in the support for school choice initiatives, charter schools, and homeschooling, which provide families with options to tailor their children's education to their specific needs and values. Additionally, conservative policymakers often advocate for vocational training programs and apprenticeships to equip individuals with practical skills that align with the demands of the labor market.

One common misconception about the conservative view on education is that it prioritizes traditional academic subjects at the expense of practical skills and vocational training. In reality, conservatives recognize the value of both traditional academic disciplines and practical training, seeking to provide individuals with a well-rounded education that prepares them for diverse career paths and life pursuits.

The conservative belief in the importance of education is deeply rooted in the conviction that a well-educated populace is essential for the preservation of individual liberties and the flourishing of a free society. By equipping individuals with the knowledge, skills, and virtues necessary to thrive, education becomes a catalyst for personal empowerment and societal advancement. As such, conservative thinkers and policymakers continue to champion educational initiatives that uphold these principles, recognizing education as a vital instrument for fostering a prosperous and flourishing society.

School Choice and Vouchers

SCHOOL CHOICE AND THE use of vouchers have been central to conservative educational policy, reflecting a commitment to expanding educational options for families and promoting competition and innovation within the education system. This chapter aims to provide a comprehensive exploration of the conservative support for school choice and vouchers, delving into the underlying principles, practical implications, and potential impact on educational outcomes.

School choice, as advocated by conservatives, refers to the ability of parents to select the most suitable educational environment for their children, whether it be traditional public schools, charter schools, private schools, or homeschooling. Vouchers, in this context, are government-issued certificates that parents can use to subsidize the cost of private school tuition or other educational expenses. This approach is underpinned by the belief that empowering parents with the freedom to choose the best educational setting for their children fosters competition, drives improvement, and better aligns the education system with the diverse needs and values of families.

Conservative proponents of school choice and vouchers argue that these mechanisms promote parental empowerment, as families are no longer bound by residential school assignments and are instead able to prioritize their children's educational needs and values. By introducing market forces into the educational landscape, school choice and vouchers are seen as catalysts for innovation and improvement, as schools are incentivized to compete for students by offering high-quality educational programs and services.

To illustrate the impact of school choice and vouchers, consider the case of Milwaukee, Wisconsin, which implemented one of the earliest and most extensive voucher programs in the United States. The Milwaukee Parental Choice Program, established in 1990, allows low-income families to use vouchers to attend private schools, including religious institutions. Proponents of the program argue that it has expanded educational opportunities for disadvantaged students, leading to improved academic outcomes and higher graduation rates.

Furthermore, the proliferation of charter schools, which are publicly funded but operate independently, has provided additional options for families seeking alternative educational models. Charter schools often emphasize specialized curricula, innovative teaching methods, and greater flexibility in decision-making, offering parents diverse educational choices outside the traditional public school system.

While conservative proponents laud the benefits of school choice and vouchers, critics express concerns about potential drawbacks and equity issues. Some argue that these policies may exacerbate educational inequality by diverting resources away from traditional public schools, particularly in low-income communities, and perpetuating a two-tiered system that disproportionately benefits affluent families. Additionally, opponents highlight the risk of selective admissions and exclusionary practices in private schools, which could further marginalize vulnerable student populations.

From a broader ideological perspective, detractors question the reliance on market-based solutions in education, expressing reservations about the commodification of schooling and the potential erosion of the public education system. These critics advocate for comprehensive investments in traditional public schools, equitable funding mechanisms, and efforts to address systemic challenges rather than embracing market-oriented reforms.

To substantiate the impact of school choice and vouchers, empirical evidence from various studies and analyses can be referenced. Research on voucher programs in cities like New York, Washington, D.C., and New Orleans has yielded mixed findings, with some studies reporting modest gains in student achievement and others indicating negligible or negative effects. Such divergent outcomes underscore the complexity of evaluating the efficacy of school choice and voucher policies, highlighting the need for nuanced assessments that consider contextual factors and implementation variations.

Furthermore, data on parental satisfaction and engagement in school choice initiatives can provide insights into the perceived benefits and challenges experienced by families navigating educational options. Understanding the preferences and experiences of parents, particularly those from underserved communities, is essential for comprehensively evaluating the impact of school choice and vouchers on educational access and quality.

In discussing the nuances of school choice and vouchers, it is important to clarify key terms such as educational savings accounts (ESAs), tax-credit scholarships, and opportunity scholarships, which represent additional mechanisms for expanding educational choice. ESAs, for instance, allow families to use state funds to cover various education-related expenses, including tuition, tutoring, and educational materials. Similarly, tax-credit scholarships enable individuals and corporations to receive tax credits for donations to scholarship-granting organizations, which in turn provide financial assistance to students attending private schools.

The conservative support for school choice and vouchers reflects a commitment to enhancing educational opportunities, fostering innovation, and empowering parents to make informed decisions about their children's education. While proponents emphasize the benefits of increased choice and competition, it is essential to consider the potential impact on equity, student outcomes, and the broader educational landscape. By engaging with diverse perspectives and empirical evidence, a comprehensive understanding of school choice and vouchers can inform ongoing discussions about the future of education and the pursuit of educational excellence for all students.

Curriculum and Textbook Standards

THE GOAL OF CONSERVATIVE efforts to influence curriculum and textbook standards is to ensure that educational materials align with conservative values, providing students with a balanced and accurate understanding of history, civics, and social issues.

To achieve this goal, conservative advocates would need to collaborate with educators, policymakers, and textbook publishers to influence the content and presentation of curriculum materials and textbooks. They would also need to be well-versed in the specific content and standards of the subjects in question.

In the pursuit of influencing curriculum and textbook standards, conservative advocates would engage in a multi-faceted approach that involves engaging with educational institutions, participating in policy discussions, and collaborating with content creators to ensure that conservative perspectives are adequately represented in educational materials.

- Conservative advocates would seek to engage with school boards, educational administrators, and teachers to advocate for the inclusion of conservative principles in curriculum development. This could involve providing input during curriculum review processes, offering resources and expertise, and proposing specific content recommendations.

- Conservative advocates would actively participate in policy discussions at the local, state, and national levels to influence the adoption and implementation of curriculum and textbook standards that reflect conservative values. This may involve lobbying policymakers, providing expert testimony, and collaborating with like-minded organizations to advocate for specific content requirements.

- Conservative advocates would collaborate with textbook publishers, content creators, and educational technology providers to ensure that conservative perspectives are accurately represented in textbooks, digital resources, and educational materials. This could involve reviewing and providing feedback on draft materials, offering expertise on specific subject matter, and advocating for the inclusion of diverse viewpoints.

- When engaging with educational institutions, it is important for conservative advocates to build relationships with educators and administrators, approaching discussions with a spirit of collaboration and constructive dialogue.

- In policy discussions, it is crucial for conservative advocates to present evidence-based arguments and articulate the educational value of including conservative perspectives in curriculum and textbook standards.

- When collaborating with content creators, conservative advocates should be prepared to provide specific recommendations and examples of content that aligns with conservative values, while also being open to constructive feedback and compromise.

Conservative advocates can validate the impact of their efforts by monitoring changes in curriculum and textbook standards, assessing the inclusion of conservative perspectives in educational materials, and gathering feedback from educators and students about the impact of these changes on their learning experiences.

In the event of resistance or pushback against efforts to influence curriculum and textbook standards, conservative advocates may need to engage in sustained advocacy, build broader coalitions of support, and leverage public opinion to advocate for the inclusion of conservative values in educational materials.

Conservative efforts to influence curriculum and textbook standards are driven by a commitment to ensuring that students receive a balanced and accurate education that reflects conservative values. By engaging with educational institutions, participating in policy discussions, and collaborating with content creators, conservative advocates can contribute to shaping the educational landscape to align with their principles. Through ongoing monitoring and validation of their efforts, they can ensure that conservative perspectives are effectively integrated into curriculum and textbook standards, contributing to a more comprehensive and diverse educational experience for students.

JACK DONAHUE

Teacher Tenure and Performance

IN THE REALM OF EDUCATION policy, the issue of teacher tenure and performance evaluation has been a subject of fervent debate, with conservative voices advocating for significant reforms to the current system. Teacher tenure, which grants educators a level of job security after a probationary period, has come under scrutiny due to concerns about its impact on teacher quality and student outcomes. Conservative views emphasize the importance of performance-based evaluations as a means to ensure that educators are held accountable for their effectiveness in the classroom. This chapter delves into the conservative perspective on teacher tenure and performance, exploring the rationale behind their stance and the implications of their proposed reforms.

Conservative advocates assert that the current tenure system creates barriers to removing underperforming teachers, leading to detrimental effects on student achievement. They propose that implementing performance-based evaluations would provide a more effective means of assessing and improving teacher quality, ultimately benefiting students and the education system as a whole.

One of the primary arguments put forth by conservative advocates is the correlation between teacher quality and student outcomes. Research studies have consistently demonstrated the impact that effective teachers have on student learning, with high-quality instruction leading to improved academic performance and long-term success. Conversely, the presence of underperforming teachers has been shown to hinder student progress and contribute to educational disparities, particularly in disadvantaged communities.

In examining the relationship between teacher quality and student achievement, studies have revealed that students who are taught by highly effective teachers experience greater academic growth and are better positioned for future success. Furthermore, the detrimental impact of ineffective teachers on student learning has been found to exacerbate existing achievement gaps, perpetuating inequality within the education system. These findings underscore the critical importance of ensuring that all students have access to high-quality instruction, thereby necessitating a comprehensive evaluation of teacher performance.

Critics of performance-based evaluations often highlight concerns about the subjectivity and potential bias in assessing teacher effectiveness. They argue that standardized test scores, commonly used as a metric in performance evaluations, may not accurately capture the full scope of a teacher's impact on student learning. Additionally, there are apprehensions about the potential for evaluations to disproportionately disadvantage educators working in challenging environments, where external factors can significantly influence student outcomes.

In response to these objections, conservative advocates emphasize the need for a balanced approach to performance evaluations, one that considers multiple measures of teacher effectiveness. While acknowledging the limitations of relying solely on standardized test scores, they advocate for the inclusion of classroom observations, student feedback, and evidence of professional development and collaboration. By incorporating a holistic assessment of a teacher's performance, the potential for bias and subjectivity can be mitigated, ensuring a fair and comprehensive evaluation process.

Further support for the conservative perspective on teacher tenure and performance can be found in case studies of successful education reforms that have prioritized accountability and effectiveness. Jurisdictions that have implemented performance-based evaluations and streamlined tenure processes have witnessed improvements in teacher quality and student outcomes, providing tangible evidence of the positive impact of these policy changes.

The conservative agenda regarding teacher tenure and performance is firmly rooted in the commitment to enhancing educational quality and student success. By advocating for performance-based evaluations and reforms to the tenure system, conservative voices aim to address the crucial link between teacher effectiveness and student achievement, ultimately striving for a more equitable and effective education system. Through evidence-based policy proposals and a dedication to accountability, conservative advocates seek to elevate the teaching profession and ensure that all students have access to the high-quality instruction they deserve.

Promoting STEM Education

IN EXAMINING CONSERVATIVE strategies for promoting science, technology, engineering, and mathematics (STEM) education, it is essential to compare and contrast various approaches and initiatives to gain insights into their nuances and broader implications. By analyzing these strategies, we can evaluate their effectiveness in addressing the challenges and opportunities within the field of STEM education.

The entities being compared are the traditional STEM education approach and the conservative agenda for promoting STEM education. The traditional approach typically emphasizes curriculum development, teacher training, and increasing student interest in STEM fields. On the other hand, the conservative agenda focuses on market-based solutions, such as public-private partnerships, school choice, and policies that prioritize workforce readiness.

THE CONSERVATIVE AGENDA

The purpose of comparing these two approaches is to gain a comprehensive understanding of the strategies employed to promote STEM education. By exploring the rationale behind each approach, we can assess their intended insights and potential impact on students, educators, and the broader STEM community.

The benchmarks for comparison will include the effectiveness of increasing student interest in STEM fields, the ability to prepare students for STEM careers, and the capacity to address equity and diversity within STEM education. These criteria will set the parameters for analysis and enable a balanced assessment of the two approaches.

The traditional approach to promoting STEM education often centers on curriculum enhancements, extracurricular programs, and outreach initiatives aimed at sparking student interest in STEM subjects. In contrast, the conservative agenda emphasizes market-based solutions, such as incentivizing private sector investment in STEM education, fostering partnerships between educational institutions and industry, and advocating for school choice policies that prioritize STEM-focused curricula.

While the traditional approach focuses on generating student interest in STEM fields through enrichment programs and outreach, the conservative agenda prioritizes aligning STEM education with workforce needs and market demands. This distinction highlights the different priorities and strategies employed to promote STEM education, with the traditional approach emphasizing educational enrichment and the conservative agenda emphasizing workforce readiness.

The comparison reveals that the traditional approach to promoting STEM education aims to foster a love for learning and exploration in STEM fields, often through hands-on experiences, mentorship programs, and exposure to role models in STEM careers. Conversely, the conservative agenda seeks to align STEM education with the current and future needs of the job market, emphasizing practical skills and workforce readiness.

The implications of these differences are profound, as they reflect contrasting philosophies on the purpose of STEM education. The traditional approach prioritizes the cultivation of curiosity, critical thinking, and problem-solving skills, while the conservative agenda places greater emphasis on preparing students for specific careers and industries.

The contemporary relevance of this comparison is evident in the evolving landscape of the STEM workforce. As technology and innovation continue to drive economic growth and societal progress, the demand for a highly skilled STEM workforce is increasing. Both approaches have relevance in addressing this demand, with the traditional approach nurturing the next generation of innovators and the conservative agenda focusing on producing a workforce aligned with industry needs.

The comparison of the traditional approach and the conservative agenda for promoting STEM education underscores the diverse strategies employed to address the challenges and opportunities within the field. Both approaches offer valuable insights and potential contributions to advancing STEM education, and a comprehensive understanding of their nuances is essential in shaping effective policies and initiatives for the future.

Addressing Political Bias in Education

IN RECENT YEARS, CONSERVATIVE concerns about political bias in education have gained prominence, sparking debates about the role of academic institutions in promoting intellectual diversity and ideological balance. This issue has become particularly salient as reports of perceived liberal bias and censorship on college campuses have emerged, raising questions about the impact of such bias on students' intellectual development and the exchange of diverse viewpoints within educational settings.

The primary issue at hand is the presence of political bias, predominantly of a liberal nature, in educational institutions. This bias encompasses not only classroom instruction but also extends to administrative policies, faculty hiring practices, and campus culture. It manifests in the form of selective presentation of information, suppression of conservative perspectives, and the promotion of specific ideologies, ultimately limiting the free exchange of ideas and hindering the development of critical thinking skills among students.

The consequences of unchecked political bias in education are multifaceted and far-reaching. Firstly, it can lead to the indoctrination of students, where they are exposed predominantly to one ideological perspective, limiting their ability to critically engage with diverse viewpoints and stunting their intellectual growth. This can result in a lack of preparedness to navigate the complexities of a diverse and ideologically varied society. Additionally, the suppression of conservative perspectives can create an environment where students feel silenced or marginalized, leading to a lack of intellectual diversity and the stifling of open dialogue.

To address this challenge, a multifaceted approach is necessary. First and foremost, educational institutions must commit to fostering an environment that upholds the principles of intellectual diversity and freedom of expression. This entails actively promoting a culture where all perspectives, including conservative ones, are valued and encouraged. Additionally, implementing transparent and unbiased hiring processes for faculty and staff is essential to ensure that diverse viewpoints are represented within the academic community.

The implementation of these solutions requires a comprehensive review of institutional policies and practices to identify and rectify instances of bias. This may involve developing clear guidelines for classroom discussions and ensuring that educational materials present a balanced view of contentious issues. Moreover, providing platforms for open dialogue and debate, such as hosting speaker series with diverse perspectives, can help create an inclusive and intellectually stimulating environment.

In instances where institutions have actively embraced intellectual diversity, the outcomes have been promising. For example, universities that have established programs to promote viewpoint diversity have seen an increase in students' exposure to a wide range of ideas and perspectives, leading to enhanced critical thinking and a more robust intellectual environment. Moreover, graduates from these institutions have demonstrated a greater ability to engage in civil discourse and navigate ideological differences, contributing to a more harmonious and intellectually vibrant society.

While the aforementioned strategies are crucial, it is also important to consider alternative solutions. One such approach involves the establishment of independent oversight committees to monitor and address instances of political bias in education. These committees can serve as neutral arbiters, ensuring that academic institutions uphold the principles of intellectual diversity and free expression. Additionally, incentivizing the inclusion of diverse viewpoints in curriculum development and academic research can further promote a more balanced and intellectually enriching educational experience.

Addressing political bias in education is pivotal to ensuring that academic institutions provide a well-rounded and intellectually stimulating environment for students. By actively promoting intellectual diversity, fostering open dialogue, and implementing transparent and unbiased policies, educational institutions can cultivate a generation of critical thinkers equipped to engage with the complexities of an ideologically diverse world. Embracing a commitment to intellectual diversity not only enriches the educational experience but also prepares students to become active and informed participants in society, contributing to a more cohesive and intellectually vibrant community.

The Future of Education Reform

IN THE WAKE OF INCREASING concerns about the impact of political bias and ideological imbalance in educational institutions, particularly in the realm of higher education, the call for conservative education reform has gained momentum. As we delve into the complexities of this issue, we are confronted with a thought-provoking question: How can conservative education reform efforts effectively address the challenges posed by political bias and promote intellectual diversity within educational settings?

To contextualize this question, it is imperative to recognize the pivotal role of education in shaping the intellectual landscape of society. Educational institutions serve as the crucible where diverse perspectives converge, fostering the development of critical thinking skills and the exchange of ideas. However, when political bias infiltrates these environments, it threatens the very essence of intellectual growth and ideological diversity, thereby impacting the future of our society.

The central issue that conservative education reform seeks to address is the pervasive presence of political bias, predominantly of a liberal nature, within educational institutions. This bias permeates not only the content of classroom instruction but also extends to administrative policies, faculty hiring practices, and the overall campus culture. Its manifestations are manifold, ranging from the selective presentation of information to the suppression of conservative viewpoints, ultimately hindering the free exchange of ideas and impeding the development of critical thinking skills among students.

In presenting the real solution to this multifaceted challenge, conservative education reform endeavors to transform educational institutions into bastions of intellectual diversity and free expression. This transformative approach involves fostering a culture where all perspectives are valued and encouraged, creating an environment that stimulates critical thinking and open dialogue. It necessitates a comprehensive review of institutional policies and practices to rectify instances of bias and the implementation of transparent and unbiased hiring processes for faculty and staff.

To exemplify the potential outcomes of embracing intellectual diversity, we must showcase instances where institutions have actively promoted viewpoint diversity and witnessed tangible results. Universities that have undertaken initiatives to cultivate intellectual diversity have witnessed an increase in students' exposure to a wide range of ideas and perspectives, leading to enhanced critical thinking and a more robust intellectual environment. Graduates from these institutions have demonstrated a greater ability to engage in civil discourse and navigate ideological differences, contributing to a more harmonious and intellectually vibrant society.

While the aforementioned strategies are pivotal, it is also imperative to consider alternative solutions. One such approach involves the establishment of independent oversight committees to monitor and address instances of political bias in education. These committees can serve as neutral arbiters, ensuring that academic institutions uphold the principles of intellectual diversity and free expression. Additionally, incentivizing the inclusion of diverse viewpoints in curriculum development and academic research can further promote a more balanced and intellectually enriching educational experience.

Conservative education reform offers a transformative vision for the future of education, one that is rooted in the promotion of intellectual diversity and the cultivation of critical thinking skills. By actively fostering an environment that upholds the principles of intellectual diversity and freedom of expression, educational institutions can metamorphose into beacons of open dialogue and diverse perspectives. Embracing a commitment to intellectual diversity not only enriches the educational experience but also prepares students to become active and informed participants in society, contributing to a more cohesive and intellectually vibrant community.

As the clarion call for conservative education reform reverberates through the halls of academia, it beckons us to envision a future where educational institutions serve as the crucible for the exchange of diverse ideas and the cultivation of critical thinking. The future of education reform hinges on the collective endeavor to foster an environment where all perspectives are valued, empowering students to navigate the complexities of an ideologically diverse world with intellectual acumen and open-mindedness. The path to this future is illuminated by the unwavering commitment to promoting intellectual diversity within educational settings, ensuring that the seeds of critical thinking and diverse perspectives flourish and bear fruit in the fertile soil of academia and beyond.

Healthcare and Social Welfare

The Role of Government in Healthcare

Understanding the role of government in healthcare is essential for comprehending the complexities of the healthcare system. It is crucial to delve into the key terms and concepts that shape conservative perspectives on this matter.

To explore the conservative perspective on the role of government in healthcare, it is important to define and understand the following key terms:

1. Limited Government

Limited government refers to the principle that the government's role should be restricted to specific, enumerated functions. In the context of healthcare, this means that the government's involvement should be minimal, with a focus on creating an environment that allows for market-driven solutions and individual choices.

This concept can be likened to the idea of a referee in a sports game. The referee has a defined role in ensuring that the game is played fairly and within the rules, but does not actively participate in the game itself. Similarly, a limited government in healthcare is meant to provide a framework for fair and transparent market competition, without directly controlling or dominating the healthcare sector.

2. Free Market

The conservative view on healthcare emphasizes the importance of a free market approach. This entails minimal government intervention, allowing for competition, innovation, and efficiency in the delivery of healthcare services. A free market in healthcare enables individuals to make choices based on their needs and preferences, fostering a more patient-centric system.

The concept of a free market in healthcare can be likened to the principles of supply and demand in economics. In a free market, healthcare providers compete to attract patients by offering high-quality services at competitive prices, similar to how businesses compete in other industries. This competition can drive improvements in service quality and efficiency, benefiting patients and the overall healthcare system.

3. Individual Responsibility

Conservatives emphasize the importance of individual responsibility in healthcare. This principle underscores the idea that individuals should take ownership of their health and healthcare decisions. By promoting individual responsibility, conservative healthcare policies seek to empower individuals to make informed choices about their healthcare needs and lifestyles.

The concept of individual responsibility in healthcare can be compared to the idea of personal finance. Just as individuals are responsible for managing their finances and making decisions about saving, spending, and investing, they are also encouraged to take an active role in managing their health and making healthcare choices that align with their personal values and priorities.

4. Subsidiarity

Subsidiarity is a principle that advocates for decision-making and governance at the most local or decentralized level possible. In the context of healthcare, subsidiarity supports the idea that healthcare decisions and policies should be determined at the level closest to the individuals and communities affected, rather than being centralized at the federal level.

The concept of subsidiarity in healthcare can be likened to the idea of local governance in communities. Just as local governments are often best positioned to understand and address the unique needs of their communities, subsidiarity in healthcare allows for tailored approaches to healthcare delivery and decision-making that align with the specific needs and preferences of individuals and local healthcare providers.

5. Patient Empowerment

Conservative healthcare policies prioritize patient empowerment, aiming to provide individuals with the information, resources, and control necessary to make informed healthcare decisions. By empowering patients, conservative approaches to healthcare seek to shift the focus towards patient-centered care and personalized health management.

The concept of patient empowerment can be compared to the idea of consumer empowerment in other industries. Just as empowered consumers have the ability to make choices based on their preferences and needs, patient empowerment in healthcare enables individuals to actively participate in their healthcare journey, make decisions about treatment options, and engage with healthcare providers as partners in their care.

6. Personal Choice

Personal choice is a fundamental principle in conservative healthcare ideology, emphasizing the importance of allowing individuals to make decisions about their healthcare options based on their personal values, needs, and circumstances. This principle supports the idea that individuals are best positioned to make choices that align with their unique healthcare preferences and beliefs.

The concept of personal choice in healthcare can be likened to the idea of freedom of expression in society. Just as individuals have the freedom to express their opinions and make choices in various aspects of life, personal choice in healthcare allows individuals to express their preferences and make decisions about their healthcare without undue influence from external entities.

7. Fiscal Responsibility

Fiscal responsibility is a key aspect of conservative healthcare policy, emphasizing the importance of prudent financial management and accountability in healthcare spending. This principle supports the idea that efficient use of resources and responsible budgeting are essential for maintaining a sustainable healthcare system.

The concept of fiscal responsibility in healthcare can be compared to the principles of budgeting and financial planning in personal or business contexts. Just as individuals and organizations strive to manage their finances responsibly to achieve long-term stability and growth, fiscal responsibility in healthcare aims to ensure that healthcare resources are allocated efficiently and sustainably to meet the needs of patients and the healthcare system.

8. State Flexibility

Conservative healthcare policies often advocate for state flexibility, promoting the idea that states should have the autonomy to design and implement healthcare policies that align with the unique needs and preferences of their populations. This approach emphasizes the importance of tailoring healthcare solutions to local contexts and allowing states to experiment with innovative approaches to healthcare delivery.

The concept of state flexibility in healthcare can be likened to the idea of regional autonomy in governance. Just as different regions may have distinct cultural, economic, and social characteristics that influence their governance needs, state flexibility in healthcare recognizes the diverse healthcare challenges and opportunities across the country, allowing for customized approaches to healthcare policy and delivery.

9. Healthcare Market Competition

Conservative healthcare perspectives prioritize market competition as a means to drive efficiency, innovation, and quality in healthcare services. By fostering competition among healthcare providers and insurers, conservative policies aim to create incentives for improving the value and accessibility of healthcare options for patients.

The concept of healthcare market competition can be compared to the principles of competition in other industries. Just as competition in business can lead to better products, services, and prices for consumers, healthcare market competition encourages providers to strive for excellence in delivering healthcare services, ultimately benefiting patients and the overall healthcare system.

10. Regulatory Efficiency

Conservative healthcare policies emphasize the importance of regulatory efficiency, seeking to minimize bureaucratic barriers and red tape in healthcare delivery. By streamlining regulations and promoting a more efficient regulatory environment, conservative approaches aim to reduce administrative burdens and costs, allowing healthcare providers to focus on delivering high-quality care to patients.

The concept of regulatory efficiency in healthcare can be likened to the principles of streamlined processes and efficiency in other sectors. Just as businesses and organizations seek to optimize their operations and minimize unnecessary bureaucracy to improve productivity and effectiveness, regulatory efficiency in healthcare aims to create a more agile and responsive healthcare system that prioritizes patient care over administrative hurdles.

The conservative perspective on the role of government in healthcare is shaped by these key concepts, which collectively advocate for a healthcare system that prioritizes individual choice, market competition, fiscal responsibility, and patient empowerment. By understanding these principles and their real-world implications, we can gain deeper insights into the conservative agenda for healthcare policy.

Market-Based Solutions

IN THE REALM OF HEALTHCARE policy, conservative ideology often advocates for market-based solutions as a means to address the complexities and challenges within the healthcare system. This chapter delves into the conservative support for market-based solutions in healthcare, emphasizing the importance of competition, individual choice, and regulatory efficiency in shaping a patient-centric and sustainable healthcare framework.

Market-based solutions in healthcare revolve around the application of free market principles to drive efficiency, innovation, and quality in the delivery of healthcare services. The core concept centers on creating an environment where competition among healthcare providers and insurers leads to improved value and accessibility of healthcare options for patients. By fostering a marketplace where individuals have the freedom to make informed choices based on their healthcare needs and preferences, market-based solutions aim to shift the focus towards patient-centered care and personalized health management.

Conservative healthcare policies often advocate for minimal government intervention, allowing market forces to shape the healthcare landscape. This approach aligns with the principle of limited government, emphasizing that the role of the government in healthcare should be restricted to specific, enumerated functions, thus creating a framework for fair and transparent market competition without direct control or dominance over the healthcare sector.

To illustrate the impact of market-based solutions in healthcare, consider the case of a hypothetical healthcare market where multiple providers compete to attract patients by offering high-quality services at competitive prices. In this scenario, patients have the freedom to choose their healthcare providers based on factors such as service quality, convenience, and affordability. This competition drives improvements in service quality and efficiency, benefiting patients and the overall healthcare system.

Furthermore, market-based solutions can be exemplified by the concept of health savings accounts (HSAs), which empower individuals to make tax-free contributions to an account dedicated to healthcare expenses. By giving individuals greater control over their healthcare spending and decision-making, HSAs align with the conservative principle of individual responsibility, emphasizing the importance of personal choice and financial empowerment in healthcare.

While conservative ideology strongly advocates for market-based solutions, it is important to acknowledge that differing perspectives exist regarding the extent of market influence in healthcare. Critics of market-based solutions often raise concerns about potential disparities in access to care, particularly for vulnerable populations. Additionally, the impact of market competition on healthcare quality and affordability may vary across different regions and demographic groups, prompting discussions about the need for targeted interventions to address disparities and ensure equitable access to healthcare services.

Supporting the case for market-based solutions in healthcare, data and facts can provide valuable insights into the correlation between market competition and healthcare outcomes. Studies have shown that areas with higher levels of competition among healthcare providers tend to exhibit lower healthcare costs and improved quality of care. For instance, research conducted by the Commonwealth Fund has highlighted the positive association between market competition and healthcare efficiency, emphasizing the potential benefits of a competitive marketplace in driving positive healthcare outcomes.

Additionally, empirical evidence can be presented to showcase the impact of regulatory efficiency on healthcare delivery. By streamlining regulations and minimizing administrative burdens, healthcare providers can focus on delivering high-quality care to patients, leading to enhanced patient satisfaction and improved healthcare outcomes.

In the context of market-based solutions, it is essential to clarify the complex term of regulatory efficiency. Regulatory efficiency refers to the optimization of administrative processes and the reduction of bureaucratic barriers in healthcare delivery. By enhancing the efficiency of regulatory frameworks, healthcare providers can navigate regulatory requirements more effectively, resulting in a more agile and responsive healthcare system that prioritizes patient care over administrative hurdles.

Market-based solutions in healthcare embody the conservative principles of individual choice, competition, and regulatory efficiency. By fostering a marketplace that empowers individuals to make informed healthcare decisions and encourages competition among healthcare providers, market-based solutions aim to improve the quality, accessibility, and affordability of healthcare services. While acknowledging differing perspectives on the role of market influence in healthcare, the conservative support for market-based solutions underscores the potential for patient-centered care and innovative healthcare delivery models within a competitive marketplace.

The conservative agenda for healthcare policy emphasizes the transformative potential of market-based solutions in addressing the complexities of the healthcare system. By advocating for competition, individual choice, and regulatory efficiency, conservative ideology seeks to create a sustainable and patient-centric healthcare framework that empowers individuals and drives positive healthcare outcomes. Understanding the nuances of market-based solutions in healthcare is essential for comprehending the conservative perspective on healthcare policy and its implications for shaping the future of healthcare delivery.

The Affordable Care Act

THE AFFORDABLE CARE Act (ACA), commonly known as Obamacare, has been a subject of intense debate within the realm of healthcare policy. This chapter explores conservative criticisms of the ACA and offers alternative healthcare proposals that align with conservative principles. By analyzing the complexities of the ACA and contrasting them with conservative healthcare ideologies, this chapter aims to provide insights into the nuanced implications of healthcare reform in the United States.

THE CONSERVATIVE AGENDA

The Affordable Care Act represents a landmark healthcare reform initiative introduced during the Obama administration, aiming to expand access to affordable healthcare coverage for millions of Americans. Its key provisions include the establishment of health insurance marketplaces, the expansion of Medicaid eligibility, and the implementation of consumer protections such as prohibiting insurance companies from denying coverage based on pre-existing conditions.

Conservative criticisms of the Affordable Care Act stem from ideological differences in approaches to healthcare policy. Conservatives advocate for market-based solutions, limited government intervention, and individual choice, emphasizing the importance of preserving free market principles in healthcare delivery.

The comparison of the Affordable Care Act and conservative healthcare ideologies serves to elucidate the underlying philosophical disparities in healthcare policy. By delineating the distinct approaches to healthcare reform, this analysis aims to shed light on the divergent perspectives on the role of government, market dynamics, and individual empowerment in shaping the healthcare landscape.

The benchmarks for comparison encompass the fundamental principles of the Affordable Care Act and conservative healthcare ideologies. These criteria include the role of government intervention, the influence of market forces, the emphasis on individual responsibility, and the overarching impact on healthcare accessibility, quality, and affordability.

The Affordable Care Act sought to expand healthcare coverage through the implementation of health insurance marketplaces and the expansion of Medicaid, aiming to reduce the number of uninsured individuals. Conservative healthcare ideologies, on the other hand, prioritize market-based solutions and minimal government intervention, advocating for increased competition and individual choice as drivers of healthcare quality and accessibility.

The ACA's reliance on government mandates and subsidies to expand coverage contrasts with the conservative emphasis on market competition and consumer-driven healthcare. While the ACA aimed to increase government oversight in healthcare, conservative principles underscore the importance of limited government involvement to foster a more dynamic and responsive healthcare market.

One of the primary distinctions between the Affordable Care Act and conservative healthcare ideologies lies in the approach to individual responsibility and decision-making in healthcare. The ACA's implementation of individual mandates and employer mandates represented a departure from conservative principles, as it compelled individuals and businesses to participate in the healthcare system through regulatory requirements.

Conservative healthcare ideologies prioritize individual choice and personal responsibility, advocating for initiatives such as health savings accounts and increased consumer autonomy in healthcare decision-making. This contrast reflects differing perspectives on the role of government in shaping individual healthcare choices and financial obligations.

The comparison between the Affordable Care Act and conservative healthcare ideologies reveals the divergent paths in healthcare reform. The ACA's emphasis on expanding government oversight and regulatory requirements reflects a belief in the central role of government in ensuring healthcare accessibility and equity. Conversely, conservative criticisms underscore the potential adverse effects of government intervention on market dynamics and individual freedoms in healthcare decision-making.

Insights into the nuances of these approaches highlight the trade-offs between government-led initiatives and market-driven solutions in healthcare reform. The ACA's focus on expanding coverage and regulating insurance practices intersects with concerns about rising costs, limited choice, and regulatory burdens. Conservative alternatives, rooted in market principles, raise questions about the balance between government safety nets and individual empowerment in healthcare.

The comparison between the Affordable Care Act and conservative healthcare ideologies remains pertinent in contemporary discussions surrounding healthcare reform. As debates continue on the efficacy and sustainability of the ACA, contrasting conservative proposals offer alternative perspectives on addressing the complexities of the healthcare system. With ongoing shifts in political landscapes and policy priorities, understanding the implications of these differing approaches is essential for shaping the future of healthcare policy.

The conservative criticisms of the Affordable Care Act underscore the ideological disparities in healthcare reform. By contrasting the ACA's reliance on government intervention with conservative principles of market-based solutions and individual choice, this analysis elucidates the intrinsic differences in healthcare ideologies. Ultimately, the comparison serves to provide insights into the broader implications of healthcare reform, offering a nuanced understanding of the divergent paths in shaping the future of healthcare delivery in the United States.

JACK DONAHUE

Medicaid and Social Safety Nets

AS THE DISCUSSION ON healthcare policy continues, it is imperative to delve into the conservative perspectives on Medicaid and the broader concepts of social safety nets. This segment aims to offer a comprehensive exploration of conservative viewpoints on Medicaid, emphasizing the balance between providing a safety net and promoting self-sufficiency. By dissecting the nuances of Medicaid and its implications for individuals and society, this analysis seeks to shed light on the conservative approach to ensuring healthcare accessibility and financial stability.

The following list encapsulates key points central to conservative perspectives on Medicaid and social safety nets, providing a structured framework for an in-depth examination of each element:

Medicaid serves as a critical component of the social safety net, offering healthcare coverage for low-income individuals and families. From a conservative standpoint, it is essential to acknowledge the significance of safety nets while scrutinizing their impact on individual incentives and fiscal implications. Medicaid represents a safety net designed to provide essential healthcare services, but its expansion and sustainability warrant thoughtful consideration to ensure long-term effectiveness.

Conservative perspectives on Medicaid underscore the importance of balancing compassion with fiscal responsibility. While acknowledging the need to support vulnerable populations, conservatives emphasize the prudent allocation of resources to avoid fiscal strain and dependency. This necessitates a careful evaluation of Medicaid's scope and eligibility criteria to ensure that it effectively targets those in need while mitigating potential disincentives to self-sufficiency.

A core tenet of conservative ideology in the context of Medicaid is the promotion of self-sufficiency. This principle underpins the approach to safety nets, advocating for policies that empower individuals to transition from dependency to self-reliance. In the context of Medicaid, initiatives aimed at promoting employment, education, and personal responsibility align with conservative ideals of fostering independence and reducing long-term reliance on government support.

Conservative analyses of Medicaid delve into systemic challenges inherent in safety net programs, including issues related to program efficiency, waste, fraud, and abuse. Addressing these challenges requires a multifaceted approach that prioritizes accountability, transparency, and targeted interventions to streamline program delivery and safeguard taxpayer resources. Mitigating systemic inefficiencies is crucial to preserving the integrity and sustainability of Medicaid as a safety net.

Conservative perspectives underscore the potential for innovation in healthcare delivery within the framework of Medicaid and social safety nets. Encouraging competition, leveraging market dynamics, and exploring alternative models of care delivery align with conservative principles of empowering individuals and fostering efficient, patient-centered healthcare solutions. This emphasis on innovation aims to enhance the quality, accessibility, and cost-effectiveness of healthcare services for Medicaid beneficiaries.

Credible sources, data, and firsthand accounts substantiate the conservative viewpoints on Medicaid and social safety nets. Research studies, policy analyses, and testimonies from individuals impacted by safety net programs enrich the understanding of the complexities surrounding Medicaid and underscore the need for thoughtful, evidence-based policy considerations.

The practical implications of conservative perspectives on Medicaid and social safety nets manifest in policy proposals and initiatives aimed at reforming safety net programs. These applications emphasize the implementation of targeted reforms, evidence-based interventions, and outcome-driven policies to align safety nets with conservative principles while effectively meeting the needs of vulnerable populations.

The conservative perspective on Medicaid and social safety nets encapsulates a multifaceted examination of the role of safety nets in healthcare, the balance between compassion and fiscal responsibility, the promotion of self-sufficiency, the mitigation of systemic challenges, and the fostering of innovation. This comprehensive analysis offers insights into the conservative vision for Medicaid and underscores the complexities inherent in navigating the intersection of safety nets, healthcare delivery, and individual empowerment.

Tort Reform and Medical Liability

TO DELVE INTO THE CONSERVATIVE agenda for tort reform and medical liability reduction, it is crucial to have a fundamental understanding of the current landscape of medical malpractice, legal precedents, and economic implications associated with malpractice claims. Additionally, an awareness of the ethical considerations and patient outcomes affected by tort reform measures is essential for a holistic comprehension.

Tort reform encompasses a spectrum of legislative and policy interventions aimed at mitigating excessive litigation and liability costs in the medical domain. Conservative proposals in this realm seek to address the challenges posed by escalating malpractice insurance premiums, defensive medicine practices, and the overall impact of malpractice lawsuits on healthcare affordability and accessibility. By dissecting the nuances of tort reform, this segment endeavors to elucidate the conservative vision for a more balanced and sustainable medico-legal framework.

Conservative perspectives on tort reform underscore the need to curb frivolous lawsuits, exorbitant jury awards, and the adverse effects of defensive medicine on healthcare delivery. It is imperative to highlight the role of tort reform in fostering a more predictable and equitable legal environment for healthcare providers and patients alike. By delving into the economic ramifications of malpractice litigation, including its impact on healthcare costs and the availability of medical services, conservatives advocate for reforms that align with the principles of fairness and prudence.

In delineating specific policy proposals, conservative agendas for tort reform emphasize initiatives such as caps on non-economic damages, statute of limitations revisions, alternative dispute resolution mechanisms, and the introduction of expert panels to review malpractice claims. These proposals aim to strike a balance between safeguarding patient rights and curbing the escalation of malpractice insurance premiums, thus promoting a more sustainable and patient-centric medico-legal landscape.

Conservative analyses delve into the intricate web of factors contributing to medical liability costs, encompassing not only malpractice insurance premiums but also the broader implications for healthcare affordability, provider retention, and regional disparities in litigation. By scrutinizing the economic underpinnings of medical liability, conservatives advocate for evidence-based approaches to contain costs without compromising the quality of patient care or the accountability of healthcare professionals.

A critical facet of conservative proposals for tort reform is the ethical dimension, which necessitates a careful examination of the impact of legal interventions on patient safety, provider accountability, and the overall quality of healthcare delivery. Conservatives prioritize patient outcomes and the preservation of medical standards while advocating for reforms that mitigate the adversarial nature of malpractice litigation and foster a more collaborative and patient-focused approach to resolving medical disputes.

When exploring conservative proposals for tort reform and medical liability reduction, it is essential to approach the subject with a balanced perspective, acknowledging the complexities and trade-offs inherent in legislative interventions. Additionally, an understanding of the historical precedents and empirical evidence surrounding tort reform measures offers valuable insights into the potential ramifications of policy changes on healthcare accessibility, provider behavior, and patient rights.

Validating the efficacy of conservative proposals for tort reform and medical liability reduction necessitates a multifaceted approach, encompassing empirical research, stakeholder consultations, and comparative analyses of tort reform initiatives across different jurisdictions. By rigorously assessing the impact of proposed reforms on healthcare costs, malpractice claims, and patient outcomes, conservatives seek to substantiate the viability of their policy agenda and its potential to foster a more sustainable and equitable medico-legal framework.

The conservative agenda for tort reform and medical liability reduction encapsulates a nuanced examination of the economic, ethical, and patient-centric considerations underpinning proposed interventions. By delineating the rationale behind tort reform measures, policy proposals, and their potential impact on healthcare delivery, conservatives aim to navigate the delicate balance between legal accountability, patient welfare, and healthcare affordability.

This comprehensive analysis offers insights into the conservative vision for a more equitable and sustainable medico-legal landscape, underscoring the complexities inherent in navigating the intersection of legal reforms, medical liability, and societal welfare.

Mental Health and Addiction

MENTAL HEALTH AND ADDICTION are complex and pervasive issues that profoundly impact individuals, families, and communities. Conservative approaches to addressing these challenges are rooted in principles of personal responsibility, access to treatment, and the preservation of societal well-being. This segment aims to examine conservative perspectives on mental health and addiction, delving into the proposed policies, interventions, and ethical considerations that underpin the conservative agenda in these domains.

Conservative principles offer a comprehensive framework for addressing mental health and addiction, emphasizing the significance of individual agency, community support, and evidence-based interventions. This segment asserts that conservative approaches to mental health and addiction are founded on the promotion of personal accountability, the enhancement of treatment accessibility, and the cultivation of a supportive societal environment conducive to recovery and resilience.

Conservative policies prioritize empowering individuals to take charge of their mental health and addiction recovery through initiatives such as expanding access to mental health services, promoting community-based support networks, and fostering partnerships between public and private sectors to address the root causes of addiction.

The conservative emphasis on personal responsibility aligns with the recognition of individuals as active agents in their own well-being. By promoting a culture of resilience and self-reliance, conservative strategies seek to engender a sense of agency in individuals grappling with mental health challenges or addiction, thereby fostering a more sustainable and empowering path to recovery.

Conservative approaches also advocate for the integration of mental health education and awareness programs in schools, workplaces, and community settings, aiming to destigmatize mental health issues and cultivate a supportive and informed environment for individuals seeking assistance.

Moreover, conservative initiatives underscore the importance of evidence-based treatment modalities, the promotion of innovative therapeutic interventions, and the provision of comprehensive support services to address the multifaceted needs of individuals struggling with addiction and mental health conditions.

Critics of conservative approaches to mental health and addiction may contend that the emphasis on individual responsibility could potentially overlook systemic barriers and societal factors contributing to mental health challenges and addiction. Additionally, concerns may be raised regarding the adequacy of funding and resources allocated to mental health programs and addiction treatment under conservative policies.

In response to these contentions, it is imperative to underscore that conservative strategies do not discount the significance of systemic influences on mental health and addiction. Instead, they acknowledge the interplay between individual agency and societal factors, advocating for a balanced approach that addresses both personal accountability and the broader environmental determinants of mental health and addiction.

Furthermore, conservative policies prioritize the allocation of resources to bolster mental health infrastructure, enhance treatment accessibility, and fortify community-based support systems, thereby mitigating the potential shortcomings attributed to underfunding or resource constraints.

In reinforcing the conservative agenda for mental health and addiction, it is essential to highlight the role of faith-based organizations, non-profit entities, and community initiatives in complementing government efforts to provide holistic support to individuals grappling with mental health challenges and addiction.

Moreover, conservative proposals emphasize the significance of early intervention and prevention strategies, aiming to identify and address mental health concerns and addiction risk factors proactively, thereby averting the escalation of these issues and their associated societal impacts.

Conservative approaches to mental health and addiction underscore the principles of personal responsibility, treatment accessibility, and community engagement as foundational pillars for addressing these critical societal issues. By integrating evidence-based interventions, destigmatizing mental health concerns, and fostering a supportive environment, the conservative agenda seeks to empower individuals, fortify community resilience, and promote a holistic approach to mental health and addiction, thereby advancing the well-being of individuals and society as a whole.

The Future of Healthcare and Social Welfare

THE LANDSCAPE OF HEALTHCARE and social welfare is undergoing profound transformations, propelled by demographic shifts, technological advancements, and evolving societal needs. As the demands on healthcare systems and social welfare programs continue to intensify, conservative perspectives on these critical domains warrant careful examination. This segment aims to explore the challenges and opportunities for conservative reforms in healthcare and social welfare, elucidating the underlying principles, proposed policy initiatives, and ethical considerations that underpin the conservative agenda in these spheres.

A primary challenge confronting healthcare and social welfare systems is the escalating strain imposed by an aging population, increasing prevalence of chronic diseases, and the growing complexity of healthcare needs. The rising demand for healthcare services and long-term care, coupled with the financial pressures on social welfare programs, underscores the urgency of addressing the sustainability and effectiveness of these crucial societal pillars.

Furthermore, the existing inefficiencies and bureaucratic complexities within healthcare and social welfare frameworks present formidable obstacles to the delivery of high-quality, accessible, and affordable services to individuals and families. Inadequate coordination among healthcare providers, fragmented care delivery, and disparities in access to essential services contribute to suboptimal health outcomes and disparities in social welfare support, exacerbating the inequities within our society.

Failure to address these pressing challenges has far-reaching repercussions, encompassing both individual well-being and societal cohesion. Without meaningful reforms, healthcare systems risk becoming overwhelmed, compromising the delivery of timely and comprehensive care to those in need. Moreover, the strain on social welfare programs threatens to perpetuate disparities, impede upward mobility, and undermine the resilience of communities, perpetuating cycles of poverty and inequity.

THE CONSERVATIVE AGENDA

A conservative perspective on healthcare and social welfare reforms emphasizes the principles of individual empowerment, market-based solutions, and fiscal responsibility. Proposing a methodical and pragmatic approach, conservative strategies advocate for the promotion of patient-centered care, the enhancement of choice and competition within healthcare markets, and the cultivation of self-sufficiency and accountability within social welfare programs.

Central to conservative healthcare reforms is the advocacy for patient-centered care models that afford individuals greater autonomy and control over their healthcare decisions. By fostering a competitive marketplace that encourages innovation, quality improvement, and cost containment, conservative policies aim to expand access to high-quality care while promoting efficiency and value in healthcare delivery.

In the realm of social welfare, conservative approaches prioritize the facilitation of upward mobility through targeted interventions that promote self-reliance, economic independence, and the reduction of dependency on government assistance. Emphasizing the pivotal role of private enterprise, community organizations, and faith-based initiatives, conservative proposals seek to create pathways for individuals to attain self-sufficiency and contribute to the economic and social fabric of their communities.

The translation of conservative healthcare and social welfare reforms into tangible solutions necessitates a multifaceted approach. For healthcare, this entails the promotion of consumer-driven healthcare models that empower individuals to make informed choices regarding their health coverage, care providers, and treatment options. Additionally, fostering a regulatory environment that encourages price transparency, innovation, and competition among healthcare providers is imperative to drive improvements in care quality and cost-effectiveness.

In the domain of social welfare, the implementation of conservative reforms requires the establishment of targeted assistance programs that prioritize work, education, and skill development, incentivizing self-sufficiency and upward mobility. Moreover, fostering public-private partnerships that harness the strengths of community organizations, philanthropic entities, and businesses can augment the capacity to address social welfare needs in a manner that is responsive, efficient, and attuned to the unique circumstances of individuals and families.

The efficacy of conservative healthcare and social welfare reforms can be discerned through the examination of past outcomes and projected impacts. Historically, conservative initiatives that have embraced market-driven reforms in healthcare have demonstrated improvements in care quality, expanded choices for consumers, and moderated healthcare costs. By fostering an environment of competition and innovation, these reforms have engendered greater efficiency and responsiveness within healthcare systems, benefiting both individuals and the broader society.

In the realm of social welfare, conservative policies that have prioritized self-sufficiency and individual empowerment have shown promise in breaking cycles of dependency, fostering economic mobility, and strengthening the social fabric of communities. By aligning assistance programs with incentives for work, education, and skill-building, these reforms have facilitated positive transitions for individuals and families, reducing long-term reliance on government support and cultivating pathways to economic self-reliance.

THE CONSERVATIVE AGENDA

While conservative approaches offer compelling solutions to the challenges in healthcare and social welfare, alternative perspectives may advocate for different strategies, such as the expansion of government-sponsored healthcare systems or the augmentation of social safety nets through increased public expenditure. Evaluating these alternatives necessitates a comprehensive analysis of their potential impacts on care quality, access, and fiscal sustainability, as well as their implications for individual choice, innovation, and market dynamics within healthcare and social welfare domains.

The imperative for conservative healthcare and social welfare reforms is underscored by the urgency of addressing the escalating demands, inefficiencies, and disparities within these critical societal pillars. By championing patient-centered care, market-based solutions, and targeted interventions that promote self-sufficiency, conservative initiatives seek to fortify the resilience of healthcare systems and social welfare programs, thereby advancing the well-being of individuals and communities in an evolving societal landscape.

Environmental Stewardship

Conservative Perspectives on the Environment

As the discourse surrounding environmental stewardship continues to evolve, it is essential to examine conservative perspectives on this critical issue. The conservative approach to environmental conservation is rooted in a nuanced understanding of the balance between ecological preservation and economic growth.

Conservative environmental perspectives encompass a range of beliefs and values that emphasize the responsible use of natural resources and advocate for policies that promote sustainability without impeding economic development.

At its core, conservative environmentalism seeks to achieve a harmonious equilibrium between environmental protection and economic progress. It acknowledges the intrinsic value of nature and the importance of prudent resource management while recognizing the significance of economic growth for societal well-being.

One key element of conservative environmentalism is the emphasis on individual and local responsibility in environmental stewardship. Conservatives often argue for decentralized decision-making and the engagement of private entities and local communities in environmental initiatives, contending that local actors are best equipped to address environmental challenges in a manner that aligns with their specific needs and circumstances.

Another essential aspect of conservative environmental perspectives is the promotion of market-based solutions to environmental issues. Conservatives advocate for harnessing the power of free markets to incentivize innovation and efficiency in environmental protection, favoring mechanisms such as emissions trading and voluntary eco-labeling programs over prescriptive regulations.

Moreover, conservative environmentalism underscores the importance of scientific rigor and cost-benefit analysis in crafting environmental policies. Rather than relying solely on ideological or alarmist approaches, conservatives advocate for evidence-based decision-making that carefully evaluates the potential benefits and costs of environmental interventions.

The roots of conservative environmentalism can be traced back to the early conservation movement in the United States during the late 19th and early 20th centuries. Figures such as Gifford Pinchot and Theodore Roosevelt espoused a conservation ethic that emphasized the sustainable use of natural resources for the betterment of present and future generations, laying the groundwork for the fusion of conservative principles with environmental stewardship.

Conservative environmental perspectives are situated within a broader framework of conservative ideology, which prioritizes individual liberty, limited government intervention, and the preservation of traditional values. This framework informs conservative approaches to environmental issues, shaping the lens through which conservatives view the role of government, the private sector, and civil society in addressing environmental challenges.

In practice, conservative environmental principles have been exemplified through initiatives such as conservation easements, which allow landowners to voluntarily protect environmentally significant areas while retaining private property rights. Additionally, market-based mechanisms like cap-and-trade systems have been implemented to reduce greenhouse gas emissions, demonstrating the efficacy of market-oriented approaches to environmental regulation.

One common misconception regarding conservative environmental perspectives is the notion that conservatives prioritize economic interests at the expense of environmental protection. In reality, conservative environmentalism seeks to achieve a symbiotic relationship between environmental sustainability and economic prosperity, recognizing that long-term economic growth is contingent upon the health of the natural environment.

Conservative perspectives on the environment offer a comprehensive framework for addressing environmental challenges while fostering economic vitality and individual empowerment. By embracing principles of localism, market-driven solutions, and evidence-based policymaking, conservative environmentalism provides a robust foundation for sustainable and pragmatic environmental stewardship. Understanding and engaging with conservative environmental perspectives is essential for advancing a holistic approach to environmental conservation that integrates diverse viewpoints and promotes the long-term well-being of both society and the natural world.

Property Rights and Environmental Policy

IN DISCUSSING THE CONSERVATIVE emphasis on property rights and limited government intervention in environmental policy, it is essential to understand the underlying principles and values that shape this approach. Conservatism places a high value on individual property rights and limited government involvement in private affairs, and these principles profoundly influence conservative perspectives on environmental policy. This chapter will provide a comprehensive exploration of the conservative stance on property rights and environmental policy, delving into the foundational concepts, historical context, and practical applications of this viewpoint.

Property rights form the bedrock of conservative environmental policy, as they are seen as essential for promoting responsible stewardship of natural resources. The concept of property rights encompasses not only tangible assets but also the rights of individuals and communities to make decisions about the use and management of their property, including land, water, and other natural resources. This chapter will elucidate how the conservative emphasis on property rights intersects with environmental policy, shaping the approach to conservation, regulation, and sustainability.

Conservative environmental policy is underpinned by the belief that strong property rights are conducive to environmental protection and sustainable development. The recognition of individual and collective property rights is seen as a potent force for incentivizing responsible resource management and fostering innovation in environmental conservation. By granting ownership and control over natural assets, property rights empower individuals and organizations to make informed decisions that align with their long-term interests and the preservation of the environment.

Furthermore, the conservative perspective holds that private property ownership engenders a sense of accountability and investment in the upkeep and preservation of natural resources. Individuals who have a stake in the well-being of their property are more likely to adopt practices that safeguard the environment, whether through sustainable land use, habitat preservation, or responsible extraction of natural resources. This understanding of property rights as a catalyst for environmental responsibility forms the cornerstone of conservative environmental policy.

To illustrate the significance of property rights in environmental policy, consider the example of conservation easements, a voluntary agreement between a landowner and a land trust or government entity that restricts the development of a property to protect its natural, scenic, or agricultural features. Conservation easements exemplify the application of property rights in environmental conservation, as they enable landowners to maintain ownership of their property while voluntarily committing to its long-term preservation.

Moreover, the concept of water rights in the western United States provides a compelling illustration of how property rights influence environmental policy. Water rights, which confer the legal right to use water from a water source, have historically played a pivotal role in shaping water management practices, allocation, and conservation efforts. The allocation of water rights reflects the conservative emphasis on individual ownership and responsibility, as well as the belief that private stewardship of water resources can lead to more efficient and sustainable use.

While the conservative emphasis on property rights as a cornerstone of environmental policy is clear, it is important to acknowledge differing viewpoints on the role of property rights in environmental stewardship. Critics may argue that an exclusive focus on individual property rights could lead to unchecked exploitation of natural resources, resulting in environmental degradation and inequitable access to essential resources. This chapter will address these perspectives and present a balanced examination of the complexities surrounding property rights and environmental policy.

Supporting the conservative viewpoint on property rights in environmental policy with empirical evidence is crucial for substantiating the arguments presented. Data and facts related to the impact of property rights on natural resource management, conservation initiatives, and environmental outcomes will be incorporated to underscore the practical significance of property rights in shaping environmental policy. This evidence will underscore the role of property rights in incentivizing sustainable practices, fostering innovation, and promoting environmental resilience.

Energy Policy and Climate Change

ENERGY POLICY IS A multifaceted domain that encompasses the strategies and regulations governing the production, distribution, and consumption of energy resources. It holds immense significance for economic stability, national security, and environmental sustainability. On the other hand, climate change represents the existential challenge of our time, with far-reaching implications for ecosystems, human societies, and global stability. Understanding the conservative stance on energy policy and climate change is crucial for comprehending the nuanced complexities of these subjects and their intersections.

Conservative views on energy policy emphasize market-driven solutions, deregulation, and technological innovation as the primary means to ensure energy security, affordability, and reliability. The conservative agenda often advocates for reducing government intervention in the energy sector, promoting private investment and entrepreneurial initiatives, and leveraging domestic energy resources to achieve energy independence. This approach seeks to balance economic growth with environmental stewardship while prioritizing the interests of consumers and businesses.

Within conservative circles, the debate over climate change often centers on skepticism toward expansive government regulations and international agreements aimed at curbing greenhouse gas emissions. While acknowledging the need for environmental conservation, conservatives emphasize the importance of cost-benefit analysis in crafting climate policies and express concerns about the potential economic repercussions of stringent regulatory measures. The conservative agenda often advocates for market-driven innovations and voluntary initiatives to address climate challenges without compromising economic prosperity.

In comparing energy policy and climate change from a conservative perspective, it is essential to establish the criteria that will serve as the benchmarks for analysis. These criteria should encompass factors such as economic impact, regulatory approaches, technological innovation, global competitiveness, environmental sustainability, and societal resilience. By delineating these parameters, we can elucidate the multifaceted nature of these subjects and their interplay within the conservative framework.

When examining energy policy and climate change through a conservative lens, it becomes evident that both subjects are intrinsically linked by their implications for economic prosperity and environmental sustainability. The conservative emphasis on market-driven solutions and technological innovation resonates across both domains, as evidenced by the promotion of domestic energy production, investment in clean technologies, and voluntary initiatives to reduce emissions. Furthermore, the conservative approach to balancing economic growth with environmental conservation forms a common thread in both energy and climate policies.

Despite their interconnectedness, energy policy and climate change diverge in their emphasis on regulatory approaches and international cooperation. While conservative energy policy advocates for limited government intervention and a focus on domestic resources, climate change policies often entail international agreements, emissions targets, and regulatory frameworks that can be perceived as encroachments on sovereignty and free-market principles. This contrast underscores the complexities of addressing environmental challenges within the conservative agenda, requiring a delicate balance between economic imperatives and global environmental concerns.

The comparison of energy policy and climate change from a conservative perspective offers profound insights into the complexities of balancing economic imperatives with environmental responsibilities. It underscores the challenges of crafting policies that promote energy security, economic growth, and environmental sustainability while addressing the uncertainties and trade-offs inherent in climate change mitigation efforts. This analysis reveals the need for innovative solutions that reconcile the divergent demands of energy policy and climate change within the conservative framework.

Connecting historical or theoretical comparisons to current realities enhances the relevance of this analysis. In today's rapidly evolving geopolitical and environmental landscape, the conservative agenda on energy policy and climate change has significant implications for global energy markets, technological advancements, and international climate negotiations. By grounding this analysis in contemporary relevance, we can offer insights into the practical implications of conservative perspectives on these critical subjects.

The exploration of conservative views on energy policy and the debate over climate change provides a comprehensive understanding of the nuanced complexities inherent in these subjects. By analyzing their similarities and differences, we gain insights into the broader implications of the conservative agenda on energy and environmental policies, offering a nuanced perspective on the challenges and opportunities posed by these critical domains.

Natural Resource Management

THE CONSERVATIVE APPROACH to natural resource management encompasses a multifaceted strategy that integrates market-based solutions, private-sector initiatives, technological innovation, and regulatory frameworks tailored to promote responsible resource extraction, sustainable utilization, and environmental conservation. This chapter will explore the foundational principles underpinning conservative natural resource management, examine the policy tools and incentives deployed to achieve sustainable resource practices, and analyze the real-world implications of conservative strategies for natural resource governance.

Conservative natural resource management is rooted in the recognition of the intrinsic value of natural resources and the imperative to balance resource utilization with long-term environmental sustainability. At its core, conservative principles emphasize the importance of private property rights, market incentives, and decentralized decision-making to foster responsible resource stewardship. By upholding the principles of limited government intervention and individual responsibility, conservative approaches seek to harness the power of free markets and innovation to achieve sustainable resource management.

Conservative policies for natural resource management embrace a range of tools and incentives designed to align economic interests with environmental objectives. These may include tax incentives for conservation practices, market-based mechanisms such as cap-and-trade systems, and public-private partnerships to promote sustainable resource extraction and utilization. By leveraging economic incentives, conservative strategies aim to encourage responsible resource management while fostering innovation and technological advancements in resource efficiency and conservation.

Examining the real-world implications of conservative natural resource management involves analyzing case studies, policy outcomes, and empirical evidence to assess the effectiveness of conservative strategies in promoting sustainable resource practices. This entails evaluating the environmental impact of conservative policies, assessing their economic implications for resource-dependent industries, and gauging the resilience of conservative frameworks in addressing contemporary resource management challenges.

Conservation and Wildlife Protection

CONSERVATION AND WILDLIFE protection have long been central themes of environmental stewardship, drawing attention to the critical need for responsible management of natural habitats and the preservation of biodiversity. Under the conservative agenda, these efforts are approached through a lens that emphasizes private property rights, market-based solutions, and decentralized decision-making to achieve sustainable and effective conservation practices. In this chapter, we will delve into the conservative strategies and policies aimed at conserving natural habitats and protecting wildlife, examining their principles, tools, and real-world implications.

The conservative approach to conservation and wildlife protection prioritizes market-based solutions, private-sector engagement, and decentralized decision-making to achieve effective and sustainable resource management, recognizing the intrinsic value of natural habitats and biodiversity.

One of the primary pieces of evidence supporting the conservative approach to conservation and wildlife protection is the emphasis on private property rights as a driver for responsible environmental stewardship. Conservative principles uphold the idea that individuals have a vested interest in preserving and managing their own properties, leading to more effective and sustainable conservation efforts. This is evidenced by numerous case studies where private landowners have successfully implemented conservation measures to protect habitats and wildlife on their properties.

In examining the role of private property rights in conservation, it becomes evident that individuals are more likely to invest in and actively manage their property when they have a clear stake in its well-being. By empowering landowners to make decisions about conservation on their own properties, the conservative approach fosters a sense of ownership and responsibility, leading to more effective and sustainable outcomes. This has been observed in various conservation programs where private landowners have voluntarily participated in habitat protection and restoration efforts, resulting in tangible benefits for wildlife and ecosystems.

Critics of the conservative approach to conservation often argue that market-based solutions and private property rights may not adequately address the collective responsibility for protecting natural habitats and wildlife. They contend that relying solely on individual landowners' initiatives may not be sufficient to address broader conservation challenges, particularly in areas where critical habitats are under threat from development or other external pressures.

THE CONSERVATIVE AGENDA

In response to these counterarguments, it is important to note that while the conservative approach emphasizes private property rights, it also recognizes the need for collaborative efforts and partnerships to address larger conservation challenges. Market-based solutions and private initiatives can be complemented by strategic conservation easements, public-private partnerships, and conservation incentives to ensure comprehensive and coordinated conservation efforts that extend beyond individual properties.

Additional support for the conservative approach to conservation and wildlife protection can be found in the success of market-based mechanisms such as conservation banking and habitat exchanges, which have demonstrated the effectiveness of leveraging economic incentives to achieve conservation objectives. These innovative approaches have facilitated the protection and restoration of critical habitats while providing economic opportunities for landowners, aligning conservation goals with market forces.

The conservative agenda for conservation and wildlife protection presents a compelling framework that prioritizes private property rights, market-based solutions, and decentralized decision-making as key drivers for effective and sustainable resource management. By recognizing the inherent value of natural habitats and biodiversity, and empowering individuals to take an active role in conservation, conservative strategies offer a nuanced and pragmatic approach to addressing the complex challenges of environmental stewardship. Through a combination of market incentives, private initiatives, and collaborative partnerships, the conservative approach underscores the importance of individual responsibility and collective action in safeguarding natural ecosystems and wildlife for future generations.

JACK DONAHUE

Innovation and Technology in Environmental Solutions

IN TODAY'S WORLD, THE intersection of innovation, technology, and environmental solutions has become increasingly crucial in addressing the myriad challenges facing our planet. The conservative agenda recognizes the potential of innovation and technology as powerful tools for advancing environmental sustainability and offers a distinct approach to harnessing their potential for the greater good. This chapter will explore the conservative strategies and policies that promote innovation and technology as solutions to environmental challenges, emphasizing their role in driving positive change and fostering sustainable practices.

Research and development play a pivotal role in driving innovation and technological advancements in the environmental sector. Conservative strategies prioritize the promotion of R&D through public-private partnerships, tax incentives, and grants to support the exploration and development of cutting-edge technologies aimed at environmental solutions. By fostering a conducive environment for scientific inquiry and technological breakthroughs, the conservative agenda seeks to accelerate the pace of innovation in addressing environmental challenges.

Numerous case studies and reports have highlighted the positive impact of R&D investments in environmental technologies, showcasing how breakthroughs in areas such as renewable energy, waste management, and resource efficiency have stemmed from sustained commitment to research and development. Testimonials from industry experts and academic researchers further underscore the importance of R&D in driving environmental innovation and technological progress.

THE CONSERVATIVE AGENDA

The practical applications of promoting R&D in environmental technologies are far-reaching, spanning from the development of advanced renewable energy systems to the creation of novel waste-to-resource processes. By investing in R&D, conservative policies aim to unleash the potential for game-changing technologies that can mitigate environmental impacts and promote sustainable practices across various sectors.

Transitioning from the promotion of R&D, the conservative agenda extends its focus to the integration of clean technologies in industrial practices, emphasizing the pivotal role of technological adoption in driving environmental sustainability and operational efficiency.

Clean technologies encompass a wide array of innovations designed to minimize environmental impact and resource consumption in industrial processes. Conservative approaches advocate for the integration of clean technologies through incentives, regulatory frameworks, and industry partnerships, aiming to facilitate the adoption of sustainable practices within manufacturing, energy production, and resource-intensive sectors. By incentivizing the implementation of clean technologies, conservative policies seek to drive substantial reductions in emissions, resource usage, and environmental footprint across industrial operations.

Empirical evidence from industrial case studies and emissions data showcases the tangible benefits of integrating clean technologies, demonstrating significant reductions in greenhouse gas emissions, water usage, and waste generation. Testimonials from industry leaders and technology providers further underscore the positive outcomes of embracing clean technologies, highlighting the role of conservative policies in fostering a conducive environment for sustainable industrial practices.

The practical applications of integrating clean technologies extend to diverse industrial settings, from the deployment of energy-efficient manufacturing processes to the adoption of advanced air and water treatment systems. By promoting the integration of clean technologies, conservative strategies aim to drive operational cost savings, environmental compliance, and long-term sustainability across industrial sectors.

Transitioning from industrial practices, the conservative agenda directs its attention to the encouragement of private sector investment in green innovation, recognizing the pivotal role of private enterprise in driving environmental solutions and fostering entrepreneurial initiatives.

Private sector investment plays a critical role in catalyzing green innovation and technological advancements aimed at environmental sustainability. Conservative policies prioritize the encouragement of private sector investment through financial incentives, venture capital support, and regulatory frameworks that foster a conducive environment for green innovation. By leveraging private capital and entrepreneurial expertise, conservative strategies aim to spur the development and deployment of environmentally beneficial technologies, products, and services that address pressing environmental challenges.

Case studies of successful green innovation ventures and sustainable startups illustrate the transformative impact of private sector investment in driving environmental progress, showcasing the role of conservative policies in unlocking private capital for green initiatives. Testimonials from investors, entrepreneurs, and industry pioneers further underscore the significance of private sector engagement in nurturing green innovation and fostering sustainable business models.

The practical applications of encouraging private sector investment in green innovation manifest in the form of scalable environmental technologies, eco-friendly consumer products, and sustainable business models that align profitability with environmental stewardship. By incentivizing private sector investment, conservative approaches aim to catalyze a wave of green entrepreneurship and innovation, steering markets towards sustainable solutions and driving positive environmental outcomes.

Building upon the encouragement of private sector investment, the conservative agenda emphasizes the importance of fostering collaboration between government and technology entrepreneurs, recognizing the synergistic potential of public-private partnerships in advancing environmental innovation and addressing societal challenges.

Collaboration between government entities and technology entrepreneurs represents a cornerstone of conservative strategies for promoting environmental innovation and technological solutions. By fostering partnerships, joint initiatives, and innovation hubs, conservative policies aim to create a fertile ground for the co-creation and deployment of impactful environmental technologies. The convergence of governmental resources, regulatory support, and entrepreneurial ingenuity can catalyze the development and adoption of transformative solutions that address environmental challenges while fostering economic growth and job creation.

Success stories of collaborative projects and innovation accelerators underscore the substantial benefits of government-entrepreneur partnerships in driving environmental innovation, showcasing how conservative policies have facilitated the emergence of pioneering technologies and solutions through collaborative efforts.

Testimonials from technology entrepreneurs and government officials further highlight the positive outcomes of fostering collaboration, emphasizing the role of conservative approaches in bridging public and private interests for sustainable innovation.

The practical applications of fostering collaboration between government and technology entrepreneurs materialize in the form of groundbreaking environmental solutions, technological advancements, and policy frameworks that reflect the collective input of diverse stakeholders. By nurturing collaborative environments, conservative strategies aim to unleash the potential for cross-sectoral partnerships that drive meaningful environmental impact and societal benefits.

Continuing the narrative, the conservative agenda underscores the pivotal role of harnessing data and analytics for informed environmental decision-making, recognizing the transformative power of data-driven insights in shaping effective environmental policies and practices.

Data and analytics serve as indispensable tools in informing evidence-based environmental decision-making and shaping effective policies and practices. Conservative strategies prioritize the harnessing of data and analytics through technological investments, data sharing frameworks, and interdisciplinary research collaborations, aiming to empower stakeholders with actionable insights and predictive models that drive informed environmental choices. By leveraging data-driven approaches, conservative policies seek to optimize resource allocation, mitigate environmental risks, and monitor the impact of environmental interventions with precision and rigor.

Empirical evidence from environmental monitoring programs, remote sensing technologies, and data-driven policy assessments showcases the instrumental role of data and analytics in guiding impactful environmental decisions, demonstrating how conservative policies have enabled evidence-based approaches to environmental management and regulation. Testimonials from data scientists, policy analysts, and environmental practitioners further underscore the significance of harnessing data for informed decision-making, highlighting the role of conservative strategies in fostering a data-driven environmental governance framework.

The practical applications of harnessing data and analytics extend to diverse environmental domains, from precision conservation planning and climate modeling to real-time environmental risk assessment and adaptive management strategies. By prioritizing data-driven approaches, conservative policies aim to equip decision-makers with the tools and insights needed to address environmental challenges with agility, foresight, and measurable impact.

Transitioning from the utilization of data and analytics, the conservative agenda places emphasis on supporting entrepreneurship in sustainable solutions, recognizing the role of entrepreneurial ventures in driving environmental innovation and fostering dynamic solutions to complex environmental challenges.

Entrepreneurship serves as a catalyst for fostering sustainable solutions and technological innovations that address environmental challenges. Conservative strategies prioritize the support of entrepreneurship in sustainable solutions through business incubation programs, mentorship networks, and regulatory frameworks that encourage the development and scaling of environmentally beneficial ventures. By nurturing an ecosystem of sustainable entrepreneurship, conservative policies aim to unlock the potential for transformative solutions, disruptive technologies, and market-driven approaches that align economic prosperity with environmental stewardship.

Success stories of sustainable startups, eco-entrepreneurs, and green technology pioneers highlight the positive outcomes of supporting entrepreneurship in sustainable solutions, showcasing how conservative policies have fueled a wave of innovative ventures and technologies that contribute to environmental progress. Testimonials from sustainable entrepreneurs, venture capitalists, and industry experts further underscore the role of conservative approaches in fostering an entrepreneurial landscape conducive to sustainable innovation and environmental impact.

The Future of Environmental Stewardship

AS THE WORLD GRAPPLES with the complex and pressing challenges of environmental conservation, it is imperative to contemplate the future of environmental stewardship through a conservative lens. The conservative agenda, with its emphasis on innovation, technology, and sustainable practices, presents a distinct approach to addressing environmental concerns.

How can conservative strategies harness the power of innovation and technology to not only address, but also prevent, environmental challenges in the long term?

In the contemporary environmental landscape, the urgency to combat pressing ecological issues has never been more pronounced. As we confront the consequences of climate change, resource depletion, and biodiversity loss, it becomes crucial to assess how conservative policies can leverage innovation and technology to foster sustainable solutions that transcend immediate mitigation and extend to long-term environmental resilience.

THE CONSERVATIVE AGENDA

The central issue that demands our attention is the need for proactive, forward-thinking strategies that go beyond reactive measures to address environmental challenges. While conventional approaches often focus on mitigating the immediate impact of environmental issues, the conservative agenda seeks to address the root causes and prevent future crises through innovation and technology-driven solutions.

Conventional environmental approaches primarily rely on regulatory measures and short-term interventions to manage environmental challenges. While these efforts are undoubtedly essential, they often overlook the transformative potential of innovation and technology to drive sustainable change at a systemic level.

The real solution lies in harnessing the power of innovation and technology as proactive tools for environmental stewardship. Conservative strategies advocate for the promotion of research and development in environmental technologies, the integration of clean technologies in industrial practices, the encouragement of private sector investment in green innovation, fostering collaboration between government and technology entrepreneurs, harnessing data and analytics for informed environmental

Imagine a world where proactive environmental solutions driven by innovation and technology not only mitigate the detrimental effects of climate change but also create a thriving ecosystem where nature and humanity coexist harmoniously. By engaging with these concepts on an emotional level, we can cultivate a genuine commitment to environmental stewardship that transcends mere compliance and embraces a proactive, visionary approach to conservation.

Criminal Justice and Law Enforcement

The Conservative Approach to Law and Order

At the heart of the conservative perspective on law and order is the central belief that stricter laws, aggressive policing, harsh punishments, and maximum penalties serve to deter crime and promote public safety. Conservatives reject the notion that external factors like poverty, lack of education, or a difficult upbringing might lessen an individual's culpability for their crimes. Instead, the focus is on personal responsibility and just punishments that fit the crime.

Conservatives are skeptical of rehabilitation approaches that seem overly forgiving or accommodating to those who willingly commit offenses. The fear is that anything less than tough sentences fails to discourage criminality or deliver true justice. For victims and their families, strong sentencing provides a sense that there are consequences for destructive actions. From the conservative viewpoint, society has a duty to punish those who infringe on others' rights and freedoms through unlawful behavior.

Conservatives advocate for policies aligned with their law and order perspective. They push for legislation that cracks down on patterns of offense with mandatory minimums, truth-in-sentencing laws, and habitual offender statutes like "three strikes" rules requiring life sentences after three serious crimes. These types of sentencing guidelines restrict judicial discretion during punishment which conservatives view as being too lenient and inconsistent.

Conservatives also pressure leaders to fund advanced training for police forces while demanding respect and compliance with law enforcement. Use of force policies should provide leeway for police to subdue dangerous suspects. At the same time, conservatives expect individuals to take personal responsibility by cooperating fully with authorities and not resisting arrest. The approach tends to be deferential to the challenges of police work while emphasizing compliance by citizens.

Additionally, conservatives state that gun control measures mainly limit lawful owners while failing to prevent criminals from illegally obtaining firearms. Instead of additional gun regulations, conservatives push for strictly enforcing sentences for the use of a firearm in a crime, illegal weapon possession, and firearm-related violence. The goal is to punish violators to the fullest extent possible.

For drug crimes, conservatives advocate for ramping up interdiction efforts, empowering police, and imposing mandatory minimums for trafficking and distribution. While liberals may see treatment as an alternative to incarceration, conservatives see rehab as a luxury that lets dealers and users off the hook. Jail time serves as the most effective deterrent in their eyes.

However, the conservative approach is not without its criticisms. Detractors point out that harsh sentencing and overcrowded prisons have not reduced the crime rate over the past decades. The U.S. has the world's highest incarceration rate despite declining crime, indicating that the policy emphasis skews too punitive. Sky-high costs to maintain so many prisoners could be better spent on early intervention programs.

Additionally, the focus on individual responsibility ignores research on how adversity, trauma, poverty, addiction and mental illness contribute to criminal pathways. A more nuanced policy approach would incorporate preventative social services and support successful re-entry after release. Otherwise, the revolving door keeps spinning through the justice system without addressing root problems.

While holding individuals accountable remains important, data shows that rehabilitative methods combined with consequences provide better outcomes than punishment alone. Most critics agree that personal responsibility plays a central role, but that conservatives rely too heavily on an inflated "tough on crime" mentality despite contradicting evidence.

The conservative perspective emphasizes individual blame, strict sentencing, aggressive policing, and punitive incarceration as the central means to maintain law, order and justice. Opponents counter that the approach is overly simplistic, excessively harsh, and comes with significant financial and societal drawbacks that perpetuate crime cycles. The debate continues, but the conservative viewpoint remains popular with large segments of the population who want to "get tough" on criminals.

Policing and Community Relations

COMMUNITY POLICING is a fundamental aspect of law enforcement that aims to establish a positive relationship between the police and the community they serve. It focuses on proactive problem-solving and building trust and cooperation between law enforcement agencies and the communities they serve.

Conservative perspectives on community policing emphasize the importance of maintaining law and order while also fostering a strong bond between the police and the community. It is based on the belief that when the police are an integral part of the community, they can better understand its needs and concerns, thereby improving their ability to ensure public safety.

Conservatives advocate for a proactive approach to community policing, which involves engaging with citizens, addressing underlying social issues, and working collaboratively to prevent crime. This approach encourages police officers to be visible and accessible in the community, fostering open lines of communication and trust.

Conservative principles underscore the significance of empowering local law enforcement agencies to make decisions tailored to the specific needs of their communities. This approach prioritizes local control and accountability, allowing for flexibility in addressing community concerns and crime prevention strategies.

One example of successful community policing from a conservative perspective is the implementation of neighborhood watch programs. These programs involve community members taking an active role in preventing crime by working closely with law enforcement. By participating in neighborhood watch programs, citizens become the eyes and ears of law enforcement, contributing to the overall safety and security of their neighborhoods.

Additionally, the concept of "broken windows policing," which focuses on addressing minor infractions and disorderly behavior, has been employed in conservative approaches to community policing. This strategy aims to maintain order and prevent more serious crimes by addressing visible signs of disorder and decay within the community.

While conservative perspectives on community policing emphasize the role of law enforcement in maintaining order and promoting community safety, it is important to acknowledge that there are various viewpoints on the approach to community relations within different political ideologies.

Some individuals may have reservations about the conservative approach, expressing concerns about potential over-policing and the impact on certain communities. It is essential to consider these perspectives and engage in constructive dialogue to address any potential drawbacks and work towards a balanced and effective approach to community policing.

Data and statistics play a crucial role in understanding the impact of community policing efforts. Research has shown that communities with strong relationships between law enforcement and residents experience lower crime rates and improved overall community well-being. Moreover, studies have demonstrated that when citizens feel a sense of trust and partnership with law enforcement, they are more likely to report crimes and cooperate with investigations.

Furthermore, factual evidence supports the effectiveness of community policing strategies in reducing crime and enhancing public safety. By integrating data and facts into the discussion, we can gain valuable insights into the tangible benefits of conservative approaches to community policing.

When discussing community policing, it is essential to clarify complex terms such as "proactive problem-solving," "local control," and "neighborhood watch programs" to ensure that the concepts are easily understood. Proactive problem-solving involves identifying and addressing underlying issues that contribute to crime, while local control refers to the authority of local law enforcement agencies to implement tailored strategies. Neighborhood watch programs are initiatives where community members collaborate with law enforcement to prevent crime in their neighborhoods.

Conservative perspectives on community policing prioritize the establishment of strong relationships between law enforcement and the community, promoting proactive problem-solving, and emphasizing local control and accountability. By integrating examples, exploring different viewpoints, and incorporating data and facts, we have gained a comprehensive understanding of the conservative approach to community policing.

Key takeaways from this chapter include the importance of building trust and cooperation between law enforcement and the community, the effectiveness of proactive community policing strategies, and the necessity of considering diverse perspectives in shaping law enforcement policies. Understanding these key principles is essential for developing effective and sustainable community policing initiatives that align with conservative values and prioritize the well-being of communities.

Criminal Justice Reform

THE GOAL OF CRIMINAL justice reform from a conservative perspective is to promote public safety, reduce recidivism, and ensure that the criminal justice system is fair, effective, and accountable. This chapter will explore conservative proposals for criminal justice reform, focusing on strategies to achieve these objectives.

Before delving into criminal justice reform, it is essential to understand the foundational principles that guide conservative approaches to the criminal justice system. Additionally, familiarity with the current challenges and shortcomings within the system is crucial to developing effective reform strategies.

Conservative proposals for criminal justice reform are multifaceted, encompassing various aspects of the criminal justice system, including sentencing, rehabilitation, reentry programs, and the role of law enforcement. The overarching goal is to create a system that balances accountability with the opportunity for redemption and rehabilitation, ultimately reducing crime and enhancing public safety.

Conservative criminal justice reform emphasizes the importance of proportionate sentencing that takes into account the severity of the offense and the individual's criminal history. Implementing sentencing guidelines that provide judges with discretion while ensuring consistency and fairness is a key component of reform efforts. Additionally, exploring alternatives to incarceration for non-violent offenses, such as drug courts and diversion programs, can effectively address underlying issues contributing to criminal behavior.

Investing in evidence-based rehabilitation programs within correctional facilities and supporting reentry initiatives for individuals returning to society after incarceration are vital components of conservative criminal justice reform. These programs focus on addressing substance abuse, mental health, and skill development to reduce recidivism and facilitate successful reintegration into the community.

Conservative proposals for criminal justice reform emphasize the need for ongoing training for law enforcement officers to enhance de-escalation techniques, crisis intervention, and cultural competency. Furthermore, promoting accountability and transparency within law enforcement agencies through the implementation of body-worn cameras, use-of-force policies, and civilian oversight mechanisms contributes to building trust and legitimacy within communities.

Prioritizing the rights and needs of crime victims is a fundamental aspect of conservative criminal justice reform. Implementing victim-centered practices that provide support, resources, and involvement in the criminal justice process can contribute to healing and restoration for those impacted by crime.

- It is crucial to approach criminal justice reform with a comprehensive understanding of the complexities and interconnectedness of the various components within the system.

- While focusing on rehabilitation and reentry, it is important to balance support for individuals with accountability for their actions to ensure public safety.

- Engaging in collaborative efforts with stakeholders, including law enforcement, community organizations, and policymakers, is essential for successful implementation of reform initiatives.

Successful implementation of conservative criminal justice reform can be validated through the examination of recidivism rates, the effectiveness of rehabilitation programs, community engagement with law enforcement, and the experiences of individuals impacted by the reformed policies.

In the process of implementing criminal justice reform, potential challenges may arise, such as resistance to change, resource limitations, and differing perspectives on the appropriate balance between accountability and rehabilitation. Addressing these challenges requires open dialogue, evidence-based solutions, and a commitment to the overarching goal of promoting public safety and fairness within the criminal justice system.

Conservative proposals for criminal justice reform are rooted in principles of accountability, rehabilitation, and public safety. By focusing on proportionate sentencing, evidence-based rehabilitation, law enforcement training and accountability, and victim-centered approaches, conservative reform efforts aim to create a more effective and equitable criminal justice system.

Understanding the nuanced details and considerations involved in these proposals is essential for advancing meaningful and sustainable criminal justice reform.

The Death Penalty

THE DEATH PENALTY, also known as capital punishment, is a legal process where a person is sentenced to death by the state as punishment for a crime. This sentence is usually reserved for the most serious offenses, such as murder, and is a highly controversial and debated topic. The significance of the death penalty lies in its moral, ethical, and practical implications within the criminal justice system.

The purpose of comparing and contrasting the death penalty with alternative forms of punishment is to gain insights into the effectiveness, morality, and implications of capital punishment. By examining the criteria and rationale behind the use of the death penalty, this comparison aims to provide a balanced view of its role in the criminal justice system and its broader societal impact.

The benchmarks for comparison will include considerations of deterrence, retribution, justice, cost, and the potential for wrongful convictions. These parameters will serve as the framework for analyzing the complexities of the death penalty and its alternatives.

When comparing the death penalty with alternative forms of punishment, it becomes apparent that one of the primary arguments in favor of the death penalty is its potential deterrent effect on crime. Proponents argue that the threat of execution serves as a powerful deterrent, preventing individuals from committing heinous crimes. However, empirical studies have shown mixed results regarding the actual deterrent effect of the death penalty, with some suggesting that the certainty of punishment, rather than the severity, plays a more significant role in deterring crime.

In contrast, alternative forms of punishment, such as life imprisonment without parole, offer the possibility of rehabilitation and redemption. While the death penalty permanently ends the life of the offender, life imprisonment provides an opportunity for individuals to reflect, reform, and potentially contribute positively to society within the confines of a correctional facility.

Delving into the comparisons reveals that the complexities of the death penalty extend beyond its purported deterrence effect. The moral and ethical considerations of executing individuals, the potential for wrongful convictions, and the emotional toll on victims' families are important factors that require thoughtful analysis. Moreover, the societal costs associated with the lengthy appeals process and the overall administration of the death penalty raise questions about its practicality and efficiency within the criminal justice system.

Connecting historical and theoretical comparisons to current realities underscores the ongoing relevance of the death penalty debate. Recent advancements in forensic science and the exoneration of individuals from death row due to DNA evidence highlight the fallibility of the justice system and the potential for irreversible mistakes in capital cases. These real-world examples underscore the importance of critically evaluating the role of the death penalty in contemporary society.

The comparison and contrast of the death penalty with alternative forms of punishment provide valuable insights into the complexities of the criminal justice system. By examining the nuances of deterrence, retribution, justice, cost, and the potential for wrongful convictions, a comprehensive understanding of the implications of capital punishment and its alternatives can be achieved. This analysis serves as a foundation for informed discourse and policy considerations regarding the role of the death penalty in a conservative agenda for criminal justice reform.

Second Chance Programs

THE CONSERVATIVE AGENDA has long been rooted in principles of personal responsibility, accountability, and the belief in second chances. In the context of criminal justice reform, second chance programs and efforts to reintegrate ex-offenders into society align with these core conservative values. By addressing the challenges faced by individuals with criminal records and advocating for their successful reentry into communities, conservatives aim to foster a society that embraces redemption and offers pathways to productive citizenship.

This comprehensive exploration of conservative support for second chance programs encompasses several pivotal points:

Conservative support for second chance programs is grounded in the recognition that individuals who have served their sentences should have the opportunity to rebuild their lives and contribute positively to society. Rehabilitation and redemption are fundamental tenets of the conservative approach to criminal justice, emphasizing the potential for personal transformation and the capacity for individuals to change their behavior. By investing in programs that address underlying issues such as substance abuse, mental health challenges, and skill development, conservatives seek to empower ex-offenders to break the cycle of crime and embrace law-abiding lifestyles.

One of the key challenges faced by ex-offenders is the web of legal and societal barriers that hinder their successful reintegration into communities. Conservatives advocate for the removal of unnecessary obstacles that impede the ability of individuals with criminal records to secure housing, employment, and educational opportunities. This includes initiatives to reform occupational licensing laws, expand access to expungement and record-sealing mechanisms, and promote fair hiring practices that consider an individual's qualifications and potential rather than solely focusing on past criminal history.

Economic stability and self-sufficiency are critical components of successful reentry for ex-offenders. Conservative policies and programs prioritize the creation of pathways to meaningful employment, entrepreneurship, and financial independence. This may involve collaborations with businesses, community organizations, and workforce development agencies to provide training, mentorship, and job placement services tailored to the unique needs of individuals with criminal records. By equipping ex-offenders with the tools to build sustainable livelihoods, conservatives aim to reduce recidivism and strengthen the economic fabric of communities.

The conservative approach to second chance programs emphasizes the symbiotic relationship between successful reentry and public safety. By investing in evidence-based reentry initiatives, conservatives seek to address the underlying factors that contribute to criminal behavior and recidivism. This includes support for transitional housing, access to healthcare and counseling services, and the promotion of community supervision models that prioritize accountability and support. Through these efforts, conservatives aim to reduce the likelihood of reoffending and promote safer neighborhoods for all residents.

Recognizing the interconnectedness of individuals within society, conservatives emphasize the importance of strengthening familial and communal bonds as part of the reentry process. Second chance programs that focus on family reunification, parenting support, and community engagement play a vital role in restoring social connections and fostering a sense of belonging for ex-offenders. By nurturing these relationships and promoting social responsibility, conservatives aim to create environments where individuals with criminal records can thrive and fulfill their potential as productive members of society.

The effectiveness of conservative-backed second chance programs is supported by empirical evidence and firsthand accounts of individuals who have benefited from these initiatives. Research studies have shown that comprehensive reentry programs that address employment, housing, healthcare, and substance abuse treatment contribute to lower recidivism rates and positive outcomes for ex-offenders. Testimonials from program participants underscore the transformative impact of second chance opportunities, highlighting stories of personal growth, restored relationships, and meaningful contributions to communities.

In practice, conservative support for second chance programs manifests through legislative efforts, public-private partnerships, and community-based initiatives. This may involve the introduction of reentry-focused policies at the state and federal levels, collaboration with employers to create inclusive hiring practices, and the allocation of resources to support reentry service providers. By translating principles into actionable strategies, conservatives actively work to implement comprehensive reentry solutions that address the multifaceted needs of individuals with criminal records.

The interconnected nature of the points outlined underscores the holistic approach that underpins conservative support for second chance programs. Each aspect contributes to a cohesive framework that prioritizes rehabilitation, reintegration, and the restoration of individuals and communities. As the discussion transitions from promoting rehabilitation and redemption to fostering economic opportunity and enhancing public safety, the continuity of these efforts becomes apparent, reflecting the integrated nature of conservative solutions for effective criminal justice reform.

The conservative agenda for second chance programs is rooted in the belief that every individual has the capacity for redemption and deserves the opportunity to rebuild their lives after serving their sentences. By promoting rehabilitation, removing barriers to reentry, fostering economic opportunity, enhancing public safety, and restoring families and communities, conservatives seek to create a society that embraces the potential for positive transformation. Through evidence-based policies and practical interventions, conservative support for second chance programs underscores a commitment to justice, opportunity, and the restoration of dignity for individuals seeking a second chance.

Victims' Rights and Restorative Justice

VICTIMS' RIGHTS AND restorative justice are essential components of the conservative agenda. This discussion will explore the conservative perspective on the rights of victims, the principles of restorative justice, and the significance of these concepts in the broader context of criminal justice reform.

The conservative approach emphasizes the recognition of victims' rights and advocates for restorative justice as a means of promoting healing, accountability, and community restoration within the criminal justice system.

To support this claim, it is crucial to understand the foundational principles that underpin conservative perspectives on victims' rights and restorative justice. Central to this perspective is the acknowledgment of the profound impact that crime has on individuals and communities. Victims' rights are viewed as integral to the pursuit of justice and the restoration of the social fabric. Restorative justice, in turn, is seen as a means of addressing the harm caused by criminal behavior and fostering meaningful accountability and reconciliation.

Conservative support for victims' rights and restorative justice is rooted in the belief that the criminal justice system should prioritize the needs and experiences of those who have been harmed. This includes advocating for legal protections and support services that empower victims to participate meaningfully in the criminal justice process. Moreover, restorative justice principles emphasize the importance of offender accountability, the repair of harm, and the involvement of the affected parties in the resolution of criminal conflicts.

Conservatives argue that the integration of victims' rights and restorative justice practices into the criminal justice system contributes to the overall goal of promoting public safety and addressing the needs of those impacted by crime. By prioritizing the rights of victims and emphasizing approaches that seek to repair the harm caused by criminal behavior, conservatives aim to create a system that is responsive to the needs of individuals and communities affected by crime.

Critics of the conservative approach to victims' rights and restorative justice may argue that prioritizing these aspects could potentially undermine the rights of the accused and lead to punitive measures that are not conducive to rehabilitation or the broader goals of justice reform. Additionally, some may question the practical implementation of restorative justice practices within the existing criminal justice framework, expressing concerns about the potential for re-traumatization or the inadequacy of such approaches in addressing more serious or violent offenses.

In response to these counterarguments, conservatives assert that the recognition of victims' rights and the implementation of restorative justice practices are not mutually exclusive to the rights of the accused or the pursuit of rehabilitation. Rather, they argue that a balanced approach that prioritizes victims' needs while also ensuring due process and opportunities for rehabilitation is essential to fostering a justice system that is fair, effective, and responsive to the needs of all stakeholders.

Furthermore, conservatives emphasize that restorative justice practices can be tailored to accommodate the severity and nature of different offenses, and that when implemented effectively, they have the potential to address the underlying factors that contribute to criminal behavior, promote accountability, and facilitate the healing and restoration of individuals and communities affected by crime.

It is important to note that empirical research and case studies have demonstrated the positive impact of incorporating restorative justice practices into the criminal justice system, particularly in cases of non-violent offenses and community-based conflicts. These findings provide further support for the efficacy of restorative justice approaches in addressing the needs of victims, promoting offender accountability, and contributing to the prevention of future harm.

The conservative perspective on victims' rights and restorative justice is grounded in the commitment to recognizing the experiences of those impacted by crime and advocating for approaches that prioritize healing, accountability, and community restoration. By integrating victims' rights and restorative justice principles into the criminal justice system, conservatives seek to create a more responsive and inclusive framework that addresses the multifaceted needs of individuals and communities affected by crime. This approach aligns with the conservative values of personal responsibility, community well-being, and the pursuit of justice that serves the interests of both victims and society as a whole.

The Future of Criminal Justice Reform

THE CONSERVATIVE AGENDA for criminal justice reform acknowledges the need for a balanced approach that addresses the complexities of the current criminal justice system. This includes recognizing the impact of crime on individuals and communities, fostering offender accountability, and promoting public safety while also advocating for the rights of the accused and opportunities for rehabilitation. It is within this context that the future of criminal justice reform must be considered, taking into account the evolving societal dynamics, the need for effective solutions, and the imperative to uphold the principles of justice and fairness.

One of the primary challenges facing conservative criminal justice reform is the issue of recidivism. The revolving door phenomenon, wherein individuals cycle in and out of the criminal justice system, poses a significant obstacle to achieving long-term public safety and rehabilitation. This problem is compounded by the inadequacy of existing rehabilitation and reintegration programs, as well as the prevalence of systemic barriers that hinder individuals from successfully transitioning out of the criminal justice system.

If the issue of recidivism is not effectively addressed, the consequences are far-reaching. Not only does recidivism perpetuate cycles of crime and victimization, but it also strains resources within the criminal justice system and undermines the potential for meaningful rehabilitation. Additionally, the societal impact of recidivism can erode trust in the justice system and contribute to the perpetuation of cycles of poverty and inequality.

To combat the challenge of recidivism, a multifaceted approach is necessary. This includes the implementation of evidence-based rehabilitation and reentry programs that address the underlying factors contributing to criminal behavior, such as substance abuse, mental health issues, and lack of educational and vocational opportunities. Furthermore, it involves the promotion of restorative justice practices that prioritize offender accountability, victim restoration, and community involvement in the resolution of criminal conflicts.

The practical steps to put these solutions into action involve a comprehensive review and reform of existing rehabilitation and reentry programs. This includes investing in resources for education, vocational training, mental health and substance abuse treatment, and transitional support services to facilitate successful reintegration. Additionally, the integration of restorative justice principles into the criminal justice system requires training and collaboration among justice practitioners, community stakeholders, and affected parties to ensure the effective implementation of restorative processes.

Research and empirical evidence suggest that the implementation of evidence-based rehabilitation and reentry programs, coupled with restorative justice practices, yields positive outcomes. In instances where comprehensive reentry programs have been successfully implemented, there has been a reduction in recidivism rates, an increase in post-release employment and educational opportunities, and a decrease in the burden on the criminal justice system. Similarly, the application of restorative justice principles has demonstrated the potential to foster offender accountability, promote victim healing, and strengthen community cohesion.

While the proposed solutions emphasize the integration of evidence-based rehabilitation and restorative justice practices, alternative approaches must also be considered. These may include the exploration of diversion programs for non-violent offenders, the implementation of community-based sentencing options, and the expansion of mental health and substance abuse treatment services within the community.

As the conservative agenda for criminal justice reform continues to evolve, it is imperative to critically assess the effectiveness of proposed solutions and to remain responsive to the changing dynamics of the criminal justice landscape. By addressing the challenge of recidivism through evidence-based rehabilitation and restorative justice practices, conservatives can contribute to the creation of a criminal justice system that prioritizes public safety, rehabilitation, and the principles of justice and fairness. This approach aligns with the conservative values of individual responsibility, community well-being, and the pursuit of a criminal justice system that serves the interests of both victims and society as a whole.

As we move forward, it is essential to engage in robust dialogue, collaboration, and innovation to ensure that conservative criminal justice reforms are informed by evidence, guided by compassion, and dedicated to the pursuit of enduring solutions that benefit individuals, families, and communities across the nation.

Immigration Policies

The Conservative Approach to Immigration

As conservatives, the approach to immigration is rooted in the belief in secure borders and the importance of enforcing immigration laws. This stance is based on the fundamental principles of sovereignty, the rule of law, and the protection of national security and economic interests. In order to fully comprehend the conservative perspective on immigration, it is essential to clarify key words that are central to understanding this complex and contentious issue.

Understanding the terminology and concepts surrounding immigration is crucial for engaging with the conservative approach to this topic. By delving into the key words and their real-world implications, we can gain a deeper understanding of the conservative perspective on immigration.

1. Sovereignty: In the conservative approach to immigration, sovereignty is a foundational concept. It emphasizes the notion that a nation has the inherent right to govern itself, control its borders, and make decisions that are in the best interest of its citizens. From a conservative perspective, the recognition and protection of national sovereignty are critical for maintaining a stable and secure society.

2. Rule of Law: The conservative belief in the rule of law underscores the importance of upholding and enforcing immigration laws. By adhering to legal processes and regulations, conservatives aim to ensure that individuals entering the country do so in a manner that respects the established legal framework. This approach seeks to

maintain order, fairness, and accountability within the immigration system.

3. National Security: For conservatives, national security is a paramount concern in the context of immigration. The protection of the nation's borders and the enforcement of immigration laws are viewed as essential components of safeguarding the country from potential threats, including terrorism, criminal activity, and other risks to public safety. The conservative approach to immigration prioritizes measures that enhance national security while balancing humanitarian considerations.

4. Economic Interests: Conservative perspectives on immigration underscore the significance of considering the economic impact of immigration policies. This includes evaluating the potential contributions of immigrants to the workforce, the preservation of job opportunities for citizens, and the overall economic stability of the country. By aligning immigration policies with economic interests, conservatives aim to promote sustainable growth and prosperity for the nation.

5. Immigration Laws: In the conservative approach, immigration laws serve as the framework for managing and regulating the entry, residence, and rights of individuals seeking to immigrate to the country. These laws are designed to establish clear guidelines, maintain order, and uphold the principles of sovereignty, the rule of law, and national security. From a conservative standpoint, the enforcement of immigration laws is essential for preserving the integrity of the immigration system and ensuring that immigration processes are conducted lawfully and responsibly.

To better understand the conservative approach to immigration, it is helpful to relate these key terms to real-world scenarios and familiar concepts that illustrate their relevance and implications.

Consider a homeowner who takes pride in maintaining the security and integrity of their property. Just as the homeowner has the right to control access to their home and establish rules for visitors, sovereign nations have the right to govern their borders and enforce immigration laws. This analogy highlights the conservative emphasis on sovereignty and the protection of national borders as essential components of responsible governance.

Moreover, the concept of the rule of law can be illustrated through the enforcement of traffic regulations. Just as traffic laws exist to ensure safety, order, and accountability on the roads, immigration laws serve a similar purpose within the context of national borders. Upholding immigration laws aligns with the conservative commitment to maintaining lawful and orderly processes for individuals seeking entry into the country.

National security can be likened to the measures taken to protect a community from potential threats. Just as community members work together to safeguard their neighborhoods, conservatives advocate for policies and practices that prioritize the security of the nation and its citizens. This connection underscores the conservative perspective on immigration as a vital aspect of safeguarding the well-being and interests of the country.

Economic interests in the context of immigration can be illustrated through the principles of responsible budgeting and financial planning. Just as individuals and households strive to make sound economic decisions that promote stability and prosperity, conservatives advocate for immigration policies that consider the economic impact on the nation. This parallel emphasizes the conservative focus on fostering sustainable economic growth and opportunity for both citizens and immigrants.

In linking these key terms to real-world concepts, we gain a deeper appreciation for the conservative approach to immigration and its implications for governance, security, and prosperity.

The conservative perspective on immigration is multifaceted, encompassing considerations of sovereignty, the rule of law, national security, economic interests, and immigration laws. By delving into the definitions and real-world connections of these key terms, we can begin to unravel the complexities of the conservative approach to immigration and its implications for national policy and governance.

Border Security and Immigration Enforcement

THE CONSERVATIVE APPROACH to border security and immigration enforcement is rooted in the belief in secure borders and the importance of upholding and enforcing immigration laws. This stance is based on fundamental principles, including sovereignty, the rule of law, and the protection of national security and economic interests. To provide a comprehensive understanding of conservative strategies for securing the border and enforcing immigration laws, it is essential to delve deeper into the concepts and perspectives related to this critical issue.

Securing the border and enforcing immigration laws are integral components of conservative strategies aimed at safeguarding the nation's sovereignty, upholding the rule of law, and protecting the well-being of its citizens and economic interests. This chapter will thoroughly examine the conservative approaches to border security and immigration enforcement, shedding light on the underlying principles, strategies, and implications.

The concept of border security encompasses a range of measures designed to prevent unauthorized entry into the country and to safeguard the integrity of national borders. Conservative approaches emphasize the deployment of physical barriers, enhanced surveillance technologies, and increased manpower to deter and apprehend individuals attempting to unlawfully enter the country. The enforcement of immigration laws involves upholding regulations and policies governing the entry, residence, and rights of individuals moving to the country. Conservatives advocate for strict adherence to immigration laws, including robust vetting processes, deportation of individuals who violate immigration regulations, and the establishment of clear guidelines for legal immigration pathways.

Legal Immigration and Pathways to Citizenship

LEGAL IMMIGRATION IS a foundational component of the conservative agenda, emphasizing the significance of merit-based immigration systems and the adherence to immigration laws. This chapter will explore the conservative stance on legal immigration, the merits of a fair and merit-based system, and the potential implications for the nation's economy and social fabric.

Conservative principles on legal immigration are rooted in the belief that immigration should be regulated to ensure that it benefits the nation and its citizens. The conservative approach seeks to prioritize legal immigration pathways, emphasizing the need for individuals to abide by immigration laws and contribute to the country's prosperity and growth. Conservative views emphasize the importance of upholding the rule of law and maintaining the integrity of the immigration system.

Conservative perspectives advocate for a merit-based immigration system that prioritizes individuals with skills, talents, and qualifications that are deemed beneficial to the nation's economy and society. This approach aims to attract individuals who can contribute to the country's innovation, workforce, and overall development. By emphasizing merit-based immigration, conservatives seek to ensure that immigration policies align with the nation's long-term interests and economic needs.

Exploring the economic and social implications of conservative views on legal immigration is crucial. Conservatives argue that a fair and merit-based immigration system can bolster the economy by attracting skilled workers, entrepreneurs, and professionals who contribute to innovation and productivity. Moreover, conservatives assert that such a system can enhance social cohesion by fostering the integration of immigrants who share the nation's values and are committed to assimilating into the fabric of American society.

When discussing conservative views on legal immigration, highlight the economic benefits of attracting skilled and qualified individuals who can contribute to key sectors of the economy, including technology, healthcare, and entrepreneurship.

While advocating for a merit-based system, it is essential to consider potential unintended consequences, such as the impact on family reunification and the need to balance skill-based immigration with the preservation of family ties.

Delving into the conservative perspective on legal immigration and pathways to citizenship reveals a nuanced approach that prioritizes the nation's long-term interests, economic prosperity, and the preservation of the rule of law. By examining the principles and strategies that underpin conservative views on legal immigration, readers can gain a deeper understanding of the conservative agenda in shaping immigration policies and pathways to citizenship.

Temporary Work Visas and Guest Worker Programs

LEGAL IMMIGRATION IS a multifaceted issue that encompasses various pathways for individuals to enter and contribute to the United States. Among these pathways, temporary work visas and guest worker programs play a significant role in addressing the nation's labor needs and fostering economic growth. Conservative perspectives on these immigration avenues underscore the importance of balancing economic demands with the protection of American workers and the preservation of national sovereignty. By exploring conservative views on temporary work visas and guest worker programs, we aim to delve into the complexities of these systems, analyze their implications, and provide insights into the broader conservative approach to immigration policy.

Temporary work visas and guest worker programs are essential components of the U.S. immigration system, allowing foreign nationals to enter the country for a limited duration to fill specific labor needs. These programs serve as mechanisms for addressing shortages in certain industries, promoting cultural exchange, and facilitating international cooperation. Conservative perspectives on these programs emphasize the need for prudent regulation, accountability, and a keen focus on protecting American workers and national security.

The purpose of comparing temporary work visas and guest worker programs from a conservative viewpoint is to illuminate the underlying principles that guide conservative immigration policy. By examining these programs through a conservative lens, we seek to uncover the rationale behind conservative approaches to managing temporary labor migration, safeguarding domestic labor markets, and addressing the broader economic and social implications of temporary foreign worker programs.

In analyzing temporary work visas and guest worker programs, the criteria for comparison will revolve around the economic impact, regulatory framework, and the prioritization of domestic workers. Additionally, the assessment will consider the potential implications for national security and the preservation of American values and culture.

Temporary work visas, such as the H-1B and H-2B visas, are designed to address specific labor shortages in the United States. The H-1B visa program, for instance, caters to highly skilled workers in specialty occupations, including fields such as technology, engineering, and academia. Conservatives recognize the value of attracting top talent to contribute to American innovation and competitiveness. However, they emphasize the need for stringent oversight to prevent abuse and ensure that these visas do not undermine opportunities for American workers.

Guest worker programs, such as the H-2A and H-2B programs, provide opportunities for foreign workers to fill seasonal or temporary jobs in agriculture, hospitality, and other industries. Conservatives acknowledge the importance of these programs in addressing labor shortages, particularly in sectors vital to the American economy. Nonetheless, they stress the need for robust verification processes to protect American workers from displacement and prevent the exploitation of guest workers.

While both temporary work visas and guest worker programs serve to address labor needs, they differ in their focus and intended outcomes. Temporary work visas primarily target high-skilled professionals, aiming to attract individuals with specialized knowledge and expertise. In contrast, guest worker programs cater to a broader spectrum of industries and often address seasonal or temporary labor demands that may not require advanced skills or qualifications.

The comparison between temporary work visas and guest worker programs reveals the nuanced approach that conservatives advocate for in managing labor migration. Conservatives recognize the importance of attracting talent and meeting labor demands while ensuring that American workers are not displaced or disadvantaged. By scrutinizing the regulatory frameworks and oversight mechanisms of these programs, conservatives aim to strike a balance between economic pragmatism and safeguarding the interests of domestic workers.

The examination of temporary work visas and guest worker programs holds contemporary relevance as the United States grapples with evolving labor dynamics and economic challenges. With ongoing debates about immigration reform and the role of foreign workers, understanding conservative perspectives on these programs can offer insights into potential policy directions and the broader implications for the American workforce and economy.

Immigration and National Security

THE RELATIONSHIP BETWEEN immigration and national security has been a topic of significant interest and debate, particularly from a conservative perspective. Conservatives often emphasize the importance of protecting the nation from potential threats while balancing the need for legal immigration and the contributions of immigrants to the country's prosperity. This chapter aims to delve into the conservative viewpoint on how immigration impacts national security, examining claims using concrete evidence rooted in credible and verified information.

Conservatives assert that immigration policies have a direct impact on national security, with a focus on border security, vetting processes, and the potential risks associated with illegal immigration and refugee resettlement.

One of the primary pieces of evidence supporting the conservative claim is the significant role that border security plays in safeguarding national security. Conservatives argue that securing the borders is crucial in preventing unauthorized entry, human trafficking, and the potential infiltration of individuals with malicious intent.

The depth of this evidence can be explored by examining the statistics and incidents related to illegal border crossings, drug smuggling, and the apprehension of individuals with criminal backgrounds attempting to enter the country unlawfully. Additionally, analyzing the impact of porous borders on the ability to track and apprehend individuals who pose a threat to national security can further strengthen this evidence.

Counterarguments may present the perspective that stringent border security measures could hinder the legitimate flow of trade and tourism, potentially affecting the economy and international relations. Furthermore, critics might argue that the focus on border security overshadows other critical aspects of national security, such as cybersecurity and domestic threats.

In response, conservatives could clarify that while they emphasize border security, they also recognize the need for efficient trade and travel facilitation. Moreover, they may highlight that border security is just one component of a comprehensive national security strategy and does not negate the importance of addressing other threats.

Supporting evidence can be provided through case studies or expert analysis demonstrating how weaknesses in immigration policies and border security have been exploited in the past, leading to potential national security vulnerabilities.

The conservative perspective on the relationship between immigration and national security underscores the essential role of robust immigration policies and border security measures in protecting the nation from external threats. By examining concrete evidence and addressing counterarguments, the validity of this assertion is reinforced, offering insights into the conservative approach to safeguarding national security through immigration policy.

Assimilation and Cultural Integration

THE CONSERVATIVE AGENDA places a strong emphasis on assimilation and cultural integration for immigrants, viewing these processes as crucial for the successful integration of newcomers into the fabric of society. The upcoming list will outline key points that underscore the significance of assimilation and cultural integration from a conservative standpoint, shedding light on the principles and mechanisms that underpin these fundamental concepts.

The adherence to common values and norms stands as a foundational principle in the conservative approach to assimilation and cultural integration. This encompasses embracing and upholding the core principles that form the cultural and societal bedrock of the host nation. The understanding and acceptance of these values, including respect for the rule of law, individual freedoms, and the preservation of democratic institutions, are deemed essential for immigrants to integrate successfully into their new communities.

Conservatives underscore the importance of immigrants aligning their beliefs and behaviors with the foundational values that define the national identity. This entails embracing the principles of freedom, equality, and justice, while also recognizing the importance of personal responsibility and the pursuit of individual and collective prosperity. By embracing these values, immigrants can forge a sense of belonging and solidarity within their adopted society, fostering a cohesive and harmonious social fabric.

Empirical studies and firsthand accounts from successful immigrant integration initiatives demonstrate the positive outcomes associated with embracing common values and norms. Respected social scientists and scholars have documented how the shared adherence to fundamental values and norms has facilitated the smooth integration of immigrants into their host communities, fostering a sense of unity and mutual understanding.

Practical applications of this principle can be witnessed in community-based programs that promote civic education and cultural exchange, enabling immigrants to familiarize themselves with the values and norms of their adopted society. Additionally, initiatives that provide platforms for immigrants to engage in open dialogue and exchange ideas about shared values have proven instrumental in promoting cultural integration and social cohesion.

Having established the significance of embracing common values and norms, the focus now shifts to the fostering of linguistic proficiency as a pivotal component of conservative assimilation and cultural integration strategies.

The Future of Immigration Policies

IMMIGRATION HAS INCREASINGLY become one of the most polarizing and complex policy debates. Over many decades, America has witnessed a range of immigration philosophies, with each administration proposing significantly different frameworks and legislation. Looking forward, the biggest questions revolve around border protection, migrant pathways, and assimilating diverse ethnicities. The outcomes of these issues will dramatically shape the demographic makeup and economic vitality of the nation for generations to come.

Conservatives perspectives frame much of the forthcoming debate as the Right wields legislative power and continues growing in influence. At the base, conservatives advocate for an orderly, legal, measured process that serves national interests. From this lens, American citizens should remain the priority, as well as discerning immigrants who demonstrate respect for the nation's founding ideals and assimilate well. Thus, conservatives view critical aspects of immigration reform through cautious, America First principles rather than radical transformations.

Conservatives will continue pushing for substantive upgrades in border security as a foundation for reform. Significant investments in customs and border patrol personnel, advanced technologies, surveillance systems, and physical barriers must take precedence before increasing legal avenues of entry under the conservative platform. With southern border apprehensions hovering around two million annually, curbing illegal crossings will dominate the debate. Most conservatives refuse expansions in guest worker permits or asylum acceptance rates without seeing marked improvements in border fortification first.

Future legislation could establish a mandatory E-Verify system requiring employers to electronically check the legal working status for all hires backed by harsh penalties for violations. Additionally, conservatives may limit eligibility for welfare, food assistance or subsidized health coverage to citizens only. These initiatives would reduce financial incentives luring illegal migrants. Realistically containing unlawful immigration flows will depend on allocating substantial resources for frontline defenses.

Part of the plan involves transitioning to merit-based admissions emphasizing skilled applicants who demonstrate talent, self-sufficiency, educational credentials and a commitment to American values. Canada and Australia exemplify points-based systems factoring English fluency, in-demand occupations, age, and cultural fit. This approach curbs preferences for family reunification or diversity lotteries seeking to evenly distribute populations. Conservatives argue purely humanitarian admissions cater to the world's poor when struggling Americans reside here legally. Qualified, vetted applicants willing to assimilate and enrich communities deserve prioritization.

In the same vein, guest worker visas should focus temporary entry solely on agriculture, seasonal jobs, and advanced fields with domestic labor shortages rather than increased permanent settlement. The future portends gradually phasing out birthright guarantees to children of illegal migrants as well. Against the backdrop of automation transforming workforces globally, merit-driven reform prevents overburdening public services through indiscriminate admission policies. An influx of lower-skilled entrants creates unnecessary competition with vulnerable American laborers, conservatives contend. Overall, the vision hinges on excellence, personal responsibility, and earning one's way into this nation.

Finally, as ethnic demographics shift, conservatives emphasize cultural integration as imperative for national unity and the rule of law. Allowing segregated sub-cultures erodes social cohesion long-term. This puts the onus on new arrivals to embrace English, self-sufficiency, constitutional rights and responsibilities, and pride in adopting longstanding American customs. Some conservatives even support limiting admissions from any single country in a given year to promote diversity rather than establishing ethnic enclaves. They may also push to restrict foreign language accommodations. The objective is having an integrated population unified behind core national principles. With emergence of hyphenated identities and multiculturalism, conservatives will double down on assimilation.

In essence, the future of conservative-driven reform involves substantially blocking illegal crossings, elevating meritorious skilled workers over family or diversity priorities, eliminating magnets drawing marginal candidates, and concentrating on cultural integration of those welcomed through narrower legal channels. As populism, nativism and civic nationalism gain momentum domestically and globally, crafting an increasingly selective, security-focused approach grows more probable. The trajectory indicates immigration policies growing more consequential for both national identity and economic priorities. With the system at a crossroads, conservative visions will significantly shape the landscape for generations to come.

Cultural Challenges and Shifts

The Conservative Perspective on Cultural Change

American society has undergone seismic cultural shifts over the past half century in norms, values, identities, behaviors, and power dynamics between genders, ethnicities, and across institutions. While liberal activists champion this cultural evolution as expanding equality and overturning oppressive traditions, conservatives largely view these changes with skepticism or alarm. The conservative worldview perceives tradition as integral to social cohesion and many new cultural trends as decays rather than progress. Their critiques and apprehensions frame much of the debate about cultural change.

At the core, conservatives value continuity, caution, and preserving time-tested customs and hierarchies. They see radical or hurried cultural changes driven by liberal agendas as reckless experiments that ignore hard-learned lessons. Outcomes from such changes may take generations to fully manifest. Conservatives believe foundational institutions like family, faith, education, law enforcement, the military, and free enterprise require stability and gradual tweaks when necessary. They view activists uprooting traditions or overhauling fundamental systems as deluded, if not dangerous.

Nowhere has the divide proven more contentious than evolving gender roles and sexual identities influencing family structures. What used to constitute stable households has fragmented with divorced, single parents, same-sex couples raising kids through adoption or fertility treatments, transgender identities, and notions of toxic masculinity—all departing from conservative ideals. They see time-honored gender roles, heterosexual nuclear families, and traditional masculinity/femininity as healthiest for nurturing functional adults and coherent communities.

Dismantling those cornerstones risks harming children and eroding social bonds in the name of misguided liberation movements, per the conservative lens. Radically reengineering the family and gender unit through activist interference courts disaster. And governments enlarging the social safety net to assist single parents enables irresponsible life choices in conservative critiques. They believe undoing cultural damage from deteriorating family values necessitates reviving the nuclear family norm.

Likewise, conservatives raise alarms about fading patriotism and national pride amid younger generations. They consider assimilation into a coherent American identity vital for domestic harmony and believe multiculturalism Balkanizes citizens through divisive hyphenated identities. Conservatives also accuse liberal elites of sowing anti-American sentiment by over-emphasizing historical flaws while ignoring the nation's virtues and successes. A warped, overly negative view of the country now permeates academia, media, and pop culture. This threatens citizens losing faith in founding ideals, according to conservatives.

The direction risks slowly dissolving national pride and civic bonds. Conservatives counter by urging renewed emphasis on assimilation, traditional holidays, democratic values education, and honorable portrayals of historical figures and events to rebuild patriotism. They see urgent need to reverse shame in American exceptionalism before erosion of shared identity and ideals reaches a point of no return in coming decades. Allowing the culture to degrade nationalist pride through activism risks weakening society's foundations.

At the broadest level, conservatives equitable expanding cultural progressivism with abandoning Judeo-Christian values that long defined mainstream morality. Rapid secularization and declining religious affiliation especially among younger demographics troubles conservatives greatly. A widening permissiveness around issues like abortion, sexuality, addiction, and euthanasia contradicts biblical teachings. Conservatives believe Sartean philosophy exalting existence over essence and individual choice above universal truths will plunge civilization into nihilistic decadence.

By weakening moral guardrails and absolving personal responsibility, cultural drift toward subjective relativism leaves little defining right from wrong, truth from lies, and barbarism from civilized order in the conservative read. Attempts at radically revising social contracts beyond marginal groups spell grave threats to the moral fabric and ethical foundations conservatism views as essential to healthy, sustainable societies. Fighting unrelenting cultural change presents conservatives with arguably their most pressing battle.

At its core, conservatism values social continuity, cohesion, assimilation into dominant cultural norms, and gradual adaptations when necessary to maintain civic harmony and stability. Consequently, many conservatives meet accelerated liberal cultural engineering led by activists over the past half century with visceral unease or condemnation rather than celebration. To their dismay, recent generations increasingly support expanded notions of identities, family structures, gender roles,normalized vulgarity, secular lifestyles, and fluid morals once considered fringe. Reversing such mounting cultural progressivism grows more improbable with time. Yet with tradition and moral guardrails perceived as vital by conservatives, resigning to rapid cultural change remains impossible. The schism will surely intensify in coming decades.

The Influence of Pop Culture

POPULAR CULTURE HAS always played a significant role in shaping societal values and norms. Whether through music, movies, television, fashion, or social media, pop culture permeates our daily lives and influences our thoughts, beliefs, and behaviors.

The concept of popular culture encompasses a wide range of phenomena that capture the attention and interest of the general public. From viral TikTok dances to blockbuster superhero films, popular culture reflects the collective tastes and preferences of a society at a given time. The influence of pop culture extends beyond mere entertainment, as it often serves as a mirror reflecting social, political, and cultural dynamics. Moreover, the rapid globalization and digital interconnectedness of the modern world have amplified the reach and impact of popular culture, making it an even more formidable force in shaping societal values.

To illustrate the impact of popular culture, we can examine the phenomenon of celebrity endorsements and their influence on consumer behavior. When a popular figure endorses a product or a cause, their influence can sway public opinion and consumer choices. For instance, a celebrity promoting sustainable fashion can significantly impact the purchasing decisions of their followers, leading to a broader shift in consumer preferences. Similarly, the portrayal of certain lifestyles, relationships, and societal norms in popular media can shape the perceptions and aspirations of individuals, especially the younger generation.

When considering the influence of pop culture, it is essential to recognize that different demographic groups may respond to cultural trends in distinct ways. For instance, the portrayal of gender roles and stereotypes in popular media may elicit varying responses based on age, socio-economic status, and cultural background. Additionally, conservative perspectives on traditional values and moral principles may clash with certain trends within popular culture, leading to debates about the preservation of societal norms.

To support our exploration, it is pertinent to examine relevant data and statistics that highlight the pervasive nature of popular culture. Studies show that the average American spends a significant amount of time consuming media, with television, social media, and streaming platforms being primary sources of entertainment and information. Furthermore, market research data demonstrates the economic impact of popular culture, showcasing the immense revenue generated by industries such as music, film, and fashion.

In this context, it is important to clarify the term "conservative responses to cultural trends." When we refer to conservative responses, we are addressing the reactions and critiques put forth by individuals, organizations, or movements that advocate for traditional values, principles, and societal norms. These responses may encompass concerns about the erosion of moral standards, the commodification of culture, or the promotion of ideologies that deviate from established traditions.

The influence of popular culture on societal values is undeniable, and its impact reverberates across various aspects of our lives. As we navigate the complexities of cultural trends, it is essential to critically analyze the messages and values conveyed through popular media. Furthermore, conservative responses to cultural trends underscore the ongoing dialogue about the preservation of traditional values and the need to uphold moral integrity in the face of cultural shifts. Understanding the intricate interplay between popular culture and conservative perspectives is crucial for comprehending the dynamics of contemporary society.

Identity Politics and Tribalism

IN THE CONTEMPORARY landscape of political and social discourse, the rise of identity politics and tribalism has sparked intense debates and controversies. This chapter aims to explore conservative critiques of identity politics and the importance of individualism within the context of these prevailing phenomena. By comparing identity politics and tribalism, we seek to offer insights into their nuances and broader implications, shedding light on their complexities and potential impact on societal values and norms.

Identity politics revolves around the idea that an individual's identity, particularly their race, gender, sexual orientation, and other social categories, significantly influences their experiences and perspectives. It emphasizes the need for recognizing and addressing systemic discrimination and inequality based on these identities. Tribalism, on the other hand, refers to the strong loyalty and allegiance to a particular social group, often leading to the prioritization of group interests over broader societal concerns.

The rationale behind comparing identity politics and tribalism is to elucidate the underlying similarities and differences between these concepts and to discern their implications for individual agency and societal cohesion. By juxtaposing these phenomena, we aim to provide a balanced view of their impact on social dynamics and the potential challenges they pose to fostering a cohesive and inclusive society.

In comparing identity politics and tribalism, the benchmarks for analysis will include their impact on social cohesion, individual agency, and the potential for fostering inclusive and equitable societies. Additionally, we will consider their implications for political discourse and the challenges they may pose to consensus-building and cooperation across diverse groups.

Both identity politics and tribalism center around the idea of group identity and solidarity. They emphasize the significance of shared experiences and the need to address systemic inequalities and injustices faced by specific social groups. Moreover, both phenomena often lead to the formation of distinct social and political movements aimed at advocating for the rights and interests of marginalized communities.

While identity politics focuses on acknowledging and addressing systemic discrimination and inequality, tribalism often leads to the prioritization of group interests over broader societal concerns. Identity politics seeks to empower marginalized groups and amplify their voices, whereas tribalism can result in the exclusion of those who do not align with the dominant group's interests and perspectives.

The comparison of identity politics and tribalism reveals the intricate interplay between collective identity and individual agency. While both phenomena stem from the need for social belonging and recognition, they manifest in divergent ways that can either foster inclusivity or exacerbate divisions within society. Understanding these nuances is crucial for navigating the complexities of contemporary social and political dynamics.

The comparison of identity politics and tribalism holds significant relevance in the current socio-political landscape, especially amidst heightened discussions about systemic discrimination, social justice movements, and the polarization of public discourse. By drawing parallels and distinctions between these phenomena, we can gain a deeper understanding of their implications for social cohesion and the pursuit of equitable and inclusive societies.

As we delve into the intricacies of identity politics and tribalism, it becomes evident that these phenomena intersect with broader societal dynamics, influencing the ways in which individuals navigate their identities and engage with the larger social fabric. The nuances and complexities of these concepts underscore the need for thoughtful analysis and dialogue to address the challenges and opportunities they present in shaping our collective future.

The Culture War

THE CONCEPT OF THE culture war has been a central theme in contemporary political and social discourse. As the clash between traditional values and progressive ideologies intensifies, it is imperative to dissect the elements that define this conflict and the conservative efforts to defend traditional values. The upcoming list delves into the key points that underpin the culture war, offering a comprehensive exploration of the battlegrounds and strategies employed by conservatives in this ideological struggle.

The cultural landscape serves as a battleground for competing ideologies, each vying for dominance and influence over societal norms and values. Conservatives have been deeply engaged in the struggle to preserve traditional cultural narratives and historical legacies amidst the rising tide of progressive reinterpretations. The battle for cultural hegemony encompasses the spheres of art, media, education, and public discourse, where conservative voices seek to counter the narrative shifts that challenge established traditions and values.

Central to the conservative agenda in the culture war is the defense of traditional family structures, which are perceived as foundational to societal stability and the well-being of future generations. Conservatives advocate for the preservation of the nuclear family model, emphasizing the roles of marriage, parental authority, and familial values. The erosion of these traditional structures, often attributed to changing social attitudes and policies, is viewed as a threat to the fabric of society and is met with staunch resistance from conservative advocates.

Religious freedoms stand as a cornerstone of conservative efforts in the culture war, reflecting the enduring commitment to the constitutional protection of religious expression and practice. The clash between conservative religious values and progressive ideologies has manifested in debates surrounding issues such as same-sex marriage, gender identity, and reproductive rights. The defense of religious freedoms encompasses legal battles, advocacy for conscience exemptions, and the assertion of religious values in public spaces, reflecting the determination to safeguard traditional moral convictions in the face of societal shifts.

Conservative efforts in the culture war extend to the preservation of national identity and patriotism, with a focus on affirming the historical narratives, symbols, and traditions that symbolize national pride and unity. The defense of national identity encompasses resistance to narratives that critique or challenge aspects of the nation's history and values, emphasizing the importance of civic education, historical accuracy, and respect for national symbols. Patriotism, as articulated by conservatives, serves as a unifying force that fosters a sense of collective identity and shared purpose.

The preservation of free speech and academic freedom stands as a critical battleground in the culture war, reflecting the conservative commitment to unfettered expression and open intellectual inquiry. Conservatives have raised concerns about ideological conformity and censorship within academic institutions and public discourse, advocating for the protection of diverse viewpoints and the free exchange of ideas. The defense of free speech is intertwined with efforts to counteract the influence of cancel culture, political correctness, and restrictions on dissenting opinions, aiming to ensure that conservative perspectives are not marginalized or silenced in the cultural sphere.

The battle for cultural hegemony is evidenced by the debates surrounding the portrayal of historical figures and events in educational curricula, the representation of traditional values in popular media, and the contestation of artistic expressions that challenge established norms.

In the defense of traditional family structures, testimonials from conservative advocates highlight the enduring significance of parental authority, the nurturing environment provided by traditional families, and the concerns over the societal impact of alternative family models.

The preservation of religious freedoms is supported by legal cases that have brought to light conflicts between conservative religious beliefs and anti-discrimination laws, as well as the testimonies of individuals whose religious convictions have been challenged in public and private spheres.

The emphasis on upholding national identity and patriotism is underscored by the public response to controversies surrounding national symbols, historical commemorations, and debates over the teaching of national history and values in educational institutions.

The protection of free speech and academic freedom is evidenced by instances of censorship and ideological bias in academic and public settings, as well as the testimonies of individuals who have faced repercussions for expressing conservative viewpoints in various cultural and educational contexts.

The defense of traditional family structures has practical applications in policy advocacy, family support initiatives, and community-based programs that promote the values and benefits of traditional family dynamics.

The preservation of religious freedoms translates into legal efforts to secure exemptions for religious organizations and individuals, as well as the development of educational resources that articulate the importance of religious liberty in a diverse society.

Upholding national identity and patriotism finds practical applications in civic education initiatives, historical preservation efforts, and the promotion of public events and commemorations that reinforce a sense of national pride and unity.

Protecting free speech and academic freedom is practically applied through legal challenges to censorship and ideological bias, the establishment of alternative educational platforms that embrace diverse perspectives, and the promotion of open dialogue in public forums and media outlets.

As we transition from the battle for cultural hegemony to the defense of traditional family structures, the interconnectedness of these conservative efforts becomes apparent in their shared objective of preserving traditional values and narratives amidst societal change. Furthermore, the practical applications of these endeavors illustrate the multifaceted nature of conservative engagement in the culture war, extending beyond ideological advocacy to tangible initiatives that shape cultural and social landscapes.

In our exploration of the preservation of religious freedoms, the intersection of legal challenges, cultural narratives, and societal attitudes illuminates the complex dynamics that underpin conservative endeavors to safeguard religious liberties. This seamless transition underscores the interconnected nature of conservative efforts to defend traditional values within the broader context of the culture war.

Moreover, as we delve into the conservative commitment to upholding national identity and patriotism, the continuity of themes related to historical narratives, civic education, and public discourse becomes evident. This seamless transition reinforces the integral role of national identity in the conservative agenda within the cultural battleground, shaping the contours of the overarching culture war.

Finally, in our examination of protecting free speech and academic freedom, the seamless transition from legal battles to practical applications illustrates the multifaceted approach adopted by conservatives in their pursuit of unfettered expression and open intellectual inquiry. The interconnectedness of legal advocacy and practical initiatives underscores the depth and breadth of conservative engagement in shaping cultural and intellectual landscapes amidst the culture war.

As the culture war unfolds on multiple fronts, the comprehensive exploration of the conservative agenda reveals the depth of the ideological struggle and the intricate strategies employed to defend traditional values in the face of evolving societal dynamics. The seamless transitions between each point underscore the interconnected nature of conservative efforts, reflecting a cohesive and multifaceted approach to shaping cultural narratives and societal norms within the broader context of the culture war.

JACK DONAHUE

Conservatism in the Arts

THE HISTORY OF CONSERVATIVE perspectives on the arts is deeply rooted in the cultural and societal transformations that have unfolded over the centuries. To truly grasp the conservative agenda in the realm of arts, it is essential to journey back to pivotal moments in history that have shaped the understanding and appreciation of artistic expressions within conservative frameworks.

Art, as an expression of human creativity and emotion, has been an integral part of human societies since ancient times. From the majestic sculptures of ancient civilizations to the intricate paintings of the Renaissance, art has served as a mirror reflecting the values, beliefs, and aspirations of its creators and the societies in which it flourished. The historical tapestry of art is woven with threads of tradition, symbolism, and cultural significance, elements that have resonated deeply with conservative ideologies throughout history.

The Renaissance period stands as a defining epoch that has left an indelible mark on conservative perspectives on the arts. This period witnessed a resurgence of classical ideals, a celebration of beauty, and a revival of traditional artistic techniques. Conservative thinkers and patrons of the arts during the Renaissance era championed the preservation of classical aesthetics and sought to revive the moral and ethical dimensions of art, viewing it as a means to convey timeless truths and uphold societal values.

Moreover, the Enlightenment era brought about profound shifts in the perception and patronage of the arts, as emerging liberal ideologies began to challenge established traditions and religious influences in artistic expression. The conservative response to these changes manifested in efforts to safeguard artistic traditions, preserve religious themes in art, and maintain a reverence for established artistic canons that reflected the moral and cultural heritage of their societies.

Drawing clear lines from the historical context to contemporary challenges, it is evident that the conservative agenda in the arts continues to grapple with the tensions between traditional artistic values and the evolving landscape of artistic expression. In the modern era, the proliferation of avant-garde movements, postmodern deconstructions, and the embrace of provocative and controversial artistic statements has posed significant challenges to conservative sensibilities regarding the role of art in society.

Conservative perspectives on the arts today are deeply concerned with the erosion of traditional artistic standards, the glorification of shock value over artistic merit, and the politicization of art that undermines its aesthetic and cultural significance. The contemporary art world's embrace of relativism and the rejection of objective standards have placed conservative advocates at odds with prevailing artistic trends that they perceive as detrimental to the preservation of cultural heritage and moral values.

Conveying the importance of historical understanding in tackling modern-day issues, the historical context provides crucial insights into the enduring significance of art as a vehicle for the transmission of cultural, moral, and spiritual values. Understanding the conservative perspectives on the arts in historical contexts illuminates the enduring quest for artistic expressions that resonate with timeless truths, uphold societal values, and contribute to the cultivation of a virtuous and cohesive societal fabric.

The need to comprehend the historical underpinnings of conservative attitudes toward the arts becomes particularly pertinent as contemporary debates surrounding cultural preservation, artistic censorship, and the role of art in shaping public consciousness unfold. By delving into the historical milestones that have influenced conservative perspectives on the arts, a nuanced understanding of the enduring tensions between traditional artistic values and modernist or postmodernist tendencies emerges, shedding light on the contemporary challenges faced by conservative advocates in the cultural sphere.

Leading the reader from the historical overview into the contemporary exploration of the conservative agenda in the arts, the seamless transition from historical contexts to modern-day challenges lays the foundation for a comprehensive examination of the role of art in promoting conservative values. As we embark on this exploration, it becomes evident that the conservative agenda in the arts represents a steadfast commitment to preserving artistic traditions, upholding cultural heritage, and fostering artistic expressions that align with enduring moral and societal values.

The Future of Conservative Cultural Engagement

IN THE RAPIDLY EVOLVING landscape of cultural narratives, conservatives face the significant challenge of engaging with and shaping the cultural discourse in a manner that aligns with their values and principles. This necessitates a deep understanding of the current cultural climate and the various influences that shape it.

Conservative cultural engagement spans across various forms of artistic expression, entertainment, media, and education. It encompasses the promotion of traditional values, the preservation of cultural heritage, and the encouragement of artistic endeavors that reflect timeless truths and moral virtues. However, in the face of shifting societal attitudes and the dominance of progressive narratives, conservatives find themselves navigating uncharted territory, where their perspectives are often marginalized or dismissed.

The primary issue at the heart of conservative cultural engagement lies in the struggle to assert their influence and relevance in an increasingly liberal and progressive cultural landscape. Conservative voices are frequently overshadowed or silenced in artistic and cultural spheres, leading to a lack of representation and a dilution of conservative values in mainstream discourse. This poses a significant challenge to the preservation of traditional cultural values and the promotion of conservative ideologies through artistic and cultural channels.

If the issue of conservative cultural engagement remains unaddressed, the consequences are far-reaching. The erosion of conservative influence in cultural narratives can lead to the dilution of traditional values, the marginalization of conservative perspectives, and the perpetuation of one-sided, ideologically driven cultural representations that do not reflect the diversity of societal viewpoints. This can result in a cultural landscape devoid of traditional moral and ethical considerations, leading to a loss of cultural cohesion and a disconnect between artistic expressions and enduring societal values.

To address the challenges of conservative cultural engagement, it is imperative to adopt a multifaceted approach that encompasses strategic initiatives to reclaim conservative influence in cultural narratives. This involves proactive measures to promote and support artistic endeavors that align with conservative values, as well as efforts to amplify conservative voices in the cultural and artistic spheres.

One of the fundamental solutions lies in fostering a renaissance of conservative cultural production, where artists, writers, filmmakers, and creators are encouraged to produce works that reflect conservative values, traditions, and moral virtues. This involves the cultivation of a supportive ecosystem that provides platforms, funding, and recognition for conservative artists and creators, enabling them to contribute to the cultural discourse from a conservative perspective.

Implementing this solution requires the establishment of institutions, grants, and programs dedicated to nurturing conservative artistic talent and promoting conservative cultural narratives. It involves the creation of conservative-themed artistic events, exhibitions, and festivals that celebrate and showcase the richness of conservative artistic expressions. Additionally, collaborations with educational institutions and media outlets can facilitate the dissemination of conservative cultural content to wider audiences.

Moreover, the integration of conservative perspectives into mainstream cultural institutions, such as museums, theaters, and educational curricula, can play a pivotal role in broadening the reach and impact of conservative cultural engagement. By actively engaging with these institutions, conservatives can influence the representation and interpretation of cultural artifacts and narratives to align with traditional values and principles.

The implementation of these strategies holds the potential to yield significant outcomes in the realm of conservative cultural engagement. A resurgence of conservative artistic and cultural production can lead to the creation of a diverse and vibrant cultural landscape that reflects the richness of conservative traditions and values. This can result in a more inclusive cultural narrative that acknowledges and respects the diversity of ideological perspectives, fostering a more balanced and representative cultural discourse.

Furthermore, the amplification of conservative voices in cultural and artistic spheres can lead to a reclamation of influence and relevance, providing an opportunity to shape the cultural narrative in a manner that upholds traditional values and promotes a deeper understanding of conservative perspectives. As a result, the broader societal impact of conservative cultural engagement can contribute to the preservation of cultural heritage, the promotion of moral and ethical considerations, and the cultivation of a more cohesive and inclusive societal fabric.

While the proposed solutions are essential in addressing the challenges of conservative cultural engagement, it is valuable to consider alternative approaches that complement and enhance these strategies. This may involve engaging with emerging digital platforms and social media to amplify conservative cultural content, leveraging technology to reach wider audiences and counter the dominance of progressive narratives in the virtual realm.

Additionally, fostering collaborations with international conservative cultural movements and organizations can facilitate the exchange of ideas, resources, and experiences, creating a global network of conservative cultural engagement that transcends geographical boundaries. This can amplify the impact of conservative cultural narratives on a broader scale, contributing to a more comprehensive and interconnected conservative cultural movement.

The future of conservative cultural engagement rests on the proactive pursuit of strategies that reclaim, promote, and amplify conservative influence in cultural narratives. By fostering a renaissance of conservative cultural production, integrating conservative perspectives into mainstream cultural institutions, and exploring alternative avenues for engagement, conservatives can pave the way for a more inclusive and representative cultural landscape that reflects the diversity of societal viewpoints and upholds enduring values and traditions.

The Role of Education in Cultural Preservation

IN ORDER TO COMPREHEND the significance of education in cultural preservation, it is essential to have a foundational understanding of the conservative principles and the value system that underpins cultural heritage. Additionally, a familiarity with the landscape of educational institutions and their potential influence on shaping societal attitudes towards cultural preservation would be beneficial.

The role of education in cultural preservation encompasses a multifaceted approach that involves instilling a sense of pride in cultural heritage, fostering critical thinking about traditional values, and promoting the preservation of historical narratives. Educational institutions serve as crucibles for transmitting knowledge, shaping perspectives, and cultivating a deep-seated reverence for the cultural legacy that forms the bedrock of conservative values.

Educational institutions play a pivotal role in shaping the narrative of cultural preservation by integrating the study of history, literature, and the arts into their curricula. By incorporating the exploration of cultural traditions, historical events, and literary works that encapsulate conservative values, educational programs can cultivate a rich tapestry of cultural literacy that fosters an appreciation for traditional heritage.

Incorporating ethical and moral education within the framework of academic instruction enables educational institutions to instill timeless virtues and principles that are integral to cultural preservation. By imparting lessons on integrity, responsibility, and respect for tradition, students can develop a deep understanding of the ethical underpinnings of cultural heritage, thus becoming stewards of conservative values.

Facilitating cultural exchange programs that expose students to diverse cultural landscapes and traditions can broaden their perspectives and deepen their appreciation for cultural diversity. By fostering an environment of cross-cultural understanding, educational institutions can nurture a sense of global citizenship while reinforcing the importance of preserving one's own cultural heritage.

Encouraging the study and practice of traditional arts and crafts within educational settings not only preserves cultural heritage but also imparts practical skills that are deeply rooted in conservative values. By promoting the preservation of traditional craftsmanship, educational institutions contribute to the continuity of cultural practices and the transmission of generational knowledge.

Introducing students to the principles of historical preservation and archival studies equips them with the tools to safeguard and document cultural artifacts, historical records, and narratives that are emblematic of conservative cultural heritage. By instilling the importance of preserving historical legacies, educational institutions nurture a sense of custodianship over the collective memory of a society.

Validating the successful integration of cultural preservation within educational contexts can be achieved through the assessment of students' attitudes towards cultural heritage, the documentation of preservation initiatives within educational institutions, and the evaluation of the impact of cultural education on the broader community.

Should challenges arise in implementing cultural preservation initiatives within educational settings, it is essential to foster open dialogue, engage with diverse stakeholders, and adapt strategies to address evolving cultural landscapes and educational needs.

The role of education in cultural preservation stands as a linchpin in the conservation of conservative values and the safeguarding of cultural heritage. By prioritizing the integration of cultural preservation within educational paradigms, societies can ensure the continuity of traditional values and the perpetuation of a rich and diverse cultural legacy for future generations.

Media and Information

____

The Conservative Perspective on Media Bias

The conservative perspective on media bias is a subject that has garnered significant attention in recent years. Critiques from conservative individuals and organizations emphasize the importance of a free and independent press, highlighting the potential impact of biased reporting on public perception and the democratic process.

Understanding the terms associated with media bias is crucial for engaging with the conservative critique of this issue. By delving into the definitions and implications of these key words, we can gain a more nuanced understanding of the conservative perspective on media bias.

As we delve into the definitions of the key terms, we can offer concise and informative explanations to provide depth and context to our discussion of media bias from a conservative perspective. It is through these definitions that we can begin to unravel the complexities of this issue and its implications for media and society.

Connecting these complex words to well-known concepts is essential to aid comprehension and relatability. By grounding these terms in familiar contexts, we can bridge the gap between theoretical definitions and practical application, fostering a deeper understanding of the conservative critique of media bias.

The first key term to address is "media bias." This term refers to the perceived partiality or inclination of journalists and news outlets to present news in a way that aligns with their own political beliefs or preferences. In the conservative critique, media bias is often viewed as a pervasive issue that skews reporting in favor of liberal or progressive ideologies, resulting in a lack of balanced and objective coverage of events and issues.

Next, we must examine the concept of "free and independent press." This term underscores the importance of a media landscape where journalists are free to report without fear of censorship or undue influence. Conservatives emphasize the foundational role of a free and independent press in holding those in power accountable and providing the public with accurate and unbiased information.

Another critical term to consider is "agenda setting." This term refers to the media's power to influence which issues and topics receive attention and prominence in public discourse. Conservatives argue that media bias can lead to a distortion of the information landscape, as certain viewpoints and narratives are given disproportionate coverage, while others are marginalized or ignored.

In discussing the conservative perspective on media bias, it is essential to address the term "confirmation bias." This concept highlights the tendency of individuals to seek out and interpret information in a way that confirms their preexisting beliefs. Conservatives argue that media bias can exacerbate confirmation bias, leading to a reinforcement of partisan viewpoints and a lack of exposure to alternative perspectives.

As we link these terms to real-world or familiar concepts, it becomes evident that the conservative critique of media bias is deeply intertwined with broader discussions about the role of media in shaping public opinion and maintaining a healthy democratic society. The consequences of biased reporting and agenda setting extend beyond the realm of journalism, influencing public discourse, political engagement, and societal cohesion.

The conservative perspective on media bias emphasizes the need for a media landscape that upholds the principles of objectivity, fairness, and accountability. By scrutinizing the definitions and implications of key terms such as media bias, free and independent press, agenda setting, and confirmation bias, we gain a clearer understanding of the conservative critique of media bias and its broader impact on society.

As we continue our exploration of the conservative perspective on media bias, it is crucial to delve deeper into the specifics of how media bias manifests and the potential consequences of biased reporting on public perception and democratic processes. By unpacking these complexities, we can gain a more comprehensive understanding of the conservative viewpoint on media bias and its implications for media and society.

The Rise of New Media

IN RECENT YEARS, THE landscape of media and information dissemination has undergone a significant transformation with the emergence and proliferation of new media platforms. These platforms, encompassing a wide array of digital technologies and social networking sites, have not only reshaped the way information is consumed but have also had a profound impact on conservative discourse and the challenges they pose to traditional media.

The rise of new media has revolutionized the way individuals access and engage with information, creating an environment where news and opinion are readily available at the swipe of a finger. This transformation has fundamentally altered the dynamics of conservative discourse and has presented both opportunities and challenges for traditional media outlets.

New media platforms, such as social media, podcasts, and online news sites, have provided conservatives with alternative avenues to share their perspectives and connect with like-minded individuals. These platforms offer a level of accessibility and immediacy that was previously unparalleled, allowing conservative voices to reach broader audiences and bypass traditional gatekeepers of information.

For instance, conservative commentators and pundits have utilized platforms like Twitter, now known as X, and YouTube to directly engage with their followers, share their insights, and counter what they perceive as biased narratives in mainstream media. The ability to create and disseminate content in real-time has empowered conservatives to shape the public discourse in ways that were not feasible through traditional media channels alone.

However, the impact of new media on conservative discourse is not without its complexities. While these platforms offer unprecedented opportunities for conservatives to amplify their voices, they also present challenges in terms of information reliability, echo chambers, and the proliferation of misinformation.

According to a Pew Research Center study, a significant portion of Americans now turn to social media for news, with 55% of U.S. adults indicating that they get their news from social media often or sometimes. This shift in news consumption patterns underscores the influential role of new media platforms in shaping public opinion and discourse, including within conservative circles.

It is essential to clarify the concept of echo chambers, which refers to the phenomenon where individuals are primarily exposed to information that aligns with their existing beliefs, creating a reinforcement of those beliefs and a limited exposure to differing perspectives. New media platforms have the potential to exacerbate echo chambers within conservative circles, as users curate their feeds and interactions to align with their ideological leanings.

The rise of new media platforms has significantly impacted conservative discourse by providing alternative channels for expression and engagement. However, these platforms also present challenges related to information reliability, echo chambers, and the spread of misinformation. Understanding the dynamic interplay between new media and conservative discourse is crucial in navigating the evolving media landscape and its implications for society.

As we delve deeper into the impact of new media on conservative discourse, it becomes increasingly apparent that the evolution of media platforms has fundamentally altered the dynamics of information dissemination and public engagement. The next chapter will further explore the multifaceted implications of new media on conservative discourse, shedding light on the evolving nature of media influence and the challenges it presents to traditional media structures.

Fake News and Disinformation

TO COMBAT FAKE NEWS and disinformation effectively, it is crucial to first identify the underlying causes and implications of these issues within the conservative discourse. We will then explore a range of strategies, including media literacy, critical thinking, and responsible information consumption, to empower individuals to discern and counteract fake news and disinformation.

Fake news and disinformation are pervasive in the digital age, posing significant challenges to the conservative discourse. It is imperative to differentiate between legitimate journalism and fabricated or misleading content. Readers must develop the ability to discern the credibility of sources and critically evaluate the information they encounter.

Educating individuals about media literacy and cultivating critical thinking skills are essential components of combating fake news and disinformation. This involves equipping individuals with the tools to analyze and verify information, discern biases, and recognize manipulative tactics employed by purveyors of false information.

Engaging in responsible information consumption entails actively seeking out diverse perspectives, verifying the accuracy of information before sharing it, and refraining from perpetuating false narratives. It is crucial to encourage a culture of responsible sharing and dissemination of information within conservative circles.

Collaborative fact-checking initiatives play a pivotal role in countering fake news and disinformation. By supporting and engaging with reputable fact-checking organizations, individuals can contribute to the verification and debunking of false information, thereby fostering a more informed and discerning community.

In recent years, Fox News, the home of the Conservative Voice must be fact checked repeatedly. In their fervor to collect Convervative eyeballs, they have begun running stories not only futher in the outfield, but outside the realm of believability.

Upholding the principles of ethical journalism and transparent reporting is instrumental in combatting fake news and disinformation. Encouraging responsible and ethical practices within media outlets, as well as holding journalists and news organizations accountable for their reporting, contributes to the preservation of factual and reliable information.

As we navigate the complexities of combating fake news and disinformation within the conservative discourse, it becomes evident that a proactive and informed approach is paramount in addressing these challenges. The effective implementation of strategies such as media literacy, critical thinking, responsible information consumption, and collaborative fact-checking initiatives holds the potential to mitigate the detrimental impact of fake news and disinformation on conservative discourse. In the subsequent chapters, we will continue to delve into the multifaceted landscape of media influence and the evolving dynamics of information dissemination within conservative circles.

Social Media and Censorship

SOCIAL MEDIA PLATFORMS have become integral to modern society, serving as conduits for communication, information dissemination, and public discourse. However, the conservative perspective on social media censorship and the importance of free speech online has sparked widespread debate, shedding light on the complexities and implications of online content regulation. This chapter aims to analyze the conservative concerns regarding social media censorship and the broader implications for free speech in the digital age.

Social media platforms, such as Facebook, Twitter (X), and YouTube, have emerged as influential channels for individuals and organizations to express their views, share information, and engage in public dialogue. Conversely, social media censorship refers to the regulation or restriction of content by these platforms, often based on community guidelines, terms of service, or government regulations. The significance of these entities lies in their pivotal role as modern-day public forums, where diverse perspectives converge and societal narratives are shaped.

The comparison of conservative perspectives on social media censorship and the importance of free speech online seeks to illuminate the underlying concerns and values driving the discourse.

By examining the benchmarks for comparison and setting the parameters for analysis, this chapter aims to offer insights into the nuances and broader implications of content regulation on social media platforms and its impact on conservative voices.

The benchmarks for comparison in this analysis encompass the principles of free speech, the impact of content moderation on conservative viewpoints, and the potential ramifications of social media censorship on public discourse. By delineating these criteria, we can delve into a balanced assessment of the conservative concerns in the context of online content regulation.

Conservative concerns about social media censorship converge with the fundamental value of free speech, emphasizing the right to express opinions and engage in open dialogue without undue restrictions. The alignment of these concerns with the principles of free speech underscores the significance of preserving open platforms for the exchange of ideas and perspectives.

Conversely, the practices of content moderation on social media platforms introduce distinctions as they entail the regulation of content deemed inappropriate, harmful, or in violation of community guidelines. This contrast highlights the complexities of balancing free expression with the need to mitigate misinformation, hate speech, and harmful content within online spaces.

The comparison of conservative concerns about social media censorship and the principles of free speech reveals nuanced implications for online discourse. It underscores the tension between promoting open dialogue and the responsibility of platforms to mitigate the spread of harmful or misleading content. Moreover, it sheds light on the challenges faced by conservative voices in navigating the evolving content regulation landscape.

The contemporary relevance of this comparison lies in its connection to ongoing debates and regulatory actions surrounding social media platforms and their impact on public discourse. By examining historical precedents and theoretical frameworks, we can enhance the relevance of this analysis to current realities, offering valuable insights for navigating the evolving landscape of online content regulation.

Before sharing a meme, make sure it makes sense. A commong Conservative meme concerns the pipeline and the tag, "Make this go virtual." This is generally laughed at by Liberals, as the proper term is viral. If you make or share Conservative memes, make sure the grammar is perfect.

As we delve into the conservative concerns regarding social media censorship and the importance of free speech online, it becomes evident that the implications of content regulation extend beyond individual platforms to encompass broader societal values and the dynamics of public discourse. In the subsequent sections, we will continue to explore the multifaceted interactions between conservative perspectives and the evolving landscape of online content regulation.

Conservative Media Outlets

AS WE DELVE INTO THE landscape of conservative media outlets and their role in shaping conservative narratives, it becomes imperative to understand the intricate dynamics, challenges, strategies, and outcomes that define their influence. This chapter aims to provide a detailed examination of a specific instance, outlining challenges, strategies, and results to derive broader insights and encourage further engagement.

The contemporary media landscape is marked by a multiplicity of platforms and voices, each vying for attention and influence. Within this dynamic ecosystem, conservative media outlets occupy a significant space, offering alternative perspectives and narratives that resonate with a substantial segment of the population. Understanding the role and impact of these outlets in shaping conservative narratives requires an in-depth exploration of their strategies, challenges, and outcomes.

The central figures in this case study encompass a diverse array of conservative media outlets, including television networks, online publications, radio programs, and social media personalities. Each entity brings its unique approach and voice to the conservative discourse, catering to distinct audiences and amplifying conservative viewpoints on a range of issues. The backgrounds of these outlets are often rooted in a commitment to upholding traditional values, limited government intervention, and free-market principles, providing a platform for conservative voices to articulate their perspectives.

One of the core challenges facing conservative media outlets lies in navigating the evolving dynamics of media consumption and audience engagement. With the proliferation of digital platforms and the fragmentation of media consumption habits, these outlets must adapt their strategies to capture and retain audience attention amidst a competitive landscape. Additionally, the perception of conservative media as partisan or ideologically driven poses a challenge in reaching audiences beyond their traditional base and fostering open dialogue across diverse viewpoints.

To address these challenges, conservative media outlets have employed a range of strategies aimed at enhancing audience engagement, leveraging digital platforms, and diversifying content formats. Embracing social media, podcasting, and video streaming has expanded their reach and facilitated direct interaction with audiences.

The outcomes of these approaches are evidenced in the sustained relevance and impact of conservative media outlets, as well as their ability to shape public discourse and influence policy debates. Audience engagement metrics, such as viewership ratings, website traffic, and social media interactions, underscore the resonance of conservative narratives and the effectiveness of targeted content delivery. Moreover, the amplification of conservative perspectives on key issues, such as limited government, individual freedoms, and national security, reflects the enduring influence of these outlets in shaping public opinion.

The case study of conservative media outlets offers insights into the evolving dynamics of media consumption and the enduring relevance of narrative-driven platforms. It also invites reflection on the challenges and opportunities inherent in shaping conservative narratives within a rapidly changing media landscape. Critically assessing the impact of these outlets on public discourse and political dynamics fosters a deeper understanding of their role in shaping conservative ideologies and mobilizing grassroots movements.

The specifics of this case study are integral to understanding the broader themes of media influence, ideological resonance, and the dynamics of conservative narratives in contemporary society. By examining the strategies and outcomes of conservative media outlets, we gain valuable insights into the enduring significance of narrative-driven platforms in shaping public opinion and political discourse.

As we contemplate the influence and strategies of conservative media outlets, it prompts us to consider the evolving role of media in shaping societal narratives and political dynamics. How can the insights gleaned from this case study inform broader discussions on media influence and ideological resonance in the digital age? This question invites further exploration and engagement with the complexities of conservative media and its enduring impact on public discourse.

Media Literacy and Critical Thinking

IN AN ERA DOMINATED by an unprecedented deluge of information and media content, the ability to discern and critically evaluate the messages and narratives presented is of paramount importance. Media literacy and critical thinking skills serve as indispensable tools in navigating the complex and often convoluted landscape of modern media. This chapter seeks to elucidate the significance of cultivating these skills and their pivotal role in shaping informed perspectives amidst the cacophony of media narratives.

The following list outlines the key facets of media literacy and critical thinking, shedding light on their essential components and practical implications:

The multifaceted nature of media messaging encompasses not only the explicit content presented but also the underlying subtexts, implicit narratives, and intended emotional resonances. Understanding the nuances of media messaging entails a comprehensive examination of not just what is being conveyed, but how it is being conveyed. Visual elements, language choices, and narrative structures all play a role in shaping the audience's reception and interpretation of the message.

Media content is inherently imbued with the perspectives, values, and biases of its creators and distributors. Critical thinking involves the ability to identify these biases, question underlying assumptions, and discern the potential impact of these biases on the portrayal of events, issues, and individuals. By honing the skill of deconstructing biases, individuals can develop a more discerning approach to consuming media and avoid falling prey to one-sided or distorted narratives.

Amidst the proliferation of information sources, ranging from established news outlets to user-generated content on social media, the ability to assess source credibility is indispensable. Media literacy empowers individuals to scrutinize the reliability, expertise, and potential agendas of information sources, enabling them to differentiate between verifiable, fact-based reporting and unsubstantiated or biased claims. This skill forms the bedrock of informed decision-making and the construction of well-founded opinions.

Media literacy equips individuals with the discernment to recognize and resist manipulative tactics employed in media content. Propaganda, misinformation, and persuasive techniques often seek to shape perceptions, evoke emotional responses, and influence behavior. By unraveling these manipulative strategies, individuals can safeguard themselves against undue influence and make informed judgments based on factual and reasoned assessment.

A critical aspect of media literacy revolves around fostering a healthy skepticism toward information and narratives encountered in the media sphere. Encouraging individuals to question, probe, and seek corroborating evidence promotes a mindset of inquiry that is essential in discerning the veracity and implications of media content. Embracing skepticism as a constructive approach to media consumption engenders a culture of conscientious engagement and intellectual autonomy.

Media literacy extends beyond the realm of analytical scrutiny to encompass the cultivation of empathy and perspective-taking. Understanding diverse viewpoints, cultural contexts, and individual experiences portrayed in media narratives fosters a more nuanced and compassionate engagement with the world. By empathizing with diverse perspectives, individuals can transcend simplistic categorizations and develop a more holistic understanding of complex societal issues.

The culmination of media literacy and critical thinking manifests in the ability to engage in constructive discourse that transcends echo chambers and polarization. By incorporating diverse perspectives, substantiated evidence, and respectful dialogue, individuals can contribute to a more informed and inclusive public discourse. This engagement serves to fortify media literacy by inviting ongoing reflection, exchange of ideas, and collective sense-making.

The necessity of media literacy and critical thinking is underscored by numerous studies and testimonials that attest to the transformative impact of these skills. Research has consistently demonstrated the correlation between media literacy education and enhanced critical thinking, analytical skills, and civic engagement. Testimonials from individuals who have honed their media literacy and critical thinking capacities often highlight the newfound confidence in navigating media narratives and the ability to discern credible sources amidst the deluge of information.

The practical applications of media literacy and critical thinking reverberate across diverse domains, from educational settings to professional environments and civic participation. In educational contexts, integrating media literacy into curricula equips students with the skills necessary to critically evaluate media content, cultivate empathy, and engage in respectful discourse. In professional settings, these skills enable employees to navigate information sources, discern credible data, and communicate effectively across diverse audiences. Moreover, in the realm of civic participation, media literacy empowers individuals to make informed decisions, scrutinize political messaging, and contribute to informed public deliberations.

The interplay of media literacy and critical thinking intertwines seamlessly, with each point building upon the preceding one to form a comprehensive framework for navigating the media landscape. These interconnected skills collectively enable individuals to decipher, evaluate, and engage with media content in a manner that transcends passive consumption, fostering an active and discerning approach to media narratives.

As we delve into the intricacies of media literacy and critical thinking, it becomes evident that these skills are not merely theoretical constructs but practical tools that empower individuals to navigate the multifaceted world of media with acumen and discernment. In the ensuing exploration, we will unravel the manifold dimensions of media literacy and critical thinking, illuminating their profound impact on individual agency, societal discourse, and the democratic fabric of our information-rich age.

The Future of Media and Information

AMIDST THE RAPID PROLIFERATION of digital media and the rise of social networking platforms, how can conservatives effectively navigate the evolving landscape of information dissemination and consumption to ensure the preservation and propagation of conservative values and ideologies?

In the current epoch, marked by the omnipresence of digital media and the widespread dissemination of information through diverse channels, the question of how conservatives can navigate and shape the evolving media landscape is of paramount importance. The power of media in shaping public opinion, influencing societal narratives, and mobilizing political movements cannot be overstated. As such, it is imperative for conservatives to critically engage with these transformations to safeguard and advance their principles in an era characterized by unprecedented information dissemination and consumption.

The central issue that arises from the proliferation of digital media and the democratization of information dissemination is the potential dilution and distortion of conservative narratives and ideologies. The unfiltered and often unvetted nature of content on social media platforms can lead to the amplification of misinformation, the marginalization of conservative perspectives, and the erosion of trust in traditional media sources. This poses a significant challenge to the propagation of conservative ideas, as it becomes increasingly arduous to ensure the veracity and integrity of conservative narratives amidst the cacophony of digital discourse.

Confronted with the deluge of information on digital platforms, many individuals, including conservatives, often resort to echo chambers and confirmation bias, seeking out content that aligns with their existing beliefs and ideologies. This tendency to gravitate towards like-minded communities and narratives can inadvertently foster polarization, hinder critical engagement with diverse perspectives, and perpetuate the spread of unsubstantiated or biased information. Moreover, the reliance on sensationalism and clickbait tactics by certain media outlets further exacerbates the challenge of discerning reliable and credible sources of information.

The unique solution to navigating the evolving media landscape lies in the cultivation of media literacy and critical thinking skills within conservative circles. By equipping individuals with the tools to discern credible sources, deconstruct biased narratives, and engage in constructive discourse, conservatives can reclaim agency in shaping the information ecosystem. Additionally, the strategic utilization of digital media platforms to amplify conservative voices, foster meaningful dialogue, and counter misinformation can serve as a potent means to counteract the challenges posed by the digital age.

The emotional stakes inherent in the proliferation of digital media and information consumption are undeniable. The erosion of trust in traditional media sources, the amplification of polarizing narratives, and the dissemination of misleading or outright false information can evoke feelings of disillusionment, frustration, and apprehension. By embracing media literacy and critical thinking as powerful tools to counteract these challenges, individuals can reclaim a sense of agency, empowerment, and optimism in navigating the complex landscape of digital media, thereby fueling a renewed sense of purpose in safeguarding conservative values and ideologies.

Technology and Innovation

The Conservative Perspective on Technology

While liberals often enthusiastically embrace emerging technologies for perceived benefits to equality, conservatives adopt more hesitant postures based on threats to stability, privacy, and traditional commerce. Rapid modern technological shifts tied to digital media, automation, artificial intelligence, biohacking and more foreshadow profound economic and societal transformations conservatives seek to temper with prudent regulation and ethical safeguards. Though not outright technophobes, conservatives demonstrate far less tolerance for radical change or utter faith in technological panaceas promising utopian futures compared to progressive advocates.

The acceleration of automation across sectors from manufacturing to white collar professions poses one of the most disruptive tech-driven threats for the coming decade in the conservative lens. Transitioning to driverless transit, automated factories and warehouses, AI-augmented services, and other innovations leaves concerns about structural unemployment and uncertainty. While progressives tout possibilities for freeing humans from economic coercion and liberating creative pursuits, conservatives see dire risks to the very capitalist foundations America relies upon for economic dynamism.

Rapid automation could hollow out livelihoods faster than workforce transitions to new jobs materialize. And guaranteed basic incomes to offset mass job losses undermine the work ethic conservatism views as essential for societal health. Approaching the technological tightrope cautiously, conservatives will advocate adapting antitrust and fair trade policies to ensure mega tech firms better serve public interests versus self-interest alone. Preserving upward mobility and viable paths to prosperity must check utopian automation zealotry.

Equally worrying, networked devices, location tracking, biometrics, predictive analytics, facial recognition and abundance of personal data online fed into machine learning algorithms threaten citizens' reasonable privacy expectations and civil rights. Techno-solutionists eagerly mining data for convenience, profit and optimized social engineering ignore or dismiss mounting privacy costs, as conservatives caution.

While technology evangelists envision personalized services, pre-crime threat detection and Emotion AI spotting deception before crimes occur, such preemptive surveillance offends conservative principles of limited government overreach into private lives and due process. Legislation must ensure privacy, consent and human agency despite advancing intrusive capacities expanding state and corporate visibility into intimate life details, they contend. Personal responsibility, not preemptively restricting all, secures ordered liberty.

Looking farther ahead, transformative biohacks allowing genetic enhancements, bionic/AI hybrid implants, eliminating diseases through re-engineered organs present monkeys' paw scenarios where intended benefits spiral into dehumanization and unforeseen tragedies in conservative critiques. Humans reconstituting human nature itself courts metaphysical calamity, akin to the Tower of Babel myth exemplifying vain overreach. From cloning to life extension pursuits to creating conscious machines surpassing limited human faculties, hubristic quests for godlike technological powers offend conservative dispositions.

While Silicon Valley technologists cheer CRISPR gene editing and pioneering cyborgs as ushering post-human transcendence, conservatives recoil at redesigning life and what makes humans exceptional into tools for optimization. However wondrous, abandoning prudent boundaries risks erasing humanity's essence and dignity for uber functionality. No matter how close science brings individuals to immortality, fallibility and interdependence should temper indulging Promethean aspirations. Conservative philosophies ground techno-futurism in ancient wisdom and ethics.

Overall the conservative tech ethos strongly favors free enterprise innovation and solutions remedying human constraints. But idealism must bend toward moral realism. Thus, conservatives adopt more circumspect postures than wide-eyed futurists awaiting AI utopias, designer babies, augmented superintelligence and defeating mortality. Custom, community and soul matter beyond any transformative gadgets materialist science conjures. Some grim futures portend dehumanized dystopias where convenience displaces meaning. So conservatives preach carefully charting courses balancing ingenuity with timeless wisdom through tumultuous technological currents ahead.

Innovation and Entrepreneurship

THE CONSERVATIVE BELIEF in the power of innovation and entrepreneurship to drive economic growth is deeply rooted in the fundamental principles of free markets, individual freedom, and limited government intervention. At the core of this belief lies the understanding that innovation and entrepreneurship are the driving forces behind economic progress and prosperity.

To fully comprehend the conservative agenda regarding innovation and entrepreneurship, it is essential to first establish the foundational principles that underpin this perspective. Conservatives emphasize the importance of individual initiative, personal responsibility, and the free market as catalysts for economic growth and advancement. This ideology forms the basis for their staunch support of innovation and entrepreneurship as primary drivers of economic prosperity.

Innovation, as viewed through the conservative lens, encompasses the process of introducing new ideas, products, or methods that lead to enhanced efficiency, productivity, and economic value. This can manifest in various forms, such as technological advancements, process improvements, or the development of new business models. Entrepreneurship, on the other hand, embodies the spirit of risk-taking, creativity, and initiative to establish and grow new ventures, thereby contributing to job creation and wealth generation. These concepts are intricately interwoven, as innovation often fuels entrepreneurial endeavors, while entrepreneurship serves as a vehicle for bringing innovative ideas to fruition.

Conservatives advocate for policies and environments that foster a culture of innovation and entrepreneurship, recognizing the crucial role they play in driving economic growth. By championing free-market principles, minimal government intervention, and a conducive regulatory framework, conservatives aim to cultivate an environment where individuals and businesses are incentivized to innovate and pursue entrepreneurial opportunities. This approach not only stimulates economic activity but also promotes competition, which is essential for driving innovation and delivering value to consumers.

A compelling example of the conservative belief in the power of innovation and entrepreneurship can be observed in the technology sector. Silicon Valley, renowned for its innovative prowess and entrepreneurial spirit, epitomizes the conservative principles in action. The region's ecosystem thrives on a culture of risk-taking, creativity, and technological advancement, fueled by minimal government interference and a robust free-market environment. Companies such as Apple, Google, and Amazon exemplify the transformative impact of innovation and entrepreneurship on economic growth, job creation, and global competitiveness.

Furthermore, the success stories of small business owners and startups across various industries serve as poignant illustrations of the conservative ideology in practice. By removing barriers to entry, reducing regulatory burdens, and fostering an environment conducive to innovation, conservatives aim to empower aspiring entrepreneurs to pursue their visions and contribute to economic expansion.

While the conservative perspective staunchly advocates for minimal government intervention and the primacy of free markets in driving innovation and entrepreneurship, it is important to acknowledge that alternative viewpoints exist. Critics argue that an unrestricted free-market approach may lead to potential negative externalities, such as income inequality, environmental degradation, and social disparities. They advocate for a more interventionist role of government in regulating and guiding innovation and entrepreneurship to address these concerns.

In contrast, conservatives contend that excessive government intervention stifles innovation and entrepreneurship by impeding individual freedom, imposing regulatory burdens, and distorting market dynamics. They argue that a balanced approach, which safeguards against market abuses while preserving the incentives for innovation and entrepreneurship, is essential for sustainable economic growth and societal progress.

Empirical evidence consistently supports the conservative stance on the pivotal role of innovation and entrepreneurship in driving economic growth. Studies have shown that economies with higher levels of entrepreneurial activity and innovation tend to exhibit greater resilience, higher productivity, and increased job creation. Additionally, nations with favorable conditions for entrepreneurship and innovation, characterized by flexible labor markets, strong property rights, and minimal regulatory barriers, have consistently outperformed their counterparts in terms of economic dynamism and prosperity.

In discussing the conservative belief in the power of innovation and entrepreneurship, it is imperative to clarify certain complex terms that are often associated with this discourse. One such term is "creative destruction," a concept introduced by economist Joseph Schumpeter, which refers to the process whereby new innovations and entrepreneurial activities render existing products, industries, or technologies obsolete. While this phenomenon may initially disrupt established markets, it ultimately leads to enhanced productivity, efficiency, and overall economic progress.

The conservative agenda regarding innovation and entrepreneurship underscores the profound impact of these forces on economic growth and societal advancement. By championing free-market principles, individual freedom, and minimal government intervention, conservatives seek to cultivate an environment where innovation and entrepreneurship can flourish, driving job creation, wealth generation, and technological progress. Embracing a balanced approach that safeguards against market abuses while preserving the incentives for innovation and entrepreneurship is essential for fostering sustainable economic growth and prosperity. As we navigate the complexities of the modern economy, it is imperative to recognize the indispensable role of innovation and entrepreneurship in shaping our collective future.

Regulation and Technological Advancement

BEFORE DELVING INTO the conservative perspective on regulating new technologies, it is essential to have a foundational understanding of the principles that underpin conservative ideology. This includes a recognition of the emphasis on free-market principles, limited government intervention, and the promotion of individual freedom and responsibility as catalysts for economic growth and societal progress. Furthermore, a basic understanding of the dynamics of technological innovation and the potential risks associated with emerging technologies will be beneficial for comprehending the conservative approach to regulation.

To provide a broad overview, we will first outline the rationale behind conservative approaches to technological regulation. This will involve discussing the inherent tension between fostering innovation and ensuring safety and ethical considerations. We will then delve into the key principles that guide conservative perspectives on regulatory frameworks for new technologies, emphasizing the importance of minimizing regulatory burdens and preserving the incentives for technological advancement.

The conservative approach to regulating technological advancements encompasses several key considerations. We will explore the principles of risk-based regulation, the promotion of voluntary industry standards, and the role of market forces in guiding technological development. Additionally, we will examine the importance of regulatory flexibility and adaptability in the face of rapid technological change, highlighting the need for responsive and proportionate regulatory measures that do not stifle innovation.

THE CONSERVATIVE AGENDA

As we navigate the detailed steps of conservative approaches to regulating new technologies, it is important to bear in mind the delicate balance that must be struck between regulatory oversight and fostering innovation. We will emphasize the potential unintended consequences of overly stringent regulation, such as stifling technological progress and impeding economic growth. Conversely, we will also highlight the risks associated with inadequate regulation, including potential safety hazards and ethical concerns. Practical tips for policymakers and regulatory bodies will be provided to navigate these complexities effectively.

To validate the effectiveness of conservative regulatory approaches to technological advancements, we will examine case studies and empirical evidence that demonstrate the outcomes of implementing conservative principles in regulatory frameworks. This will involve analyzing the impact of regulatory policies on technological innovation, economic growth, and societal well-being, providing tangible examples of successful conservative regulatory practices.

While conservative approaches to regulating new technologies prioritize minimizing regulatory burdens, it is important to acknowledge potential challenges and criticisms. We will address common concerns raised regarding the conservative stance on technological regulation, including issues related to consumer protection, environmental impact, and ethical considerations. By offering potential solutions and responses to these challenges, we aim to provide a balanced perspective on the intricacies of conservative regulatory frameworks for technological advancements.

Now, let's delve into the detailed steps of conservative approaches to regulating new technologies, exploring the principles and considerations that shape conservative perspectives on technological regulation.

JACK DONAHUE

Privacy and Data Security

IN THE REALM OF PRIVACY and data security, conservative concerns are paramount, reflecting a deep-seated commitment to safeguarding individual liberties and protecting against potential abuses of power. In this chapter, we will explore the conservative agenda surrounding privacy and data security, delving into the nuances of these critical concepts and examining the need for robust data security measures in an increasingly interconnected and technologically driven world.

Privacy and data security are foundational elements of individual autonomy and the protection of personal information in the digital age. Privacy encompasses the right to control one's personal information and the freedom from unwarranted intrusion, while data security pertains to the safeguarding of data from unauthorized access, use, or manipulation. Both concepts are integral to preserving individual freedoms and mitigating the risks associated with the pervasiveness of digital technologies in modern society.

The rationale behind comparing privacy and data security is to elucidate the interconnected nature of these concepts and the imperative to balance the preservation of privacy with the implementation of robust data security measures. By juxtaposing these subjects, we aim to unravel the complexities of safeguarding personal information in an era of rapid technological advancements and proliferating data breaches. Furthermore, this comparison seeks to underscore the significance of conservative perspectives in formulating comprehensive strategies for privacy protection and data security.

The benchmarks for comparison in evaluating privacy and data security will revolve around the fundamental principles of individual autonomy, the scope of permissible data collection and utilization, the role of regulatory frameworks, and the efficacy of security measures in safeguarding personal information. These criteria will serve as the parameters for analyzing the dynamics between privacy and data security, offering a comprehensive perspective on the conservative approach to addressing these critical issues.

When examining privacy and data security through a conservative lens, it becomes evident that both concepts share a common foundation in preserving individual autonomy and upholding the sanctity of personal information. Conservatives emphasize the importance of limiting government intrusion and advocating for privacy rights, while also recognizing the need for robust data security measures to protect against unauthorized access and potential breaches. By drawing parallels between privacy and data security, conservative perspectives underscore the inseparable nature of these concepts and the necessity to address them cohesively.

Despite the inherent alignment between privacy and data security, distinctions emerge in their respective emphases. Privacy places a primary focus on the individual's right to control their personal information and limit its dissemination, while data security underscores the technical and organizational measures implemented to protect data from unauthorized access and breaches. Conservatives navigate the nuances of these distinctions by advocating for comprehensive privacy laws and regulations that are complemented by stringent data security measures, ensuring a holistic approach to safeguarding personal information.

The comparison between privacy and data security yields profound insights into the conservative approach to addressing these critical issues. By recognizing the symbiotic relationship between privacy rights and data security measures, conservatives advocate for a balanced approach that respects individual autonomy while acknowledging the imperative to fortify data protection mechanisms. This analysis underscores the intricate interdependence of privacy and data security within the conservative framework, highlighting the need for comprehensive strategies that harmonize these essential components.

The contemporary relevance of privacy and data security cannot be overstated, particularly in an era characterized by widespread digital interconnectedness and the proliferation of data-driven technologies. Conservatives are at the forefront of advocating for legislative and regulatory measures that align with the evolving landscape of privacy and data security, recognizing the imperative to adapt to emerging technological challenges while preserving individual freedoms and mitigating potential risks.

As the digital ecosystem continues to evolve, privacy and data security remain pivotal concerns for conservatives, reflecting a steadfast commitment to safeguarding individual liberties and protecting against potential abuses of power. By comprehensively addressing these issues and integrating robust data security measures, conservatives uphold the fundamental tenets of privacy and data protection, fostering a climate of trust and security in an increasingly interconnected world.

Conservative Perspectives on Big Tech

AS WE DELVE INTO CONSERVATIVE critiques of big tech companies and their influence on society and politics, it becomes imperative to underscore the significance of understanding the multifaceted impact these entities have on our daily lives. This list will provide a comprehensive exploration of key concerns and reservations held by conservative voices, shedding light on the intricate dynamics at play.

THE CONSERVATIVE AGENDA

In the conservative critique of big tech, several pivotal points emerge, each offering a distinct vantage point on the influence and implications of these tech giants. The following list previews the critical issues to be expanded upon:

a. Big tech companies, such as Google, Facebook, Amazon, and Apple, have amassed unprecedented market dominance, raising concerns about their ability to stifle competition and exert undue influence on the economy. The consolidation of power in the hands of a few tech behemoths has led to calls for antitrust measures and regulatory scrutiny. The unchecked expansion of these companies has the potential to impede innovation, restrict consumer choice, and distort market dynamics, thereby undermining the principles of free and fair competition.

b. The sprawling reach of big tech conglomerates encompasses various sectors, from e-commerce and digital advertising to cloud computing and content distribution. Their pervasive presence in multiple facets of the digital landscape has raised apprehensions about the erosion of competitive markets and the impediment to small businesses and startups. Moreover, the acquisition of potential competitors and the strategic positioning of products and services have enabled these companies to wield substantial influence, shaping consumer behavior and dictating industry standards.

c. Numerous studies and investigations have highlighted the disproportionate control wielded by big tech firms in their respective domains. Testimonials from entrepreneurs and industry insiders further underscore the challenges posed by the overwhelming market dominance of these companies, with firsthand accounts detailing the hurdles faced in competing with and navigating the landscape shaped by tech giants.

d. The implications of unchecked monopoly power extend beyond economic realms, permeating into societal and political spheres. The capacity of big tech companies to shape public discourse, control information flow, and influence market dynamics underscores the urgency of addressing their monopolistic practices to ensure a level playing field for businesses and consumers alike.

Transitioning from the scrutiny of monopoly power and market influence to the examination of censorship and free speech concerns, the interplay between these issues reveals the intricate web of challenges posed by big tech companies and their far-reaching impact on society and politics.

a. The growing prevalence of content moderation and censorship by big tech platforms has ignited debates surrounding the freedom of expression and the boundaries of permissible discourse. Conservative voices have raised alarm over the selective censorship and de-platforming of individuals and organizations based on ideological or political affiliations, raising pertinent questions about the role of these companies in shaping public discourse and stifling dissenting viewpoints.

b. The implementation of content moderation policies by big tech companies has led to a myriad of controversies, with instances of conservative voices and viewpoints being disproportionately targeted for censorship. The opaque nature of moderation algorithms and the lack of transparency in decision-making processes have exacerbated concerns about the arbitrary and biased enforcement of community standards. Furthermore, the presence of ideological biases within these companies has fueled apprehensions about the suppression of viewpoints that diverge from prevailing narratives.

c. Instances of de-platforming, demonetization, and algorithmic demotion of conservative content creators and media outlets have been well-documented, underscoring the tangible impact of censorship on free speech and public discourse. Testimonials from affected individuals and organizations illuminate the challenges faced in navigating an environment where dissenting voices are susceptible to silencing and suppression.

d. The implications of censorship and free speech concerns extend beyond the digital realm, permeating into the broader societal fabric and political landscape. The ability of big tech platforms to shape narratives and control the dissemination of information underscores the urgency of safeguarding free expression and fostering an environment conducive to diverse perspectives and robust debate.

Transitioning from the examination of censorship and free speech concerns to the exploration of data privacy and security risks, the interconnected nature of these issues underscores the multifaceted challenges embedded within the domain of big tech companies and their influence on society and politics.

a. The unprecedented collection and utilization of user data by big tech companies have raised profound concerns about privacy infringement and data security vulnerabilities. The pervasive surveillance and data aggregation practices employed by these companies have engendered apprehensions about the erosion of individual privacy and the susceptibility of personal information to exploitation and breaches.

b. The intricate web of data collection and utilization by big tech companies transcends conventional boundaries, encompassing a wide array of online activities and behavioral patterns. The aggregation of personal data for targeted advertising, algorithmic profiling, and predictive analytics has raised ethical and legal dilemmas, particularly in the absence of robust regulations and oversight. Furthermore, data security lapses and breaches have underscored the vulnerabilities inherent in the storage and management of vast troves of user information, amplifying concerns about the potential repercussions of data exposure and misuse.

c. Numerous instances of data breaches and privacy violations involving big tech companies have underscored the tangible risks posed to user privacy and data security. Testimonials from individuals impacted by data breaches and privacy infringements provide firsthand insights into the ramifications of lax data protection measures and the imperative to fortify privacy safeguards.

d. The implications of data privacy and security risks extend beyond individual privacy concerns, permeating into broader societal and ethical dimensions. The commodification of personal data and the susceptibility to data breaches underscore the urgent need for comprehensive privacy regulations and robust security measures to mitigate the risks posed by the unchecked aggregation and exploitation of user information.

Transitioning from the exploration of data privacy and security risks to the scrutiny of political bias and manipulation, the intricate interplay between these issues reveals the far-reaching implications of big tech companies on the political landscape and democratic processes.

a. The pervasive influence of big tech companies on the dissemination of information and the shaping of public opinion has raised concerns about ideological biases and partisan manipulation. Conservative voices have highlighted instances of algorithmic biases, content suppression, and targeted manipulation aimed at amplifying specific narratives and marginalizing opposing viewpoints, thereby exerting a profound impact on the political discourse and electoral processes.

b. The algorithmic curation of content and the prioritization of specific viewpoints have contributed to the amplification of partisan echo chambers and the marginalization of dissenting perspectives. Moreover, the role of big tech companies in regulating political speech and moderating electoral content has engendered apprehensions about the potential distortion of democratic processes and the erosion of fair and balanced discourse. The alignment of these companies with particular political ideologies has further underscored concerns about the impartiality of content moderation and the susceptibility to partisan manipulation.

c. Instances of biased content curation, targeted de-platforming of political figures, and algorithmic manipulation have been the subject of extensive scrutiny, highlighting the tangible impact of political bias and manipulation on the democratic fabric. Testimonials from individuals and organizations affected by ideological biases and partisan manipulation provide firsthand accounts of the challenges posed by the unchecked influence of big tech companies on political discourse and electoral integrity.

d. The implications of political bias and manipulation extend beyond ideological considerations, permeating into the fundamental tenets of democratic governance and public trust. The capacity of big tech companies to shape political narratives and influence electoral outcomes underscores the urgency of addressing the regulatory and ethical dimensions of their influence, ensuring the preservation of fair and impartial democratic processes.

The ethical dilemmas posed by the practices and influence of big tech companies extend beyond conventional regulatory and policy considerations, encompassing profound moral and societal implications. The commodification of personal data, the proliferation of disinformation, and the erosion of privacy rights raise profound ethical questions about the impact of tech conglomerates on individual autonomy, societal values, and the fabric of truth and trust.

Emerging Technologies and Ethical Considerations

AS WE TRAVERSE THE landscape of conservative perspectives on emerging technologies, particularly artificial intelligence and genetic engineering, it is imperative to delve into the profound ethical considerations that underpin these advancements. The fusion of technological innovation with ethical contemplation yields a tapestry of complexities, presenting a formidable terrain for conservative scrutiny and deliberation. This discourse seeks to navigate the intricate intersections of conservatism and emerging technologies, shedding light on the ethical considerations that resonate deeply within conservative frameworks.

In the conservative approach to emerging technologies, the ethical implications of artificial intelligence and genetic engineering encapsulate a confluence of considerations, encompassing individual autonomy, societal values, and the sanctity of life. The fundamental proposition to be examined revolves around the imperative of preserving ethical boundaries and moral principles amidst the rapid advancements in these domains, safeguarding against the erosion of human dignity and societal integrity.

Embarking on the exploration of artificial intelligence, it is paramount to scrutinize the ethical dimensions embedded within the development and deployment of AI systems. The convergence of AI with diverse spheres of human existence engenders profound implications for privacy, autonomy, and societal well-being, necessitating a comprehensive evaluation rooted in empirical evidence and ethical reflection.

The proliferation of artificial intelligence technologies has unfurled a tapestry of ethical quandaries, ranging from privacy infringements to algorithmic biases. Within the conservative framework, the preservation of individual liberties and the inviolability of human dignity serve as bedrocks for the examination of AI's ethical terrain.

The ethical underpinnings of AI are intricately intertwined with the preservation of privacy rights and the autonomy of individuals. The exponential growth in AI-driven surveillance and data aggregation has engendered profound concerns regarding the erosion of privacy boundaries and the susceptibility of personal information to exploitation. Empirical evidence from comprehensive studies and testimonies from individuals impacted by AI-driven privacy infringements underscore the tangible ramifications of unchecked technological encroachments on privacy rights. The conservative ethical lens accentuates the imperative of fortifying privacy safeguards and curtailing the encroachment of AI into the private domains of individuals, anchoring the discourse within the realm of individual autonomy and liberty.

Delving deeper into the evidence, the ethical implications of AI extend beyond privacy infringements to encompass algorithmic biases and discriminatory outcomes. The inherent biases embedded within AI systems, often reflective of societal prejudices and disparities, raise pertinent questions about the ethical ramifications of algorithmic decision-making. Studies elucidating the disparate impact of AI algorithms on marginalized communities and empirical evidence showcasing instances of algorithmic discrimination provide substantive support for the conservative apprehensions regarding the ethical dimensions of AI. The conservative ethical framework underscores the imperative of cultivating fair and equitable AI systems that uphold the principles of justice and non-discrimination, reinforcing the ethical boundaries that safeguard societal values and individual rights.

Amidst the scrutiny of AI's ethical terrain within the conservative paradigm, counterarguments emerge, challenging the conservative apprehensions regarding the ethical implications of artificial intelligence. Proponents of AI posit its potential to ameliorate societal challenges, enhance efficiency, and foster innovation, thereby presenting a counter-narrative that accentuates the utilitarian benefits of AI technologies.

In response to the counterarguments, it is imperative to underscore that the conservative scrutiny of AI's ethical dimensions does not negate its potential for societal advancement and technological progress. Rather, it endeavors to delineate the ethical boundaries that safeguard individual autonomy, societal values, and the sanctity of human dignity amidst the proliferation of AI technologies. The conservative ethical framework seeks to engender a nuanced discourse that harmonizes technological advancement with moral imperatives, steering the trajectory of AI development towards a landscape rooted in ethical fortitude and societal integrity.

Supplementing the conservative ethical scrutiny of AI, additional substantiation emerges from empirical studies, ethical analyses, and testimonies that converge to illuminate the profound ethical considerations embedded within the realm of artificial intelligence. The multifaceted nature of AI's ethical implications necessitates a comprehensive examination fortified by diverse evidentiary pillars, underscoring the imperative of ethical reflection and empirical substantiation.

Transitioning from the ethical labyrinth of artificial intelligence to the domain of genetic engineering, the conservative ethical lens converges upon the profound considerations that underpin the manipulation of genetic material and the augmentation of biological entities. The ethical implications intertwined with genetic engineering encapsulate a myriad of concerns resonating deeply within conservative ethical frameworks, encompassing the sanctity of life, individual autonomy, and societal values.

The ethical contours of genetic engineering intersect with the preservation of the sanctity of life and the maintenance of ethical boundaries in manipulating the fundamental building blocks of biological existence. The conservative ethical framework accentuates the imperative of upholding the intrinsic value of life and the ethical constraints that safeguard against the commodification and instrumentalization of genetic material. Empirical evidence elucidating the ethical dilemmas inherent in genetic manipulation and testimonies from ethical scholars and bioethicists converge to fortify the conservative ethical scrutiny of genetic engineering, anchoring the discourse within the realm of moral imperatives and societal integrity.

Delving deeper into the evidence, the ethical implications of genetic engineering extend beyond individual considerations to encompass societal values and ecological ramifications. The conservative ethical lens scrutinizes the ethical dimensions of genetic engineering through the prism of societal well-being, ecological sustainability, and the preservation of natural order. Empirical evidence detailing the potential ecological repercussions of genetic manipulation and testimonies from conservationists and environmental scholars bolster the conservative ethical apprehensions regarding the ethical implications of genetic engineering. The conservative ethical framework underscores the imperative of fostering an ethical landscape that harmonizes technological innovation with ecological integrity and societal values, reinforcing the ethical boundaries that safeguard the sanctity of life and the well-being of ecological systems.

The conservative scrutiny of emerging technologies, particularly artificial intelligence and genetic engineering, unfolds a tapestry of ethical considerations deeply rooted in empirical evidence, ethical reflection, and societal values. The preservation of individual autonomy, societal well-being, and the sanctity of life serves as a lodestar guiding the conservative ethical examination of these technologies, reinforcing the imperative of fortifying ethical boundaries amidst the rapid pace of technological advancement. The confluence of conservative ethical scrutiny with empirical substantiation engenders a discourse that navigates the intricate terrain of emerging technologies, fostering a landscape fortified by ethical fortitude and societal integrity.

The Future of Technology and Innovation

AS WE DELVE INTO THE future of technology and innovation, it is imperative to comprehend the intricate interplay between emerging trends and the conservative agenda. The fusion of technological advancements with the conservative ethos presents a formidable terrain for scrutiny and deliberation, necessitating a comprehensive evaluation rooted in empirical evidence and ethical reflection.

The landscape of technology and innovation is replete with profound implications for societal progress, economic prosperity, and individual well-being. Against this backdrop, the conservative perspective seeks to navigate the ethical considerations and policy imperatives that resonate deeply within the realm of technological advancement, anchoring the discourse within the framework of individual autonomy, societal values, and the preservation of ethical boundaries.

One of the primary issues that warrant conservative scrutiny pertains to the ethical implications of data privacy in the era of pervasive digitalization. The exponential growth in data collection, aggregation, and utilization has unfurled a tapestry of ethical quandaries, engendering concerns regarding the erosion of privacy boundaries and the susceptibility of personal information to exploitation. The conservative ethical lens accentuates the imperative of fortifying privacy safeguards and curtailing the encroachment of technology into the private domains of individuals, anchoring the discourse within the realm of individual autonomy and liberty.

Furthermore, the ethical dimensions of algorithmic biases and discriminatory outcomes inherent within artificial intelligence technologies present a formidable challenge that necessitates conservative examination. The conservative ethical framework underscores the imperative of cultivating fair and equitable AI systems that uphold the principles of justice and non-discrimination, reinforcing the ethical boundaries that safeguard societal values and individual rights.

If these issues are not addressed, the ramifications could range from the erosion of individual liberties and the proliferation of algorithmic discrimination to the commodification and instrumentalization of genetic material. The erosion of privacy boundaries could lead to a loss of autonomy and the susceptibility of personal information to exploitation. Algorithmic biases could exacerbate societal prejudices and disparities, undermining the principles of justice and equity. Moreover, the commodification of genetic material could compromise the sanctity of life and ethical constraints, leading to potential ecological repercussions and societal upheaval.

To address these challenges, it is imperative to devise comprehensive strategies that uphold the conservative ethos while fostering technological innovation. One such solution involves the formulation and implementation of robust data privacy regulations that fortify privacy safeguards and limit the encroachment of technology into the private domains of individuals. Additionally, the cultivation of fair and equitable AI systems through stringent oversight and accountability mechanisms is essential to mitigate algorithmic biases and discriminatory outcomes.

In the domain of genetic engineering, the formulation of ethical frameworks that harmonize technological innovation with ecological integrity and societal values is imperative to safeguard the sanctity of life and the well-being of ecological systems. These solutions underscore the conservative imperative of fortifying ethical boundaries amidst the rapid pace of technological advancement, steering the trajectory of technology and innovation towards a landscape rooted in ethical fortitude and societal integrity.

The implementation of these solutions necessitates collaborative efforts from policymakers, technologists, ethicists, and societal stakeholders. It entails the formulation and enforcement of stringent data privacy regulations that underscore individual autonomy and privacy rights. Additionally, it requires the integration of ethical considerations within the development and deployment of AI systems, fostering a landscape fortified by ethical fortitude and societal integrity.

In the domain of genetic engineering, the implementation of ethical frameworks that prioritize ecological sustainability and societal well-being necessitates interdisciplinary collaboration and robust oversight mechanisms, reinforcing the ethical boundaries that safeguard the sanctity of life and the well-being of ecological systems.

The implementation of these solutions is predicted to yield tangible outcomes, ranging from the fortification of privacy safeguards and the mitigation of algorithmic biases to the preservation of the sanctity of life and ecological integrity. The cultivation of fair and equitable AI systems is anticipated to mitigate algorithmic biases and discriminatory outcomes, fostering a landscape rooted in justice and non-discrimination. Likewise, the integration of ethical frameworks within the domain of genetic engineering is projected to fortify ethical boundaries, safeguarding the sanctity of life and ecological systems amidst technological advancements.

While the proposed solutions provide a robust framework for addressing the ethical implications of technology and innovation from a conservative perspective, it is imperative to acknowledge alternative approaches. These may include the exploration of decentralized technological architectures that prioritize individual data ownership and control, as well as the promotion of ethical considerations within the design and development of AI systems and genetic engineering technologies.

The conservative agenda for technology and innovation unfolds a tapestry of ethical considerations deeply rooted in empirical evidence, ethical reflection, and societal values. The preservation of individual autonomy, societal well-being, and the sanctity of life serves as a lodestar guiding the conservative ethical examination of these domains, reinforcing the imperative of fortifying ethical boundaries amidst the rapid pace of technological advancement. The confluence of conservative ethical scrutiny with empirical substantiation engenders a discourse that navigates the intricate terrain of emerging technologies, fostering a landscape fortified by ethical fortitude and societal integrity.

Globalization and International Relations

The Conservative Approach to Globalization

As technology and trade accelerate global integration, conservatives hold deeply ambivalent views on expanding international interdependency. While acknowledging potential economic benefits from accessing foreign markets and labor, conservatives also voice reservations about threats to domestic industries, unchecked immigration flows, America ceding global influence, and sacrificing core principles for multicultural relativism. Given deep roots valuing self-sufficiency, sovereignty and exceptionalism, conservatives largely reject pure cosmopolitan globalism that relinquishes too much unilateral power. Instead they promote strategic bilateral partnerships when interests align, resisting counterproductive groupthink within international bodies.

Foremost, instead of submitting to elite directed globalism that concentrates power among unaccountable institutions while exposing middle class livelihoods to foreign wage competition, conservatives advocate economic nationalism. They favor securing the most advantageous bilateral trade deals possible through aggressive negotiations rather than accepting obligations from multiparty blocs demanding shared governance. Conservatives support incentivizing corporations to create domestic jobs with tax reforms rather than outsourcing labor. And similar to fair trade practices governing company town dynamics in America's past when workers entirely depended on employers, conservatism argues that lopsided interdependency with certain exploited developing nations warrants rebalancing based on ethical production, environmental and human rights standards.

Militarily, conservative foreign policy resists the temptations, distractions and expenditures of idealistic interventionism when core national interests do not clearly justify intervention. Conservatives harbor deep suspicions of grand Wilsonian visions to spread democratic values abroad, having witnessed the disastrous outcomes pursuing regime changes in the Middle East. They prefer pragmatic containment strategies based on ethnonationalist factions understanding only force, not fantasies that outside models of governance transplant easily. Additionally, conservatives oppose relinquishing any sovereignty to global governance bodies that constrain America's defense options and best interests.

With southern border crossings surging dramatically higher over the past two years alone, conservatives stand united against uncontrolled global migration inflows that strain public services, depress wages for native workers and risk balkanization with ethnic enclaves resisting assimilation. Each nation possesses the sovereign right to determine its own immigration policies to best serve its national interests rather than conform to external pressures. Conservatives oppose relinquishing this sovereignty to international coalitions espousing open border utopianism. And foreign aid should seek to improve living standards abroad and discourage mass exoduses rather than accelerate human dislocation.

defending economic and geopolitical interests against supranational bureaucratic overreach, conservatives harbor deeper suspicions of cultural globalization erasing traditionalism. Promotion of radical social agendas by Western progressives seeking to universalize LGBTQ values, sexual libertarianism dressed up as feminism, and secularism offends conservatives who view traditional family structures and faith as vital pillars of civilizational stability. They resent wealthy nations attached to declining birth rates and religious participation increasingly patronizing socially conservative Eastern bloc and Global South nations holding onto tradition. Conservatives will continue pushing back against cultural imperialism disguising itself as humanitarianism.

On the whole, conservatives view right-minded globalization as allowing neutral exchange of goods, reasonable people movement, and voluntary sharing of innovations - not a mechanism for concentrating power into democratically unaccountable technocratic institutions or imposing radical cultural shifts. Global cooperation guided by universal ethics serves mutual understanding but inherently regional values and interests take precedence. And transnational entanglements must not constrain national sovereignty. Thus conservatives will continue approaching relentless global integration with prudent skepticism rather than blind enthusiasm or resignation.

Trade and Economic Nationalism

IN AN INCREASINGLY interconnected global economy, the conservative perspective on trade and the balance between economic nationalism and free trade holds significant importance. The fundamental principles of conservative ideology often intersect with trade policies, reflecting a broader commitment to national sovereignty, economic stability, and the protection of domestic industries. This chapter aims to delve into the multifaceted aspects of trade and economic nationalism from a conservative standpoint, exploring the underlying concepts, perspectives, and implications.

Economic nationalism, as viewed through the conservative lens, encompasses the prioritization of domestic economic interests and the assertion of national economic sovereignty. It advocates for policies that safeguard domestic industries, protect jobs, and ensure the self-sufficiency and resilience of the national economy. This concept aligns with the conservative belief in preserving traditional institutions and fostering a strong national identity. By emphasizing economic self-reliance, economic nationalism seeks to shield the country from potential vulnerabilities arising from excessive dependence on foreign markets or resources.

From a conservative standpoint, economic nationalism is not synonymous with protectionism. Rather, it embodies a strategic approach to trade that aims to maintain a balance between international engagement and the preservation of domestic economic strength. This nuanced perspective underscores the conservative commitment to promoting self-sufficiency while acknowledging the benefits of global trade and cooperation.

Consider the case of the automotive industry, a sector that has historically been central to the economic prosperity of many nations. When examining economic nationalism within this context, we observe how conservative trade policies emphasize the preservation of domestic manufacturing capabilities and the protection of jobs in the automotive sector. By imposing tariffs on imported vehicles and components, conservative-led governments aim to incentivize domestic production, thereby bolstering the resilience of the national automotive industry.

Furthermore, the steel and aluminum tariffs introduced by the United States in 2018 provide a pertinent example of economic nationalism in action. The conservative rationale behind these tariffs was grounded in the protection of domestic steel and aluminum producers, citing national security and the preservation of critical industries as primary motivations. This real-world illustration underscores the practical application of economic nationalism within the realm of trade policy, reflecting the conservative commitment to nurturing vital domestic industries.

While economic nationalism embodies a core tenet of conservative trade ideology, it is crucial to acknowledge alternative perspectives that challenge this approach. Critics often argue that economic nationalism may lead to trade tensions, retaliatory measures, and a reduction in overall global economic welfare. Additionally, concerns regarding the potential inefficiencies and market distortions arising from protectionist measures are frequently raised.

From a conservative standpoint, however, these criticisms are weighed against the imperative of safeguarding national economic interests and preserving domestic industries. The conservative perspective acknowledges the complexities of international trade dynamics while asserting that a judicious application of economic nationalism can serve as a safeguard against overreliance on foreign markets and mitigate the risks associated with global economic volatility.

Examining trade data and statistics offers valuable insights into the implementation and impact of conservative trade policies. For instance, analyses of trade balances, industry-specific employment figures, and comparative production costs provide empirical evidence of the challenges and opportunities associated with trade and economic nationalism. By scrutinizing the economic indicators and trade patterns relevant to specific sectors or regions, policymakers can make well-informed decisions that align with conservative principles while promoting sustainable economic growth.

Furthermore, historical examples of successful integration of economic nationalism within conservative trade policies, such as the resurgence of American manufacturing in the early 20th century, offer tangible evidence of the potential benefits of prioritizing domestic economic interests. These historical precedents serve as compelling illustrations of the conservative approach to trade and economic nationalism, reinforcing the validity of these principles in contemporary economic contexts.

The concept of economic nationalism often intersects with complex economic theories and trade policy terminology. To facilitate a comprehensive understanding, it is essential to demystify these terms and provide accessible explanations. For instance, the distinction between absolute advantage and comparative advantage in trade theory can be elucidated to underscore the conservative rationale for safeguarding domestic industries despite the potential gains from international specialization. Additionally, clarifying the nuanced differences between protectionism and economic nationalism can dispel misconceptions and promote a more informed discourse on conservative trade policies.

The conservative perspective on trade and economic nationalism embodies a holistic approach that prioritizes domestic economic resilience while recognizing the benefits of global trade. By adhering to the principles of economic nationalism, conservatives seek to strike a balance between safeguarding national economic interests and promoting international cooperation. Through the integration of practical examples, comprehensive explanations, and empirical evidence, this chapter has shed light on the nuanced facets of trade and economic nationalism from a conservative standpoint, emphasizing the multifaceted considerations that underpin conservative trade policies.

As the global economic landscape continues to evolve, the conservative agenda remains steadfast in advocating for trade policies that uphold national economic sovereignty, foster domestic prosperity, and contribute to a resilient and sustainable global economy. By embracing the key takeaways presented in this chapter, readers can gain a deeper understanding of the conservative approach to trade and economic nationalism, thus contributing to a more informed and nuanced discourse on these critical issues.

Foreign Aid and International Development

THE GOAL OF CONSERVATIVE approaches to foreign aid and international development policies is to promote sustainable, effective, and accountable assistance to developing countries while safeguarding national interests and fostering self-reliance.

Before delving into conservative approaches to foreign aid and international development, it is essential to understand the underlying principles of conservative ideology, including the emphasis on sovereignty, fiscal responsibility, and the prioritization of national interests. Additionally, a comprehensive understanding of global geopolitical dynamics, economic disparities, and the diverse needs of developing nations is crucial for formulating effective conservative foreign aid strategies.

Conservative perspectives on foreign aid and international development policies are multifaceted, encompassing a range of considerations that extend beyond traditional aid paradigms. From prioritizing strategic investments to leveraging public-private partnerships, conservative approaches seek to maximize the impact of aid while upholding principles of accountability, efficiency, and reciprocity.

Conservative approaches to foreign aid and international development entail several key strategies and considerations:

1. Conservative foreign aid policies emphasize strategic allocations that prioritize countries and regions aligned with national interests and strategic objectives. By targeting assistance to areas where it can have the most significant impact, conservative approaches seek to mitigate inefficiencies and maximize the effectiveness of aid programs.

2. Central to conservative foreign aid strategies is the promotion of self-reliance and capacity building within recipient countries. This entails fostering an enabling environment for private sector growth, entrepreneurship, and institutional development, empowering nations to chart their paths towards sustainable development.

3. Conservative approaches to foreign aid often incorporate conditionality measures and robust accountability mechanisms to ensure that aid is utilized transparently and in alignment with stated objectives. This includes rigorous monitoring and evaluation frameworks, as well as mechanisms to address corruption and ensure aid effectiveness.

4. Recognizing the pivotal role of the private sector in driving economic growth, conservative foreign aid strategies emphasize the importance of fostering public-private partnerships to catalyze sustainable development. By leveraging private sector expertise, resources, and innovation, aid initiatives can yield greater long-term impact.

5. Conservative approaches to foreign aid underscore the importance of providing humanitarian assistance and crisis response in times of acute need, aligning with the principles of compassion and global solidarity while maintaining a focus on effective, targeted interventions.

THE CONSERVATIVE AGENDA

While pursuing conservative approaches to foreign aid and international development, it is imperative to consider the following tips and warnings:

- Conservative foreign aid strategies should align with national security, economic, and diplomatic interests, ensuring that aid investments contribute to broader geopolitical objectives.

- Prioritize aid initiatives that have the potential to catalyze sustainable, long-term development, fostering self-reliance and economic empowerment within recipient nations.

- Conservative approaches should guard against creating dependency dynamics through aid, instead focusing on initiatives that empower nations to take ownership of their development trajectories.

The success of conservative foreign aid and international development policies can be validated through several indicators, including:

- Measuring the tangible impact of aid investments on poverty alleviation, economic growth, and institutional capacity building.

- Soliciting feedback from recipient countries to assess the perceived effectiveness and alignment of aid programs with their development priorities.

- Evaluating the sustainability and resilience of development outcomes facilitated through conservative aid strategies.

In the event of challenges or setbacks in implementing conservative foreign aid and international development policies, it is essential to recalibrate strategies, reevaluate partnerships, and adapt to evolving global dynamics while remaining committed to the overarching goal of promoting sustainable, accountable, and impactful assistance to developing nations.

With these considerations in mind, conservative approaches to foreign aid and international development policies can serve as a framework for fostering resilient, self-reliant, and empowered societies, thereby contributing to a more prosperous and stable global community.

Multilateral Organizations and Alliances

MULTILATERAL ORGANIZATIONS and alliances are pivotal components of international relations, shaping the dynamics of global governance and cooperation. Multilateral organizations, such as the United Nations and the World Trade Organization, represent collaborative platforms where member states address shared challenges and pursue common goals. Similarly, alliances, such as NATO and the European Union, constitute strategic partnerships aimed at enhancing collective security, economic integration, and regional stability.

The purpose of comparing multilateral organizations and alliances from a conservative perspective is to gain a comprehensive understanding of their roles, functions, and effectiveness in advancing conservative principles of sovereignty, national security, and economic prosperity. By scrutinizing these entities, this analysis aims to shed light on the nuanced considerations that underpin conservative approaches to global governance and strategic partnerships.

The benchmarks for comparison between multilateral organizations and alliances encompass their governance structures, decision-making processes, adaptability to evolving geopolitical dynamics, and their impact on member states' sovereignty and national interests. Additionally, the assessment will evaluate their capacity to address contemporary global challenges, such as security threats, economic disparities, and humanitarian crises, in a manner that aligns with conservative ideologies.

Multilateral organizations and alliances share the common goal of promoting collective action and cooperation among member states. Both platforms serve as forums for diplomatic dialogue, policy coordination, and the pursuit of common objectives. However, multilateral organizations often encompass a broader scope, addressing a diverse array of global issues, while alliances tend to focus on specific regional or functional priorities, such as security or economic integration.

Where multilateral organizations emphasize inclusivity and consensus-based decision-making, alliances often prioritize strategic alignment and interoperability among member states. Additionally, multilateral organizations may face challenges in swiftly responding to crises due to their complex bureaucratic processes, while alliances are designed to facilitate rapid and coordinated action in times of need. Furthermore, multilateral organizations often emphasize universal values and norms, whereas alliances may prioritize the interests of their constituent members.

The comparative analysis reveals that multilateral organizations and alliances serve complementary yet distinct roles in international relations. Multilateral organizations offer a platform for addressing global challenges and promoting universal norms, often emphasizing cooperation and consensus-building. In contrast, alliances focus on regional or functional security concerns, fostering collective defense and interoperability among member states. From a conservative perspective, this analysis underscores the importance of maintaining a balance between global cooperation and national sovereignty, ensuring that multilateral engagements do not infringe upon the sovereign rights of individual states or undermine their national security interests.

The comparison of multilateral organizations and alliances holds particular relevance in the context of contemporary global dynamics, where the efficacy of multilateralism and the resilience of strategic alliances are under scrutiny. As the international community grapples with complex challenges, including transnational terrorism, economic interdependence, and geopolitical rivalries, understanding the distinct contributions and limitations of multilateral organizations and alliances becomes imperative for shaping effective conservative foreign policy and engagement strategies.

Expanding on the conservative perspective, it becomes evident that multilateral organizations, while essential for fostering global cooperation and addressing transnational issues, must respect the sovereignty and national interests of member states. Conservative approaches emphasize the importance of voluntary cooperation rather than supranational authority, advocating for the primacy of national sovereignty as the foundation of international relations. This underscores the need for multilateral organizations to operate within the confines of their mandates, respecting the diverse priorities and policy prerogatives of sovereign states.

On the other hand, strategic alliances, particularly in the realm of security and defense, are instrumental in advancing conservative principles of collective security and regional stability. By fostering interoperability, burden-sharing, and deterrence against common threats, alliances contribute to safeguarding the national security interests of member states while promoting a rules-based international order. From a conservative vantage point, the resilience and adaptability of strategic alliances in the face of evolving security challenges underscore their significance as pillars of stability and cooperation in an uncertain global landscape.

In the contemporary context, the juxtaposition of multilateral organizations and alliances offers conservative policymakers valuable insights into crafting foreign policy strategies that mitigate the risks of overreach while harnessing the strengths of collective action. By recognizing the distinct roles and contributions of these entities, conservative approaches to global governance can champion a balanced and pragmatic engagement that upholds national interests, preserves sovereignty, and promotes international cooperation where it aligns with the interests of sovereign nations.

The relevance of this comparative analysis extends to contemporary debates surrounding the reform of multilateral institutions and the recalibration of strategic alliances in response to emerging security threats and geopolitical realignments. By anchoring conservative foreign policy in a nuanced understanding of multilateralism and strategic partnerships, policymakers can navigate the complexities of international relations with a focus on advancing national interests, fostering stability, and promoting principled engagement on the world stage.

The conservative perspective on multilateral organizations and alliances underscores the imperative of balancing global cooperation with national sovereignty, recognizing the distinct roles and contributions of these entities in shaping international relations. By dissecting their nuances and broader implications, conservative approaches can navigate the complexities of global governance and strategic partnerships with a steadfast commitment to safeguarding national interests, fostering resilience, and promoting a prosperous and secure global community.

JACK DONAHUE

Immigration and Global Migration

AS IMMIGRATION AND global migration continue to shape the social, economic, and political landscapes of nations worldwide, understanding conservative perspectives on these phenomena is essential. This analysis aims to provide a comprehensive examination of conservative views on immigration and global migration trends, shedding light on the nuanced considerations that underpin conservative approaches to these critical issues.

Conservative perspectives prioritize the protection of national borders as a fundamental aspect of ensuring homeland security and upholding the rule of law. The emphasis is placed on preventing illegal immigration, human trafficking, and the entry of individuals with criminal intent.

Statistics from law enforcement agencies and border control authorities can demonstrate the impact of porous borders on national security and public safety. Additionally, testimonies from border patrol agents and security personnel can provide firsthand accounts of the challenges and risks associated with insufficient border security measures.

Real-world scenarios, such as the implementation of border security measures in specific regions, can illustrate the tangible effects of bolstering border security, including reduced criminal activities and enhanced control over immigration flows.

Conservative viewpoints on immigration often scrutinize its economic implications, particularly its effects on labor markets, wages, and government expenditures. Discussions revolve around the potential impacts of immigration on job opportunities for native workers, the allocation of public resources, and the overall fiscal balance.

Economic analyses, including labor market studies and fiscal impact assessments, can provide empirical evidence on the economic consequences of immigration. Testimonials from businesses, workers, and economists can offer insights into the real-world implications of immigration on job availability, wages, and public spending.

Case studies of communities or industries affected by immigration, along with comparisons of regions with varying immigration policies, can offer practical illustrations of the economic ramifications of immigration and global migration.

Conservative perspectives often emphasize the importance of preserving national identity and fostering social cohesion in the face of diverse immigration flows. Discussions focus on the integration of immigrants into the cultural fabric of the host society, promoting shared values, and addressing potential challenges related to cultural assimilation and societal harmony.

Sociological studies and cultural impact assessments can provide insights into the dynamics of cultural integration and social cohesion in the context of immigration. Testimonials from community leaders, educators, and immigrants themselves can offer firsthand perspectives on the challenges and successes of cultural and social integration.

Exemplary initiatives or programs aimed at promoting cultural exchange, language education, and intercultural understanding can serve as practical demonstrations of successful approaches to fostering social integration amidst immigration and global migration trends.

Conservative viewpoints underscore the significance of maintaining national sovereignty and control over immigration policies, while also acknowledging international responsibilities and obligations. Discussions revolve around the autonomy of nations to determine their immigration laws, address border challenges, and manage the influx of migrants, while engaging in international cooperation on humanitarian and diplomatic fronts.

Legal analyses of immigration policies, international treaties, and constitutional frameworks can provide a basis for understanding the legal dimensions of national sovereignty in the context of immigration. Testimonials from policymakers, legal experts, and representatives of international organizations can offer diverse perspectives on the delicate balance between national autonomy and global engagement in immigration matters.

Case studies of countries navigating immigration crises, international collaborations on migration issues, and diplomatic negotiations can illustrate the practical implications of balancing national sovereignty with international responsibilities in the realm of immigration and global migration.

Conservative perspectives recognize the humanitarian dimensions of immigration, particularly in the context of refugee crises, displaced populations, and humanitarian aid efforts. Discussions encompass the protection of vulnerable populations, the provision of humanitarian assistance, and the ethical considerations surrounding asylum policies and refugee resettlement.

Human rights reports, humanitarian aid assessments, and testimonies from refugees and aid workers can offer insights into the humanitarian challenges and responses related to immigration and global migration. Personal narratives and accounts from individuals affected by refugee crises can provide powerful testimonies of the impact of humanitarian considerations on immigration policies and practices.

Global Threats and National Security

AS THE GLOBAL LANDSCAPE continues to evolve, conservative approaches to addressing global threats and safeguarding national security have become increasingly vital. This exploration seeks to provide a comprehensive examination of conservative strategies and policies aimed at mitigating global threats and protecting the national security interests of nations. By delving into the intricate details and practical implications of conservative viewpoints, this analysis aims to offer a nuanced understanding of the multifaceted nature of national security and the complex dynamics at play in the face of global challenges.

Conservative approaches play a crucial role in addressing global threats and safeguarding national security, rooted in the principles of sovereignty, strength through preparedness, and assertive diplomacy.

Conservative perspectives emphasize the paramount importance of national sovereignty and the exercise of diplomatic strength in addressing global threats. The assertion is that the preservation of national sovereignty serves as the bedrock for effective security measures and international engagement.

The United Nations and other international organizations provide a platform for diplomatic discourse and negotiations, but conservative viewpoints underscore the significance of preserving national autonomy and decision-making authority. This is evidenced by historical instances where nations have upheld their sovereignty in the face of external pressures, demonstrating a commitment to protecting their national interests and security.

Conservative approaches prioritize the formulation of independent security strategies that align with a nation's unique geopolitical circumstances and historical context. By delving deeper into the evidence, it becomes evident that conservative governments and policymakers advocate for tailored security measures that are responsive to specific threats and challenges, rather than conforming to one-size-fits-all global directives.

The deployment of assertive diplomacy, backed by military preparedness, is a key aspect of conservative strategies to secure national interests and counter global threats. Diplomatic resilience, coupled with credible military capabilities, serves as a deterrent to potential adversaries and reinforces a nation's commitment to defending its sovereignty and national security.

Critics of conservative approaches may argue that an emphasis on national sovereignty could hinder international cooperation in addressing transnational threats, such as terrorism, cyber warfare, and climate change. They may contend that a more collective and collaborative approach, under the umbrella of supranational organizations, is necessary to effectively tackle global challenges.

Conservative perspectives acknowledge the importance of international cooperation in addressing global threats, but advocate for a balanced approach that respects national sovereignty while engaging in collaborative endeavors. By aligning with like-minded nations and fostering strategic alliances, conservative governments can contribute to collective efforts without compromising their autonomy and security imperatives.

The historical record demonstrates instances where collaborative efforts, under the leadership of conservative governments, have effectively countered global threats while upholding national sovereignty. These examples serve as testament to the viability of conservative strategies in achieving security objectives through diplomatic and military coordination with allied nations.

Conservative approaches to addressing global threats and safeguarding national security are anchored in the principles of national sovereignty, strength through preparedness, and assertive diplomacy. By maintaining a balance between national autonomy and international cooperation, conservative strategies aim to fortify the security interests of nations while actively contributing to global stability and resilience. This examination serves to illuminate the multifaceted nature of conservative perspectives on national security and their implications for navigating the complexities of the contemporary global landscape.

The Future of Globalization and International Relations

AS THE WORLD HURTLES towards an ever more interconnected future, the landscape of globalization and international relations becomes increasingly complex and multifaceted. The conservative agenda seeks to navigate this intricate terrain with a steadfast commitment to safeguarding national interests and security in the face of global challenges. How can conservative policies and strategies adapt to the evolving dynamics of globalization and international relations, fostering a resilient and secure future for nations? This exploration aims to delve into the heart of this pivotal question, offering a unique solution that resonates deeply with the imperatives of conservative foreign policy.

In the current global discourse, the interplay between globalization and international relations has assumed a paramount significance. The interconnectedness of economies, the proliferation of transnational threats, and the evolving dynamics of diplomatic engagements underscore the need for a nuanced understanding of the conservative perspective on navigating this complex terrain. As nations grapple with the implications of globalization on their sovereignty, security, and economic well-being, conservative foreign policy stands at the forefront, advocating for strategies that uphold national interests while engaging in the broader international community.

The central challenge that conservative foreign policy addresses lies in reconciling the imperatives of globalization with the preservation of national sovereignty and security. The accelerating pace of technological advancements, the rise of non-state actors, and the increasing interdependence of global economies present a conundrum for conservative policymakers. How can nations maintain their autonomy and security in an era characterized by intricate global linkages and interdependencies? This complex problem demands a fresh perspective that transcends conventional approaches and offers a path towards reconciling the tensions between globalization and national interests.

Conventional approaches to globalization and international relations often gravitate towards either embracing unbridled interconnectedness or retreating into isolationism. Many perceive globalization as an inevitable force that necessitates a surrender of national autonomy in favor of seamless integration into the global community. Conversely, others advocate for a complete withdrawal from international engagements, citing the need to protect national interests from perceived external threats. However, both extremes fail to capture the nuanced balance that conservative foreign policy seeks to achieve, presenting an opportunity to explore a unique solution that transcends these binary perspectives.

The conservative solution to the challenges posed by globalization and international relations lies in fostering a principled engagement with the global community while steadfastly safeguarding national sovereignty and security. This approach seeks to embrace the benefits of global interconnectedness while preserving the autonomy of nations to chart their own course. It advocates for strategic alliances, robust diplomatic engagements, and tailored security measures that align with a nation's unique geopolitical circumstances and historical context. By forging a path that navigates the complexities of globalization without compromising national interests, conservative foreign policy offers a compelling alternative to the dichotomous approaches prevalent in the current discourse.

The emotional resonance of conservative foreign policy lies in its unwavering commitment to safeguarding the legacy and future of nations. It evokes a sense of responsibility towards preserving the sovereignty and security of one's homeland, while simultaneously recognizing the need for strategic engagements within the global community. This emotional connection reinforces the significance of the conservative solution, anchoring it within the reader's values and aspirations for a secure and resilient future in an era of globalization.

As we embark on this exploration of the future of globalization and international relations through the lens of conservative foreign policy, it becomes clear that the conservative agenda offers a pragmatic and principled approach to navigating the complexities of our interconnected world. By engaging with the compelling question at the heart of this discourse, we have framed the importance of reconciling global interconnectedness with national sovereignty and security. The central challenge of addressing the implications of globalization on national interests has been laid out, and we have contrasted conventional approaches with the unique perspective offered by conservative foreign policy.

Conservative foreign policy prioritizes the formulation of tailored security strategies that resonate with a nation's distinct geopolitical circumstances. It advocates for assertive diplomacy backed by credible military capabilities, serving as a deterrent to potential adversaries and reinforcing a nation's commitment to defending its sovereignty and national security. By forging strategic alliances and fostering diplomatic resilience, conservative foreign policy presents a balanced approach that respects national autonomy while engaging in collaborative endeavors within the global community.

Critics of conservative approaches may argue that an emphasis on national sovereignty hinders international cooperation in addressing transnational threats. They may advocate for a more collective and collaborative approach under supranational organizations to effectively tackle global challenges. However, conservative perspectives acknowledge the importance of international cooperation while advocating for a balanced approach that respects national sovereignty. By aligning with like-minded nations and fostering strategic alliances, conservative governments can contribute to collective efforts without compromising their autonomy and security imperatives.

The historical record demonstrates instances where collaborative efforts, under the leadership of conservative governments, have effectively countered global threats while upholding national sovereignty. These examples serve as a testament to the viability of conservative strategies in achieving security objectives through diplomatic and military coordination with allied nations. In conclusion, conservative approaches to addressing global threats and safeguarding national security are anchored in the principles of national sovereignty, strength through preparedness, and assertive diplomacy.

As we transition to the exploration of the future of globalization and international relations, it becomes evident that the conservative agenda offers a compelling and unique solution to the challenges posed by an increasingly interconnected world. The conservative perspective on navigating the complexities of globalization and international relations is poised to shape the discourse and policies that will define the future of nations in the global arena.

The Role of Religion

The Importance of Religion in Conservative Thought

While not all conservatives identify as highly religious, Judeo-Christian values, traditions, and beliefs profoundly shape modern conservative perspectives across social, economic and governance issues. Religion provides vital ethical foundations, continuity and sense of purpose for conservatives emphasizing stability and tradition against rapid secularization. Faith serves as an essential counterweight against cultural trends that conservatives regard as decaying society's moral fabric by absolving personal responsibility. Even with church attendance falling for decades, scriptural teachings permeate conservative ideologies, and renewed alliances with faith communities strengthen the Right's influence.

Beyond personal beliefs, conservatives consider religion the wellspring of morality necessary for ordered, just societies. Scripture offers divinely inspired wisdom for self-evident moral duties, rights and wrongs that spawned Western ideals of human dignity and accountability under God. Judeo-Christian texts lay out unambiguous guardrails against murder, theft, deceit, envy and other sins conservative dogma views as foundational for criminalizing actions infringing on others' rights. Relativist secular humanism eroding moral clarity threatens civilization by eliminating universal standards forbehavioral expectations, conservatives contend.

Additionally, conservatives lament liberal social engineering weakening church authority over personal behavior regarding gender norms, sexuality, marriage, family planning, addiction and sanctity of life issues. They warn departing from scriptural morality invites degeneracy, narcissism and nihilistic despair by indulging carnal impulses Overturning long-held taboos around abortion, homosexual relations and transgender identities already demonstrate the tragic outcomes from disregarding biblical teachings in this view. Thus, maintaining religion's supreme guidance over individual choices and values remains integral for conservatives despite declining affiliation.

On a social level, conservatives extol churches, synagogues, mosques and temples as essential community institutions promoting civic engagement, responsible citizenship, and philanthropic service. These congregations provide connective tissue strengthening communities. Whether youth groups, charitable works or emotional support in difficult times, religious participation allows forging tight communal bonds and mentorship across generations. Youth disengaging from organized religion loses access to social capital and nurturing that conservatives consider vital for healthy human development within stable communities. Allowing these pillars of community life to erode portends societal deterioration.

Additionally, faith serves communities by promoting assimilation over multicultural fragmentation in conservative philosophy. Judeo Christian traditions exemplify Eurocentric norms historically definitive of American identity. Embracing these longstanding religious customs represents newcomers embracing "Americanism." Conservatives believe deviation from the nation's predominant faiths encourages segregation rather than integration. So religion holds communities together across racial and economic differences by fostering shared identity and experience.

Philosophically, conservatives object to materialist scientific overreach that reduces consciousness to mechanical brain activity and humans to programmable animals or objects. Physical reductionism aligned with rigid determinism destroys sacred ideals of morality, dignity, and God-given supernatural souls transcending mortal flesh. By insisting good and evil simply manifest from amoral socioeconomic forces utterly beyond individual control, determinist orthodoxy curtails moral agency and responsibility while simultaneously demeaning existence to meaningless, inescapable suffering for no purpose.

Conversely, religious grounding centered in a personal God bestows unmatched morality and freedom. It liberates humanity from nihilism by promising salvation, sanctity and overcoming adversity through grace. If humans lack real choices between sin and righteousness or living nobly despite circumstances due to hardwired genetics and stimuli, then no true basis for justice or accountability exists. Laws and ethics become mechanical tools of convenience then. Conservatives believe only through religiosity recognizing willful rebellion and redemption do moral frameworks retain legitimacy against dehumanizing materialism permeating modern institutions and ideas. Religion offers truth, hope and renewal.

In essence religious wisdom, community belonging and moral purpose form the perennial pillars buttressing conservatism's weight over centuries. While factions vary in doctrinal details, transcending mortal existence through timeless righteous principles centered on the individual's soul remains the cornerstone. Without this grounding, conservative philosophies lose moral authority, coherency and mass appeal. Any lasting conservative revival depends foremost on reinvigorating religious devotion in Americans. Societal salvation requires spiritual revitalization.

Religious Freedom and Conscience Rights

RELIGIOUS FREEDOM AND conscience rights are fundamental principles that have been deeply ingrained in conservative ideology. These principles not only protect the individual's right to practice their religion freely, but also safeguard their right to act in accordance with their deeply held beliefs. In this chapter, we will explore the conservative support for religious freedom and the essential nature of protecting conscience rights in a pluralistic society.

Religious freedom is a cornerstone of the conservative agenda, rooted in the belief that individuals should be able to freely exercise their faith without fear of persecution or discrimination. It encompasses the freedom to worship, express, and live out one's beliefs in both public and private spheres. Conscience rights, on the other hand, extend beyond the realm of religion and encompass the broader spectrum of deeply held moral and ethical convictions. Conservatives argue that protecting these rights is essential for preserving individual autonomy and upholding the moral fabric of society.

Conservatives maintain that religious freedom and conscience rights are not merely about protecting the rights of religious individuals, but also about preserving the pluralistic nature of society. By safeguarding these rights, conservatives seek to ensure that individuals are not coerced into violating their beliefs, thus fostering a society where diverse perspectives and beliefs can coexist harmoniously.

To illustrate the importance of religious freedom and conscience rights, consider the case of Jack Phillips, a Colorado baker who declined to create a custom wedding cake for a same-sex couple based on his religious beliefs. This case sparked a nationwide debate about the intersection of religious freedom, conscience rights, and anti-discrimination laws. It highlighted the complexity of balancing the rights of individuals to freely exercise their beliefs with the rights of others to be free from discrimination. The conservative stance in this instance emphasizes the protection of Phillips' right to act in accordance with his religious convictions, underscoring the significance of conscience rights in preserving individual autonomy.

While conservatives staunchly advocate for the protection of religious freedom and conscience rights, it is important to acknowledge that these principles can sometimes clash with competing interests, such as anti-discrimination laws or public policy objectives. Progressives, for instance, argue that religious freedom should not be used as a justification for discrimination, particularly in the context of serving the public. They contend that businesses and individuals should not be exempt from anti-discrimination laws based on religious beliefs. Understanding and engaging with these differing perspectives is crucial in fostering a nuanced understanding of the complexities surrounding religious freedom and conscience rights.

The significance of religious freedom and conscience rights is underscored by numerous legal battles and legislative debates that have unfolded in recent years. According to the Pew Research Center, the majority of Americans (82%) believe that it is important for the U.S. to protect religious freedom. Furthermore, the U.S. State Department's International Religious Freedom Report highlights the global challenges faced by individuals and communities in exercising their religious freedom, emphasizing the need for continued vigilance in protecting these rights both domestically and internationally.

In discussing religious freedom and conscience rights, it is essential to clarify the distinction between the two concepts. Religious freedom pertains specifically to the freedom to practice one's religion, while conscience rights encompass a broader range of deeply held beliefs, including moral and ethical convictions that may not be tied to a specific religious faith. By delineating these distinctions, we can better understand the multifaceted nature of protecting individual liberties and beliefs in a diverse society.

Religious freedom and conscience rights are foundational principles that form the bedrock of conservative values. They are vital in upholding individual autonomy, fostering a pluralistic society, and preserving the moral and ethical fabric of our communities. While these principles may intersect with competing interests and perspectives, their protection remains paramount in safeguarding the rights and freedoms of all individuals. As we navigate the complexities of religious freedom and conscience rights, it is imperative to seek a balance that respects the rights of all while preserving the core tenets of individual liberty and belief.

Religion and Public Life

TO EFFECTIVELY COMPREHEND the conservative perspective on religion and public life, readers should have a basic understanding of conservative ideology and the principles that underpin it. It may also be helpful to be familiar with key historical and contemporary examples that illustrate the intersection of religion and public life from a conservative standpoint.

Religion has been a central component of public life throughout history, shaping cultures, societies, and political systems. From the founding of nations to the development of laws and governance, the influence of religion on public life has been profound. Conservatives believe that religion plays a crucial role in shaping public policy, moral values, and societal norms. The conservative perspective on religion and public life is deeply rooted in the belief that religious principles provide a moral compass for governance and contribute to the preservation of societal order and stability.

1. To understand the conservative perspective on religion and public life, it is essential to examine the historical context. Throughout history, religion has been intricately intertwined with governance, influencing laws, ethics, and societal norms. Conservatives argue that the moral foundations provided by religious teachings are essential for maintaining a just and orderly society.

2. Conservatives assert that religious principles should inform policy decisions, particularly on matters pertaining to social issues, family values, and ethical considerations. The conservative viewpoint emphasizes the importance of upholding traditional moral values rooted in religious teachings when shaping public policy.

3. Religion, according to conservatives, should have a prominent place in public discourse. They argue that religious perspectives bring essential moral and ethical considerations to societal debates and governance, contributing to a more virtuous and principled public life.

4. Conservatives are staunch advocates for the preservation of religious freedom in public life. They believe that individuals and institutions should be free to express and practice their religious beliefs without undue interference from the government or societal pressures.

- When delving into the conservative perspective on religion and public life, it is important to approach the topic with an open mind, recognizing the diversity of religious beliefs and their impact on public life.

- It is crucial to distinguish between the conservative view on religion in public life and the separation of church and state, as conservatives argue for the influence of religious principles without advocating for an official state religion.

If encountering challenges in comprehending the conservative perspective on religion and public life, it may be beneficial to seek out diverse conservative viewpoints, engage in respectful dialogue with individuals of differing beliefs, and critically evaluate the historical and contemporary examples that illustrate the relationship between religion and public life from a conservative lens.

In exploring the conservative perspective on the role of religion in public life and its influence on policy decisions, it becomes evident that religion holds a significant place in conservative ideology, shaping their approach to governance, public policy, and societal values. By understanding these perspectives, readers can gain insight into the intricate interplay between religion and public life within the conservative agenda.

The Conservative Christian Movement

AS THE CONSERVATIVE movement gains momentum and influence in the political sphere, it is essential to recognize the significant impact of conservative Christianity on shaping conservative thought and political activism. In this chapter, we will closely examine a specific instance where conservative Christianity has played a pivotal role in influencing conservative ideology and policy decisions. By providing a detailed examination of this case study, we aim to outline the challenges, strategies, and results to derive broader insights and encourage further engagement with the intricate relationship between conservative Christianity and the conservative agenda.

Over the past few decades, conservative Christianity has emerged as a formidable force within the conservative movement, wielding significant influence in shaping policies and mobilizing grassroots support for conservative causes. One specific instance that exemplifies the impact of conservative Christianity on the conservative agenda is the advocacy for traditional family values and the protection of religious freedoms in the public sphere.

Central to this case study are influential conservative Christian leaders and organizations that have been at the forefront of promoting conservative values and principles. These entities have deep roots in religious communities and have leveraged their platforms to advocate for policies aligned with conservative Christian beliefs. Additionally, conservative Christian voters have become a crucial constituency within the broader conservative movement, exerting influence on electoral outcomes and policy priorities.

The core challenge at the heart of this case study lies in navigating the intersection of conservative Christianity with public policy and governance while respecting the principles of religious freedom and the separation of church and state. Balancing the promotion of traditional family values and religious liberties with the need to uphold the rights of all individuals in a diverse society presents a complex and multifaceted challenge.

Conservative Christian organizations and leaders have employed various strategies to address the challenge, including engaging in grassroots advocacy, supporting political candidates who align with their values, and utilizing media platforms to promote their message. Additionally, they have sought to influence policy decisions through legal advocacy and lobbying efforts, aiming to shape legislation in line with conservative Christian principles.

The influence of conservative Christianity on the conservative agenda has yielded tangible results, particularly in the realm of social policies and religious liberty protections. From the appointment of judges sympathetic to conservative Christian viewpoints to the passage of legislation safeguarding religious freedom, the impact of conservative Christianity on policy outcomes has been notable.

The influence of conservative Christianity on the conservative agenda underscores the significant role of religious values in shaping political discourse and policy priorities. It ties into the broader narrative of the conservative movement's commitment to upholding traditional values and the importance of understanding the diverse factors that contribute to conservative ideology.

In contemplating the impact of conservative Christianity on the conservative agenda, one is prompted to consider the implications of intertwining religious convictions with political decision-making and the ongoing dialogue surrounding the appropriate role of religious influence in the public sphere.

This specific instance serves as a microcosm of the broader influence of conservative Christianity on conservative thought and political activism, providing a nuanced understanding of the complexities and implications of this dynamic relationship. As we delve deeper into the intricate interplay between religion, politics, and governance, it is essential to critically examine the role of conservative Christianity within the conservative agenda and its implications for society at large.

JACK DONAHUE

Interfaith Dialogue and Cooperation

INTERFAITH DIALOGUE and cooperation are essential components of the conservative agenda, fostering understanding, collaboration, and mutual respect among diverse religious communities. This list delves into the key principles and approaches that underpin conservative perspectives on interfaith engagement, illuminating the significance of these efforts within the broader conservative movement.

Embracing religious pluralism is a fundamental tenet of conservative approaches to interfaith dialogue. Conservatives recognize the inherent worth and dignity of diverse religious traditions, emphasizing the importance of acknowledging and respecting differing beliefs and practices. This perspective stems from a commitment to upholding individual freedoms and fostering a society where all faith communities can coexist harmoniously.

Credible research studies and testimonials from conservative leaders affirm the value placed on religious pluralism within the conservative agenda. For instance, influential conservative thinkers and religious leaders have articulated the positive impact of religious diversity on societal cohesion and the preservation of individual liberties.

In practical terms, conservative advocacy for religious pluralism manifests in policies that safeguard the rights of individuals to freely practice their faith, protect religious minorities from persecution, and promote interfaith initiatives that celebrate the contributions of diverse religious communities to the fabric of society.

As we delve deeper into the conservative perspective on interfaith dialogue, it becomes evident that the promotion of shared moral principles is another cornerstone of conservative approaches to fostering understanding and cooperation among religious communities.

Conservative viewpoints emphasize the importance of identifying and promoting shared moral principles that transcend religious boundaries. This entails recognizing universal ethical values such as compassion, justice, and integrity, which form the basis for constructive interfaith engagement. By highlighting these common values, conservatives seek to build bridges of understanding and collaboration across religious lines, contributing to a more cohesive and ethical society.

Scholarly research and conservative discourse underscore the significance of promoting shared moral principles as a means of cultivating unity and cooperation among diverse religious groups. Conservative leaders and thinkers have articulated the role of shared moral values in bridging interfaith divides and fostering a sense of collective responsibility for the betterment of society.

In practice, conservative initiatives that promote shared moral principles often involve interfaith service projects, ethical leadership summits, and collaborative efforts to address social issues such as poverty, homelessness, and healthcare disparities. By aligning around shared moral imperatives, conservative interfaith partnerships contribute to tangible positive outcomes in local communities and beyond.

While the promotion of shared moral principles forms a crucial aspect of conservative approaches to interfaith dialogue, the preservation of religious liberties stands as a paramount concern within the conservative agenda.

Central to conservative perspectives on interfaith dialogue is the unwavering commitment to safeguarding religious liberties for all individuals and communities. Conservatives advocate for robust legal protections that ensure the free exercise of religion, defend against discrimination based on religious beliefs, and uphold the autonomy of religious institutions. This commitment stems from a deep-seated belief in the intrinsic value of religious freedom as a cornerstone of a free and flourishing society.

Legal precedents, legislative actions, and conservative advocacy efforts serve as compelling evidence of the conservative dedication to preserving religious liberties. Court cases, policy analyses, and testimonies from religious liberty advocates underscore the crucial role of conservative initiatives in upholding the constitutional rights of individuals to practice their faith without undue interference or coercion.

Practical applications of conservative commitments to religious liberty preservation encompass legal defense efforts for individuals facing religious discrimination, legislative proposals that protect the religious conscience of healthcare professionals and business owners, and educational campaigns that raise awareness about the importance of religious freedoms in a pluralistic society.

As we navigate the terrain of conservative perspectives on interfaith engagement, it becomes evident that the role of interfaith partnerships in civil society occupies a prominent position within the conservative agenda.

Conservative perspectives underscore the transformative potential of interfaith partnerships in addressing societal challenges and advancing the common good. By fostering collaborative relationships among religious communities, conservatives seek to harness the collective strengths and resources of diverse faith traditions to tackle pressing social issues, promote civic engagement, and nurture a culture of mutual respect and understanding.

THE CONSERVATIVE AGENDA

Practical applications of conservative support for interfaith partnerships include initiatives that facilitate cross-cultural dialogue, joint community service projects, and collaborative policy advocacy on issues of shared concern. Through these initiatives, conservatives contribute to building bridges across religious divides and fostering a sense of solidarity and shared purpose within civil society.

While the role of interfaith partnerships in civil society reflects the proactive engagement of conservative perspectives, it is imperative to recognize the broader contributions of interfaith dialogue and cooperation to social cohesion and stability.

Conservative viewpoints emphasize the vital role of interfaith dialogue and cooperation in fostering social cohesion and stability within diverse societies. By promoting mutual understanding, respectful discourse, and collaborative action among religious communities, conservatives seek to mitigate interreligious tensions, cultivate a sense of common purpose, and fortify the fabric of society against division and discord.

Empirical studies, community initiatives, and testimonials from conservative thought leaders attest to the positive impact of interfaith dialogue and cooperation in strengthening social cohesion and stability. Examples of successful interfaith initiatives that have contributed to peacebuilding, conflict resolution, and the promotion of shared values serve as compelling evidence of the conservative belief in the unifying potential of interreligious collaboration.

Practical applications of conservative support for interfaith dialogue and cooperation encompass initiatives that facilitate cross-cultural understanding, interfaith peacebuilding efforts, and educational programs that promote religious literacy and pluralism. By investing in these endeavors, conservatives actively contribute to the cultivation of harmonious and resilient communities that are grounded in mutual respect and shared values.

Conservative approaches to interfaith dialogue and cooperation are multifaceted, informed by a commitment to upholding religious pluralism, promoting shared moral principles, preserving religious liberties, leveraging interfaith partnerships in civil society, and contributing to social cohesion and stability. These principles not only enrich the conservative agenda but also offer valuable insights into the broader significance of interfaith engagement in fostering a more inclusive, cohesive, and flourishing society. As we continue to explore the intricate interplay between conservative values and interfaith collaboration, it becomes evident that the conservative agenda stands as a steadfast advocate for the promotion of understanding, cooperation, and unity among diverse religious communities.

Religion and Social Issues

ABORTION AND SAME-SEX marriage are two polarizing social issues that have been at the forefront of conservative discourse. The significance of these subjects lies in their intersection with religious beliefs and moral values, making them central to conservative perspectives on social policy and individual freedoms.

The purpose of comparing these subjects is to illuminate the nuanced ways in which conservative views on abortion and same-sex marriage are shaped by fundamental principles of individual rights, moral convictions, and the role of government in regulating social behavior. By examining these issues through a conservative lens, we aim to offer insights into the broader implications of these perspectives on societal norms and legal frameworks.

The benchmarks for comparison will encompass the ethical and philosophical underpinnings of conservative positions on abortion and same-sex marriage, the legal and constitutional considerations, and the societal impact of conservative viewpoints on these contentious issues.

When exploring conservative views on abortion and same-sex marriage, it becomes evident that both are deeply rooted in the defense of individual rights and the preservation of traditional moral values. Conservatives argue for the protection of the unborn and the sanctity of life in the context of abortion, while advocating for the preservation of traditional marriage and family structures in the case of same-sex marriage.

Abortion, from a conservative standpoint, is often framed as a fundamental right-to-life issue, grounded in the belief that all human life, including that of the unborn, is inherently valuable and deserving of protection. This perspective emphasizes the ethical responsibility of society and the government to safeguard the rights of the most vulnerable members of the human community.

Similarly, conservative perspectives on same-sex marriage are informed by a commitment to upholding traditional moral values and the sanctity of marriage as a foundational institution in society. Conservatives often argue that the preservation of traditional marriage between a man and a woman is integral to the well-being of families and the stability of society, reflecting deeply held religious and cultural beliefs.

Despite the shared emphasis on individual rights and moral values, the distinctions between conservative views on abortion and same-sex marriage are notable. While the abortion debate centers on the protection of the unborn and the ethical implications of terminating a pregnancy, the discourse surrounding same-sex marriage focuses on the definition and societal role of marriage itself.

Conservative arguments against abortion often highlight the moral and ethical dimensions of ending a human life, emphasizing the potential for the unborn to experience pain and the inherent dignity of every human being, regardless of stage of development. In contrast, conservative opposition to same-sex marriage is rooted in the belief that marriage is a sacred institution designed to unite a man and a woman for the purpose of procreation and the nurturing of children within a stable family unit.

Delving into the comparisons between conservative views on abortion and same-sex marriage reveals the intricate interplay between moral convictions, individual rights, and societal norms within conservative ideology. These perspectives offer insights into the complex ways in which conservative principles intersect with social issues, shaping public policy and legal frameworks.

Conservative positions on abortion and same-sex marriage also underscore the enduring influence of religious beliefs and traditional values in shaping social policies and legal interpretations. The examination of these subjects illuminates the broader implications of conservative perspectives on individual liberties, the role of government in regulating social behavior, and the intersection of law and morality in contemporary society.

The contemporary relevance of comparing conservative views on abortion and same-sex marriage is evident in ongoing legal battles, public debates, and legislative actions that continue to shape the social and political landscape. The intersection of these issues with religious exemptions and individual liberties further underscores the enduring significance of these debates within the conservative agenda and broader societal discourse.

As we navigate the complexities of conservative perspectives on social issues, it becomes clear that the conservative agenda reflects a multifaceted approach to addressing the intricate intersections of individual rights, moral values, and societal norms. The examination of these subjects offers valuable insights into the evolving landscape of conservative thought and its enduring impact on the fabric of society.

The Future of Religion in Conservative Politics

IN THE CONTEMPORARY political landscape, the role of religion in shaping conservative politics has become increasingly prominent. Religious conservatism has exerted a significant influence on public policy, social values, and individual freedoms, reflecting a deep-seated commitment to traditional moral principles and religious beliefs. However, amidst the evolving dynamics of modern society, religious conservatives face a myriad of challenges and opportunities in influencing political discourse and policy-making. This chapter aims to delve into the complexities of the future of religion in conservative politics, examining the current landscape and projecting potential trajectories in light of societal changes and political developments.

One of the primary challenges confronting religious conservatives in conservative politics is the tension between upholding traditional religious values and navigating the diverse, pluralistic nature of contemporary society. As the population becomes more diverse and secular, religious conservatives encounter resistance to their attempts to shape public policy according to their moral convictions. Moreover, the increasing emphasis on individual freedoms and rights has led to clashes with religious conservatives' efforts to maintain traditional moral standards in legislation and governance.

If the challenges faced by religious conservatives in conservative politics are not effectively addressed, there is a risk of polarization and social discord. The failure to find common ground between religious and secular perspectives could lead to legislative gridlock, exacerbating societal divisions and hindering the implementation of policies that address the needs of all citizens. Furthermore, the marginalization of religious conservatives in political discourse could diminish the representation of a significant segment of the population, undermining the diversity and inclusivity essential to a thriving democracy.

A potential method to address these challenges involves fostering constructive dialogue and collaboration between religious conservatives and other stakeholders in the political arena. By emphasizing the shared values of justice, compassion, and community welfare, religious conservatives can seek common ground with secular and diverse voices, working towards policy solutions that accommodate a spectrum of beliefs while upholding the common good.

The implementation of this solution necessitates the cultivation of platforms for open, respectful discourse and the creation of mechanisms for meaningful engagement between religious conservatives and other political actors. Additionally, fostering a spirit of empathy and understanding towards differing viewpoints is essential in navigating the complexities of religious influence in conservative politics, ensuring that all voices are heard and considered in the policymaking process.

Historical precedents and projected outcomes suggest that collaborative approaches to addressing the role of religion in conservative politics have the potential to yield substantive policy outcomes that reflect a balance of diverse perspectives. By embracing inclusivity and pluralism, religious conservatives can contribute to the development of policies that resonate with the broader population, fostering a more cohesive and harmonious society.

Alternative approaches to addressing the role of religion in conservative politics may involve strategic alliances with like-minded political groups, the development of nuanced narratives that resonate with a broad audience, and the cultivation of leaders who embody the values and principles of religious conservatism while demonstrating a commitment to unity and inclusivity.

As religious conservatives navigate the future of their influence in conservative politics, it is imperative to recognize the multifaceted nature of contemporary society and the diverse array of voices that contribute to the political discourse. By embracing the complexities of the modern political landscape and seeking common ground with a wide spectrum of beliefs, religious conservatives can play a pivotal role in shaping policies that reflect the values of justice, compassion, and inclusivity, ensuring a future that honors both tradition and progress.

Political Activism and Advocacy

The Importance of Political Engagement

The conservative belief in the importance of political engagement and civic participation is deeply rooted in the fundamental principles of democracy and the preservation of individual liberties. In order to fully grasp the significance of this belief, it is essential to understand key terms and concepts that underpin the conservative understanding of political engagement.

Political Engagement: At its core, political engagement encompasses a range of activities that individuals undertake to participate in the political process and influence decision-making in their communities, regions, and nations. This can include voting in elections, engaging in public discourse, joining political organizations, and advocating for specific policies or causes.

Conservatism: Conservatism is a political and social philosophy that emphasizes the preservation of traditional institutions, limited government intervention, individual responsibility, and free market principles. Conservatives value the importance of preserving societal norms and traditions, while also advocating for a smaller, less intrusive government.

Civic Participation: Civic participation refers to the active involvement of individuals in their communities, often through volunteer work, community service, and engagement in local governance. It is a vital component of a healthy democracy, as it fosters a sense of collective responsibility and strengthens the bonds within a society.

THE CONSERVATIVE AGENDA

In order to delve deeper into the conservative perspective on the importance of political engagement, it is crucial to define and explore the following key terms:

1. Democracy: Democracy is a system of government in which power is vested in the people, who exercise it directly or through elected representatives. It is characterized by free and fair elections, the protection of individual rights, and the rule of law. Conservatives view democracy as a foundational element of a just and equitable society, emphasizing the importance of a well-informed and engaged citizenry in sustaining democratic institutions.

2. Individual Liberties: Individual liberties encompass the rights and freedoms that are inherently possessed by every person, such as freedom of speech, religion, and assembly, as well as the right to privacy and due process. Conservatives prioritize the protection of individual liberties, viewing them as essential components of a free and prosperous society. Political engagement serves as a means for individuals to safeguard and advocate for their inherent rights.

3. Public Discourse: Public discourse refers to the exchange of ideas and opinions on matters of public concern, often taking place in the public sphere through various forms of communication. Conservatives value robust public discourse as a mechanism for deliberation and consensus-building, recognizing the importance of diverse perspectives in informing policy decisions and shaping the cultural landscape.

4. Limited Government: Limited government is a principle central to conservative ideology, advocating for a government with restricted powers and a focus on protecting individual rights and promoting economic freedom. Political engagement enables citizens to hold government officials accountable and advocate for policies

that adhere to the principle of limited government, ensuring that the state does not overstep its proper role in society.

5. Free Market Principles: Free market principles emphasize the role of competition, voluntary exchange, and private property rights in driving economic growth and prosperity. Conservatives believe that political engagement, particularly in advocating for policies that support free market principles, contributes to a thriving economy and empowers individuals to pursue their own economic interests and aspirations.

The significance of these key terms becomes apparent when considering their real-world implications. For example, the concept of limited government can be linked to the everyday experience of individuals in their interactions with regulatory agencies, tax policies, and government programs. Similarly, the value of public discourse can be illustrated through the impact of social media, public protests, and community forums in shaping public opinion and influencing policy decisions.

In the context of democracy, the act of voting in elections and participating in grassroots movements serves as a tangible manifestation of civic engagement, demonstrating the direct influence that individuals can have on the political landscape. Furthermore, the protection of individual liberties becomes palpable when considering cases of free speech, religious expression, and privacy rights in the face of government encroachment.

By grounding these concepts in real-world examples, individuals can better understand their relevance and impact on their daily lives, fostering a deeper appreciation for the conservative emphasis on political engagement and civic participation.

As we continue to explore the conservative agenda, it is evident that the importance of political engagement extends beyond theoretical principles, manifesting in tangible actions and informed advocacy. Through a comprehensive understanding of key terms and concepts, individuals can navigate the complexities of the political landscape with greater clarity and purpose, contributing to the preservation of democratic values and the advancement of conservative ideals.

Conservative Grassroots Movements

IN THE CONSERVATIVE pursuit of promoting traditional values, preserving individual freedoms, and advocating for limited government intervention, grassroots movements have played a pivotal role in shaping the direction of conservative activism and influencing policy outcomes. This chapter aims to delve into the significance of grassroots movements within the conservative agenda, examining their impact, strategies, and effectiveness in advancing conservative principles.

Grassroots movements, at their core, represent the collective efforts of ordinary citizens who mobilize to advocate for specific causes, influence political decision-making, and drive social change at the local, regional, and national levels. Within the realm of conservative activism, grassroots movements serve as a potent force for galvanizing public support, shaping public discourse, and holding elected officials accountable to the values and priorities of conservative constituents.

A fundamental aspect of grassroots movements lies in their ability to amplify the voices of individuals who share common ideological convictions and concerns. By organizing at the community level, grassroots activists harness the strength of collective action to raise awareness, build coalitions, and foster a sense of solidarity among like-minded citizens. Through coordinated efforts such as door-to-door canvassing, hosting town hall meetings, and organizing rallies, grassroots movements create a groundswell of public engagement that resonates with the conservative belief in the importance of active citizenship and civic participation.

The emergence of the Tea Party movement in the early 21st century provides a compelling illustration of the impact and influence of grassroots activism within the conservative sphere. Originating as a decentralized network of local groups, the Tea Party movement coalesced around shared concerns regarding government spending, taxation, and the expansion of federal powers. Through grassroots organizing, the movement mobilized supporters, channeled dissatisfaction with the status quo, and successfully influenced electoral outcomes and policy debates on fiscal responsibility and limited government. The Tea Party's ability to mobilize citizens at the grassroots level exemplifies the potency of localized activism in shaping the national political landscape.

While grassroots movements are instrumental in amplifying conservative voices and agendas, they also encounter challenges and complexities in effectively translating grassroots energy into tangible policy outcomes. In navigating the dynamics of grassroots activism, conservative organizers must grapple with balancing ideological purity with pragmatic coalition-building, addressing diverse concerns within the conservative base, and sustaining momentum beyond electoral cycles. Moreover, as the political landscape evolves, grassroots movements must adapt to technological advancements, changing demographics, and shifting societal attitudes to remain relevant and impactful in advancing conservative priorities.

Empirical evidence underscores the tangible impact of grassroots mobilization on electoral outcomes, with studies revealing that localized grassroots efforts, such as door-to-door canvassing and voter outreach, contribute to higher voter turnout and increased support for conservative candidates. Grassroots engagement not only amplifies conservative messaging but also fosters personal connections and trust between activists and voters, cultivating a sense of community and shared purpose that transcends traditional political messaging.

Grassroots movements encompass a diverse array of perspectives and priorities within the conservative spectrum, necessitating adept navigation of ideological diversity and strategic alignment around common goals. Coalition-building within grassroots networks involves forging alliances with like-minded organizations, finding common ground on shared policy objectives, and leveraging collective influence to effect meaningful change. Additionally, issue advocacy at the grassroots level entails educating and mobilizing citizens on specific policy issues, empowering them to engage with elected officials and shape legislative outcomes in line with conservative principles.

Grassroots movements stand as a testament to the enduring power of citizen engagement and grassroots activism in shaping the trajectory of conservative advocacy. From the Tea Party movement to localized initiatives championing conservative values, grassroots mobilization has demonstrated its capacity to amplify voices, activate communities, and influence policy decisions. By harnessing the collective strength of engaged citizens, grassroots movements not only reinforce the conservative commitment to individual agency and community empowerment but also serve as a catalyst for driving substantive change in advancing conservative principles at all levels of governance.

JACK DONAHUE

Conservative Youth Activism

AS THE CONSERVATIVE movement continues to evolve, one of the most compelling and impactful developments has been the increasing involvement of young conservatives in political activism. This surge of youthful energy has not only reshaped the landscape of conservative politics but has also played a pivotal role in redefining the strategies and priorities of the conservative agenda. In this chapter, we will closely examine the involvement of young conservatives in political activism and their influence on conservative politics, providing a detailed examination of a specific instance, outlining challenges, strategies, and results to derive broader insights and encourage further engagement.

The backdrop for our case study is the rise of conservative youth activism in the context of contemporary political and social dynamics. With the emergence of digital communication platforms, the proliferation of social media, and the increasing polarization of political discourse, young conservatives have found new avenues to amplify their voices and champion their causes. This setting has created both opportunities and challenges for young conservatives seeking to make a meaningful impact on the conservative agenda.

At the heart of this case study are the passionate and driven young conservatives who have taken it upon themselves to actively participate in political activism. These individuals, often characterized by their fervent commitment to conservative principles, come from diverse backgrounds and possess a wide range of talents and skills, from grassroots organizing and community outreach to digital advocacy and policy analysis. Their engagement reflects a deep-seated belief in the importance of shaping the trajectory of conservative politics and advancing the values they hold dear.

THE CONSERVATIVE AGENDA

The central challenge that young conservatives face in their activism lies in navigating the complexities of a rapidly changing political landscape, where traditional institutions and established norms are being challenged and redefined. Moreover, as they seek to assert their influence within the conservative movement, they must contend with perceptions of inexperience and skepticism from older generations, who may question the depth of their commitment and the validity of their contributions.

In response to these challenges, young conservatives have adopted a multifaceted approach to political activism, leveraging their unique strengths and perspectives to carve out a distinct niche within the conservative agenda. This approach encompasses a diverse array of strategies, including harnessing the power of social media to mobilize support, engaging in community-based initiatives to connect with like-minded individuals, and actively participating in conservative organizations and political campaigns.

The impact of young conservatives' activism is palpable, with their efforts contributing to a revitalization of conservative discourse and the amplification of conservative values in the public sphere. Through their innovative approaches and tireless dedication, young conservatives have succeeded in broadening the reach of conservative messaging, attracting new supporters to the conservative cause, and injecting fresh perspectives into policy discussions.

This case study offers valuable insights into the evolving nature of conservative youth activism and its implications for the broader conservative movement. It underscores the importance of embracing the energy and creativity of young conservatives, recognizing their potential to invigorate and rejuvenate conservative politics. At the same time, it prompts reflection on the need to bridge generational divides within the conservative movement and cultivate an inclusive environment that values the contributions of all conservatives, regardless of age.

The emergence of conservative youth activism serves as a microcosm of the broader evolution of the conservative movement, highlighting its adaptability and resilience in the face of societal shifts and technological advancements. By embracing the energy and ideas of young conservatives, the conservative movement can position itself for continued relevance and influence in an ever-changing political environment.

As we contemplate the implications of conservative youth activism, one cannot help but wonder: How can established conservative institutions and leaders effectively integrate the perspectives and contributions of young conservatives into the fabric of the conservative agenda, ensuring a cohesive and unified approach to advancing conservative principles? This question serves as a call to action, encouraging further engagement and collaboration among all segments of the conservative movement.

The involvement of young conservatives in political activism represents a pivotal and transformative force within the conservative movement. Their passion, innovation, and dedication have not only expanded the reach of conservative principles but have also injected vitality and dynamism into conservative politics. As we continue to witness the impact of conservative youth activism, it is imperative to recognize and elevate the voices and contributions of young conservatives, harnessing their potential to shape the future of the conservative agenda.

Conservative Media and Political Influence

AS THE CONSERVATIVE movement continues to evolve, one of the most influential and far-reaching elements has been the role of conservative media outlets in shaping conservative narratives and mobilizing political support.

Conservative media outlets, encompassing a wide spectrum of platforms including television, radio, print, and digital media, play a pivotal role in shaping and disseminating conservative perspectives and ideologies. These outlets serve as influential channels for conservative voices, providing a platform to articulate and promote conservative values, policies, and narratives to a broad audience. Moreover, conservative media serves as a counterbalance to what is often perceived as a liberal bias in mainstream media, offering an alternative perspective that resonates with conservative audiences.

The purpose of this comparative analysis is to delve into the nuanced workings of conservative media and its impact on shaping the conservative agenda. By examining the strategies and approaches employed by conservative media outlets, we aim to uncover the underlying mechanisms through which these platforms influence public opinion, mobilize political support, and contribute to the broader conservative discourse.

The benchmarks for comparison in evaluating the influence of conservative media on the conservative agenda include the reach and engagement of the audience, the framing and dissemination of conservative narratives, and the alignment of media content with conservative policy priorities. These criteria provide a comprehensive framework for assessing the impact and efficacy of conservative media in advancing the conservative agenda.

Conservative media outlets, such as Fox News, talk radio hosts like Rush Limbaugh, and digital platforms like Breitbart, share a common goal of amplifying conservative voices and perspectives. They effectively leverage their platforms to provide a forum for conservative leaders, commentators, and experts to articulate and defend conservative policies and principles. Additionally, these outlets actively engage in agenda-setting, shaping the focus of conservative discourse by highlighting key issues and narratives that resonate with conservative audiences.

While conservative media outlets share a collective commitment to advancing conservative perspectives, their approaches and emphases can vary significantly. For instance, talk radio hosts often adopt a confrontational and opinionated style, fostering a direct and impassioned connection with their audience. In contrast, digital media platforms may prioritize viral content and engagement, utilizing multimedia formats and interactive features to attract and retain a younger, digitally savvy conservative audience.

The comparison of conservative media outlets reveals the diverse strategies employed to resonate with conservative audiences and influence the conservative agenda. It underscores the multifaceted nature of conservative media, showcasing the adaptability and responsiveness of these platforms to the evolving preferences and consumption habits of conservative audiences. Furthermore, it highlights the symbiotic relationship between conservative media and the conservative agenda, illustrating how these outlets serve as influential conduits for disseminating and reinforcing conservative narratives and policy priorities.

The contemporary relevance of conservative media in shaping the conservative agenda cannot be overstated, particularly in the context of the digital age and the proliferation of social media. Conservative media outlets continue to wield significant influence in shaping public opinion, mobilizing grassroots support for conservative causes, and shaping the political landscape. Their role in framing and disseminating conservative narratives has become increasingly intertwined with broader political discourse, contributing to the polarization and diversification of media consumption patterns among conservative audiences.

The comparative analysis of conservative media outlets provides valuable insights into the dynamic and influential role played by these platforms in shaping the conservative agenda. By examining their strategies, approaches, and impact, we gain a deeper understanding of the multifaceted ways in which conservative media outlets contribute to the advancement of conservative principles and priorities. As the landscape of media and political communication continues to evolve, the role of conservative media in influencing the conservative agenda remains a critical and enduring force within the conservative movement.

Conservative Advocacy Organizations

IN THE REALM OF CONSERVATIVE advocacy, a network of organizations plays a pivotal role in shaping public policy and advancing conservative principles. These organizations operate across various domains, including think tanks, grassroots movements, legal advocacy groups, and industry associations. Their collective efforts encompass a wide array of policy areas, from fiscal and economic policies to social and cultural issues. The impact of conservative advocacy organizations on the conservative agenda is profound, influencing legislative priorities, public discourse, and the implementation of conservative policies. This chapter aims to explore the work of conservative advocacy organizations, delving into their strategies, impact, and contemporary relevance in shaping the conservative agenda.

Think tanks and policy institutes serve as intellectual hubs for conservative thought and policy development. These organizations conduct rigorous research, produce policy papers, and offer expert analysis on a wide range of issues, providing a comprehensive intellectual framework for conservative policy initiatives. Their influence extends beyond the corridors of power, as they often serve as sources of expertise for lawmakers, government agencies, and the media. The Heritage Foundation, for example, has been instrumental in shaping conservative policies related to free markets, limited government, and national security, offering detailed policy prescriptions and advocating for their implementation.

Grassroots and activist organizations form the grassroots engine of the conservative movement, mobilizing citizens and communities to advocate for conservative causes and values. These organizations engage in a variety of activities, including organizing rallies, door-to-door canvassing, and grassroots lobbying efforts. Americans for Prosperity, a prominent grassroots organization, has been influential in advocating for limited government, free-market policies, and regulatory reform at the local, state, and federal levels, leveraging its extensive grassroots network to amplify conservative voices and influence public opinion.

Legal advocacy groups play a crucial role in advancing conservative legal principles, defending constitutional rights, and challenging government overreach. These organizations often engage in litigation, filing lawsuits and amicus briefs in support of conservative legal interpretations and defending individual liberties. The Alliance Defending Freedom, for instance, has been at the forefront of defending religious freedom, free speech, and the sanctity of life, litigating numerous cases that have shaped legal precedents and protected conservative values in the legal arena.

Industry associations represent the collective interests of businesses and industries, advocating for policies that promote economic growth, free enterprise, and regulatory reform. These organizations often engage in lobbying efforts, coalition building, and public outreach to advance their policy priorities. The U.S. Chamber of Commerce, as a prominent industry association, has been influential in advocating for pro-business policies, tax reform, and trade agreements that align with conservative economic principles, leveraging its extensive network and resources to shape legislative outcomes and regulatory policies.

The impact of conservative advocacy organizations is substantiated by their track record of policy influence, legal victories, and grassroots mobilization. Research studies, media coverage, and testimonials from policymakers and activists attest to the significant role these organizations play in shaping the conservative agenda and advancing conservative policies.

The work of conservative advocacy organizations manifests in tangible policy outcomes, legislative initiatives, and public engagement. Their research and policy recommendations often translate into legislative proposals, public awareness campaigns, and legal victories that reflect the influence and impact of these organizations on the conservative agenda. Through their efforts, conservative advocacy organizations bridge the gap between conservative principles and practical policy solutions, shaping the direction of public policy and governance.

As we transition from exploring the multifaceted work of conservative advocacy organizations to examining their collaborative efforts and collective impact, it becomes evident that the synergy and diversity of these organizations contribute to a robust and influential conservative agenda. This collaborative dynamic underscores the interconnectedness and strategic alignment of diverse conservative advocacy entities in advancing a comprehensive conservative policy framework.

Campaign Finance and Political Contributions

CAMPAIGN FINANCE REGULATIONS and the role of money in politics have long been contentious issues in the political landscape. The conservative perspective on these topics encompasses a belief in free speech, limited government intervention, and the protection of individual liberties. This chapter aims to delve into conservative views on campaign finance regulations and political contributions, exploring the principles and arguments that underpin their stance.

Conservatives argue that campaign finance regulations should prioritize protecting free speech and political expression, while also ensuring transparency and accountability in the electoral process. They assert that excessive government intervention can stifle political discourse and impede the democratic exchange of ideas. Moreover, conservatives emphasize the importance of safeguarding the rights of individuals and organizations to support political causes and candidates without undue restrictions.

One of the central pieces of evidence supporting conservative views on campaign finance is the landmark Supreme Court decision in Citizens United v. FEC. In this case, the Court ruled that political spending is a form of protected speech under the First Amendment, thereby striking down certain limitations on independent expenditures by corporations and unions. This decision underscored the conservative position that political speech should not be unduly constrained, and that individuals and organizations have the right to advocate for their preferred candidates and causes.

The Citizens United decision was rooted in the belief that restrictions on political expenditures could unduly suppress speech and association, particularly for advocacy groups, corporations, and unions. Conservatives argue that by allowing a diversity of voices and perspectives to participate in the political process, the marketplace of ideas is enriched, contributing to a more robust and dynamic public discourse. Furthermore, they contend that individuals and organizations should not face onerous barriers when seeking to express their political views and support candidates who align with their values and priorities.

Conservative proponents of limited campaign finance regulations also point to the importance of protecting privacy and preventing government overreach. They argue that regulations that impose onerous disclosure requirements or restrict the ability of individuals and organizations to engage in political activities without fear of retaliation can have a chilling effect on free speech. Moreover, they highlight the potential for government intrusion into private political preferences and associations, emphasizing the need to balance transparency with the protection of individual rights.

Critics of the conservative stance on campaign finance regulations often raise concerns about the potential for undue influence and corruption resulting from unrestricted political spending. They argue that without robust regulations, wealthy individuals and powerful interest groups could disproportionately sway electoral outcomes and policy decisions, undermining the democratic principle of equal representation and fair competition. Additionally, they contend that undisclosed or unlimited contributions could give rise to a system where the voices of ordinary citizens are drowned out by the financial resources of a privileged few.

In response to these criticisms, conservative advocates assert that the focus should be on combating corruption directly through existing laws and enforcement mechanisms, rather than imposing broad restrictions that could impinge on constitutional rights. They emphasize that transparency and accountability can be achieved without infringing on free speech, and that measures such as robust disclosure requirements and anti-corruption laws can address concerns about undue influence and maintain the integrity of the electoral process.

Moreover, conservatives argue that restricting the ability of individuals and organizations to engage in political expression could have unintended consequences, such as driving political activities underground or stifling legitimate advocacy efforts. They stress that the emphasis should be on empowering citizens to make informed decisions by allowing for a diversity of voices and viewpoints to participate in the political arena, rather than constraining the ability of citizens to engage in lawful political activities.

Further bolstering the conservative position are empirical studies and analyses that have examined the impact of campaign finance regulations on electoral competition and political participation. Research has shown that overly restrictive regulations can disadvantage challengers and grassroots movements, limiting their ability to effectively communicate their messages and compete in the electoral arena. Additionally, studies have highlighted the potential for regulations to create legal uncertainty and compliance burdens, particularly for smaller organizations and advocacy groups.

Conservative views on campaign finance regulations and political contributions are rooted in a commitment to protecting free speech, promoting transparency, and preserving individual liberties. The conservative position emphasizes the importance of a vibrant marketplace of ideas, where diverse voices and perspectives can engage in the political process without undue government interference. While acknowledging the need for accountability and integrity in elections, conservatives advocate for a balanced approach that safeguards constitutional rights and fosters a robust and inclusive democratic discourse.

The Future of Conservative Political Activism

AS WE NAVIGATE THE ever-evolving landscape of political activism, it becomes increasingly crucial for conservative movements to adapt and innovate in response to emerging trends and challenges. Therefore, the question that arises is this: How can conservative political activism not only withstand the complexities of the modern political sphere but also thrive and effect meaningful change in the face of opposition and adversity?

Conservative political activism has historically been rooted in principles of limited government intervention, individual liberty, and fiscal responsibility. However, in today's fast-paced and interconnected world, the dynamics of political engagement have undergone significant transformations. The rise of social media, the increasing polarization of public discourse, and the evolving role of money in politics have all contributed to a shifting landscape that demands a reevaluation of conservative activism strategies.

The central issue that conservative political activism faces today is the need to effectively communicate its principles and policies in a way that resonates with a diverse and dynamic electorate. The challenge lies not only in articulating conservative ideas but also in countering the prevailing narratives and misconceptions that often overshadow or misrepresent those ideals. Moreover, the need to mobilize supporters, engage in effective coalition-building, and navigate the complexities of campaign finance and digital advocacy further compound the challenges faced by conservative political activists.

In the face of these challenges, conventional approaches often involve relying on traditional modes of communication and engagement, such as door-to-door canvassing, direct mail campaigns, and media appearances. While these methods have proven effective in the past, they may not fully harness the potential of emerging technologies and platforms to reach and mobilize a broader audience. Furthermore, the tendency to solely focus on policy discussions and legislative battles without adequately addressing the emotional and personal dimensions of political engagement may limit the effectiveness of conservative activism in attracting and retaining support.

The future of conservative political activism lies in embracing a multi-faceted and holistic approach that integrates traditional methods with innovative strategies to engage, educate, and inspire. This entails leveraging the power of digital and social media to amplify conservative messages, cultivate grassroots support, and counter misinformation. It also involves the development of compelling narratives that connect conservative values with real-life experiences and aspirations, resonating with individuals on an emotional and personal level.

Conservative political activists must also prioritize community outreach and coalition-building, fostering alliances with diverse groups and individuals who share common values and goals. By broadening the coalition and engaging in constructive dialogue, conservative movements can transcend partisan divides and create a more inclusive and impactful political force.

The implications of this approach are far-reaching, touching the lives of every individual who values freedom, opportunity, and personal responsibility. By strengthening conservative activism, we are not only shaping the political landscape but also safeguarding the principles that underpin our society and way of life. Every citizen has a stake in the future of our nation, and by fostering a deeper and more meaningful engagement with conservative ideas, we empower individuals to become active participants in shaping their own destinies.

Imagine a world where every voice is heard, every idea is considered, and every individual has the opportunity to make a meaningful impact. This vision is not merely a distant aspiration but a tangible reality that can be achieved through the revitalization of conservative political activism. By igniting the passion and conviction of individuals, we can build a movement that transcends political cycles and endures as a testament to the enduring values of freedom, integrity, and progress.

The conservative agenda is not merely a set of policies or legislative goals; it is a call to action, a rallying cry for individuals to stand firm in defense of their beliefs and aspirations. By tapping into the emotions and aspirations of individuals, conservative political activism can forge a deep and enduring connection with its supporters, inspiring them to become ambassadors of change in their communities and beyond.

The future of conservative political activism hinges on its ability to engage and inspire individuals on a deeply personal and emotional level. By embracing innovative strategies, fostering diverse alliances, and amplifying conservative messages through digital platforms, conservative movements can transcend existing barriers and effect transformative change in the political arena. The path ahead may be fraught with challenges, but it is also brimming with opportunities to reignite the spirit of conservatism and empower individuals to shape the future of our nation.

Looking Forward: The Future of the Conservative Agenda

Emerging Challenges and Opportunities

As the conservative movement navigates the complexities of the 21st century, it is encountering a myriad of challenges and opportunities that demand careful consideration and strategic action. To fully comprehend the landscape in which the conservative agenda unfolds, it is essential to delve into the various elements that shape its trajectory, from historical contexts to contemporary applications. In doing so, a deeper understanding of the movement's challenges and opportunities will emerge, allowing for informed and effective responses.

The conservative movement, rooted in principles of limited government, individual liberty, traditional values, and free markets, faces a diverse array of challenges and opportunities as it seeks to uphold its core tenets in the modern era. These challenges are not only formidable but also dynamic, requiring a keen awareness of the evolving socio-political landscape.

The term "conservative movement" refers to a political, social, and cultural phenomenon characterized by a commitment to upholding traditional values, maintaining a limited government role, and promoting individual liberty and free markets. It encompasses a wide range of ideologies and perspectives, united by a desire to preserve established societal structures and norms.

At the heart of the conservative movement lies a deep-rooted belief in the importance of individual freedom and personal responsibility.

This foundational principle shapes the movement's approach to governance, economics, and social issues, emphasizing the role of the individual in driving progress and prosperity.

Furthermore, the conservative movement prioritizes the preservation of traditional values and institutions, recognizing their role in providing stability and continuity within society. From family structures to religious institutions, conservatives seek to safeguard these foundational elements, viewing them as essential for the well-being of individuals and communities.

In the realm of governance, the conservative movement advocates for limited government intervention, emphasizing the importance of individual rights and freedoms. This approach is grounded in the belief that excessive government control can stifle innovation, hinder economic growth, and infringe upon personal liberties.

The origins of the conservative movement can be traced back to various historical and philosophical underpinnings, including classical liberalism, traditionalism, and a reaction against the excesses of revolutionary movements. From the writings of Edmund Burke to the intellectual contributions of Friedrich Hayek and Milton Friedman, the conservative movement has drawn upon a rich tapestry of ideas and principles to shape its worldview.

In the broader context of contemporary society, the conservative movement operates within a landscape defined by rapid technological advancements, globalization, shifting demographics, and evolving cultural norms. These external forces exert significant influence on the movement, presenting both challenges and opportunities that demand thoughtful engagement.

The application of conservative principles can be observed in various real-world scenarios, ranging from economic policies that prioritize free-market competition to social initiatives aimed at strengthening traditional family structures. Additionally, conservative perspectives on individual rights and responsibilities often manifest in debates surrounding healthcare, education, and social welfare programs.

One common misconception about the conservative movement is that it is inherently resistant to change. In reality, while conservatives emphasize the value of tradition and stability, they also recognize the need to adapt to new circumstances and address emerging challenges. This nuanced approach underscores the movement's capacity for thoughtful evolution and innovation.

As the conservative movement confronts the realities of the 21st century, it is imperative to acknowledge the multifaceted nature of the challenges and opportunities it faces. By embracing a comprehensive understanding of its principles, historical context, and contemporary relevance, the movement can navigate these dynamics with purpose and foresight, paving the way for a meaningful and impactful conservative agenda in the years to come.

Adapting to Changing Demographics

AS THE CONSERVATIVE movement continues to evolve within the dynamic landscape of the 21st century, one of the most pressing considerations is the need to adapt to changing demographics. The shifting composition of the electorate presents both challenges and opportunities, necessitating a strategic and nuanced approach to effectively engage with an increasingly diverse and multifaceted society. In this chapter, we will explore strategies for conservatives to appeal to a changing demographic, emphasizing the importance of understanding, inclusivity, and relevance in shaping the conservative agenda for the future.

The changing demographics of the American populace, marked by increasing racial and ethnic diversity, generational shifts, and evolving socio-economic dynamics, necessitate a recalibration of conservative outreach and messaging. To remain relevant and impactful, it is imperative for the conservative movement to recognize and respond to these demographic shifts with a thoughtful and inclusive approach.

The concept of adapting to changing demographics encompasses a multifaceted understanding of the diverse and evolving makeup of the American population. It involves not only acknowledging demographic shifts but also engaging with and representing the varied perspectives, experiences, and aspirations of different demographic groups within the conservative agenda.

Practical examples abound when considering the significance of adapting to changing demographics. For instance, the increasing influence of millennial and Gen Z voters, who prioritize issues such as climate change, social justice, and inclusivity, underscores the need for conservative policies and messaging that resonate with these generational values. Additionally, addressing the concerns and aspirations of growing minority communities, such as Hispanic and Asian-American voters, requires a nuanced understanding of their unique socio-cultural backgrounds and priorities.

To effectively appeal to a changing electorate, it is essential to consider a range of perspectives within the conservative movement. This includes engaging with voices from diverse communities, understanding their priorities, and integrating their perspectives into the conservative agenda. By embracing a broad spectrum of viewpoints, the conservative movement can foster a more inclusive and representative platform that resonates with a wider cross-section of the American population.

Data and statistics underscore the urgency of adapting to changing demographics. According to the U.S. Census Bureau, the nation's racial and ethnic diversity is projected to continue increasing, with non-Hispanic white populations becoming a minority by 2045. Moreover, the Pew Research Center highlights the growing influence of younger generations, with millennials and Gen Z constituting a significant portion of the electorate. These demographic trends underscore the imperative for the conservative movement to engage with and appeal to a more diverse and multi-generational electorate.

Adapting to changing demographics requires navigating complex socio-cultural dynamics and understanding the nuances of different communities. It involves moving beyond traditional political paradigms to embrace inclusivity, cultural competence, and a genuine appreciation of the varied experiences and aspirations of diverse demographic groups. By doing so, the conservative movement can foster meaningful connections and relevance across a broad spectrum of the American populace.

The imperative for conservatives to adapt to changing demographics is rooted in the recognition of a diverse and evolving electorate. By embracing inclusivity, understanding the priorities of different demographic groups, and integrating diverse perspectives into the conservative agenda, the movement can effectively appeal to a changing America. This strategic approach not only enhances the relevance of conservative principles but also paves the way for a more inclusive and impactful conservative agenda that resonates with the complexities of modern American society.

Building Broad Conservative Coalitions

HE GOAL OF BUILDING broad conservative coalitions is to unite different factions of the conservative movement under a common agenda, enhancing the movement's influence and effectiveness in shaping policies and governance.

Before embarking on the journey of building broad conservative coalitions, it is essential to have a clear understanding of the diverse conservative factions and their respective priorities. Additionally, a willingness to engage in open dialogue, compromise, and collaboration is crucial for successful coalition-building.

The process of building broad conservative coalitions involves several key steps, starting with identifying common ground among different conservative factions and gradually expanding the coalition through strategic outreach and inclusive policy-making.

Building broad conservative coalitions begins with identifying shared principles and policy goals across diverse conservative factions. This requires a comprehensive assessment of the core values and priorities that resonate with various segments of the conservative movement. By recognizing common ground, coalition-builders can lay the foundation for cohesive collaboration.

Constructive dialogue plays a pivotal role in coalition-building. It is essential to foster open communication and mutual understanding among different conservative factions, creating a platform for robust discussions and the exchange of diverse perspectives. Through respectful and inclusive dialogue, the barriers between factions can be bridged, paving the way for cooperative efforts.

Inclusivity is a driving force behind successful coalition-building. It involves actively seeking input from underrepresented conservative factions, including voices from diverse communities, youth, women, and minority groups. By embracing inclusivity, the coalition can reflect the rich tapestry of conservative values and foster a sense of belonging among all members.

A unifying agenda serves as the bedrock of broad conservative coalitions. It entails synthesizing the common priorities and policy objectives identified through dialogue and inclusivity into a comprehensive and cohesive agenda. This agenda should encapsulate the shared vision of the coalition, addressing a wide range of conservative concerns while respecting the diversity of perspectives within the movement.

Strategic outreach is vital for expanding the coalition's reach and influence. This involves actively engaging with conservative organizations, community leaders, and grassroots activists to garner support for the coalition's agenda. Furthermore, outreach efforts should extend beyond traditional conservative circles, reaching out to potential allies and supporters who may align with specific aspects of the coalition's platform.

- Patience and Persistence: Building broad conservative coalitions is a gradual and iterative process. It requires patience and persistence to navigate through differing opinions and conflicting priorities, with the understanding that consensus-building takes time.

- Flexibility and Compromise: Flexibility and a willingness to compromise are essential for successful coalition-building. While maintaining core principles, the coalition must be open to adapting its agenda and approach to accommodate the diverse perspectives within the conservative movement.

- Avoid Exclusivity: Exclusivity can undermine the strength of a broad conservative coalition. It is important to guard against excluding or marginalizing certain conservative factions, as this can fracture the unity and effectiveness of the coalition.

Once the broad conservative coalition has been formed, it is crucial to validate its impact and resonance within the conservative movement and broader society. This can be achieved through surveys, feedback mechanisms, and the assessment of the coalition's engagement with policymakers and the public.

In the event of internal disagreements or conflicts within the coalition, a structured conflict resolution process should be in place to address and mitigate tensions. This may involve mediation, facilitated discussions, or the establishment of clear decision-making protocols to navigate disagreements and maintain cohesion.

Building broad conservative coalitions is a dynamic and transformative process that unites disparate factions under a shared vision. By embracing inclusivity, fostering constructive dialogue, and crafting a unifying agenda, the conservative movement can harness its collective strength to advance a comprehensive and impactful conservative agenda that resonates with a diverse and evolving society.

Conservative Solutions for the Future

THE CURRENT STATE OF environmental conservation presents a significant challenge that requires urgent attention and innovative solutions. As the world grapples with the effects of climate change, biodiversity loss, and resource depletion, it is imperative for conservative policymakers to address these issues with a forward-thinking approach that aligns with conservative values and principles.

THE CONSERVATIVE AGENDA

The primary issue at hand is the degradation of the environment, driven by human activities such as deforestation, industrial pollution, and unsustainable resource extraction. These activities have led to the loss of vital ecosystems, the decline of species, and the disruption of natural processes, posing a threat to the balance and resilience of our planet.

Failing to address environmental degradation could lead to irreversible damage to ecosystems, jeopardize essential resources such as clean water and fertile soil, and exacerbate the frequency and intensity of natural disasters. Furthermore, the economic implications of environmental decline could strain public resources and hinder long-term prosperity.

A conservative approach to environmental conservation involves promoting stewardship, innovation, and market-driven solutions. Embracing the concept of conservation as a conservative value, policymakers can develop strategies that balance environmental protection with economic growth and individual responsibility.

Implementing conservative solutions for environmental conservation requires a multi-faceted approach. This includes incentivizing sustainable practices through market mechanisms, investing in technological advancements that promote resource efficiency, and fostering public-private partnerships to address environmental challenges.

Past examples of conservative-driven environmental policies, such as the establishment of conservation easements and the promotion of voluntary stewardship programs, have demonstrated the efficacy of market-based solutions in preserving natural landscapes and wildlife habitats. Predicted outcomes of continued conservative environmental policies include the revitalization of ecosystems, the creation of green jobs, and the sustainable management of natural resources.

While the conservative approach emphasizes market-based solutions, it is essential to acknowledge alternative strategies, such as government-led regulations and international agreements. Evaluating the effectiveness and compatibility of these alternatives with conservative principles can provide valuable insights for comprehensive environmental policy-making.

The landscape of education is evolving rapidly, shaped by technological advancements, changing societal needs, and the demand for lifelong learning. Conservative policymakers are tasked with redefining education to empower individuals, foster a skilled workforce, and uphold traditional values in a rapidly changing world.

The current education system faces challenges in preparing students for the demands of the modern workforce, adapting to diverse learning styles, and instilling fundamental values and civic responsibility. Additionally, the rising costs of higher education pose barriers to accessibility and affordability for many individuals and families.

Failing to address the shortcomings of the education system could result in a skills gap in the workforce, hinder social mobility, and weaken the foundation of civic engagement and informed citizenship. Moreover, the economic implications of an inadequately prepared workforce could limit the nation's competitiveness in a globalized economy.

Conservative solutions for redefining education emphasize choice, innovation, and parental involvement. By promoting school choice initiatives, supporting vocational and technical education, and encouraging parental empowerment in their children's education, policymakers can foster a dynamic and responsive education system.

Implementing conservative solutions for education reform involves enacting policies that expand school choice options, incentivize partnerships between educational institutions and industries, and provide resources for parental engagement in their children's education. Additionally, embracing technology as a tool for personalized learning and skill development is integral to modernizing education.

Past examples of conservative-led education reforms, such as charter school programs and apprenticeship initiatives, have yielded positive outcomes, including increased academic achievement, enhanced career readiness, and the cultivation of diverse educational pathways. Predicted outcomes of continued conservative education policies include a more adaptable and competitive workforce, increased parental involvement, and a renewed emphasis on foundational knowledge and critical thinking skills.

While the conservative approach emphasizes choice and innovation, it is important to consider alternative approaches, such as comprehensive federal education mandates and standardized curricula. Evaluating the compatibility of these alternatives with conservative principles can contribute to a well-informed and comprehensive approach to education reform.

Inspiring the Next Generation of Conservatives

AS THE CONSERVATIVE movement evolves, the imperative of engaging and inspiring the next generation of conservatives becomes increasingly paramount. The strategies outlined in this chapter seek to galvanize young individuals to embrace conservative ideals and activism, ensuring the continuity and vitality of conservative principles in the ever-changing landscape of politics and society.

The following strategies are crucial for inspiring and engaging young people in conservative ideals and activism:

1. : Nurturing a culture of inquiry and independent thought within conservative circles is essential for capturing the interest and engagement of young individuals.

2. : Harnessing the power of digital communication channels is instrumental in connecting with and mobilizing the tech-savvy younger generation.

3. : Establishing mentorship programs and leadership development initiatives can empower young conservatives to become influential voices within their communities and beyond.

4. : Encouraging active participation in civic affairs and grassroots activism instills a sense of agency and purpose in young conservatives, fostering a deeper commitment to conservative values.

- : Encouraging open discussions and debates on conservative principles and policies nurtures intellectual curiosity and sharpens critical thinking skills among young individuals. This approach fosters a deeper understanding of conservative ideals and encourages active engagement in political discourse.

- : Research studies have shown that environments that promote intellectual diversity and critical thinking skills contribute to the development of well-informed and thoughtful individuals who can positively impact their communities and society as a whole.

- : Conservative organizations and educational institutions can create forums, seminars, and discussion groups to facilitate intellectual exploration and debate, providing young people with opportunities to delve into conservative philosophy and its practical applications in various societal issues.

- : Leveraging digital platforms and social media enables conservative organizations and leaders to reach a wider audience of young individuals, disseminating conservative ideas, values, and policy positions in an accessible and engaging manner.

- : Studies have shown the significant influence of social media in shaping political opinions and mobilizing individuals, making it a potent tool for connecting with and inspiring young conservatives.

- : Developing compelling digital content, organizing online campaigns, and fostering online communities can effectively engage young conservatives, providing them with a platform to express their views, connect with like-minded peers, and contribute to the conservative movement.

- : Creating mentorship programs and leadership development initiatives within conservative circles empowers young individuals to learn from experienced leaders, acquire essential skills, and cultivate their potential as future conservative influencers.

- : Research has demonstrated the positive impact of mentorship on personal and professional growth, highlighting its importance in nurturing emerging leaders and fostering a sense of community and support among young conservatives.

- : Establishing mentorship networks, leadership training workshops, and internship opportunities within conservative organizations and political entities can provide young conservatives with guidance, exposure, and practical experience, nurturing their leadership capabilities and commitment to conservative causes.

- : Encouraging young individuals to actively engage in civic affairs and grassroots activism instills a sense of responsibility, agency, and community involvement, compelling them to champion conservative values and effect positive change in their local and national spheres.

- : Historical examples and contemporary movements have illustrated the transformative power of grassroots activism in shaping public discourse, policy decisions, and societal norms, highlighting its significance in inspiring and mobilizing young conservatives.

- : Organizing community service initiatives, political awareness campaigns, and volunteer opportunities provides young conservatives with tangible avenues to participate in civic life, fostering a sense of purpose and commitment to the conservative agenda.

These items will help carry Conservatism through the 21st century and beyond.

The Global Future of Conservatism

THE GLOBAL FUTURE OF conservatism is intricately linked to the evolving political, cultural, and societal landscapes across different regions and nations. Understanding the dynamics of conservative movements in various contexts and their potential for international cooperation is crucial for shaping the trajectory of conservative ideologies and policies on a global scale. Examining and comparing the conservative agendas of different countries and regions offers valuable insights into the nuances and broader implications of conservatism as a political force in the contemporary world.

THE CONSERVATIVE AGENDA

The purpose of this comparative analysis is to shed light on the diverse manifestations of conservatism worldwide and to discern the underlying commonalities and disparities. By delving into the varying approaches, challenges, and achievements of conservative movements in different parts of the world, this exploration aims to provide a comprehensive understanding of the global future of conservatism and the possibilities for cross-border collaboration and solidarity among conservative entities.

In evaluating the global future of conservatism, the criteria for comparison encompass ideological foundations, policy priorities, electoral strategies, and the sociocultural contexts within which conservative movements operate. By scrutinizing these dimensions, we seek to delineate the multifaceted nature of conservative agendas and the factors that shape their trajectories within distinct national and international frameworks.

When comparing conservative movements across different countries, it becomes evident that despite the diversity of political systems and cultural backgrounds, certain fundamental principles and objectives underpin the conservative ethos. The emphasis on traditional values, individual freedoms, limited government intervention, and free-market economics often serves as a unifying thread across various conservative agendas. Moreover, the commitment to upholding national sovereignty and safeguarding traditional institutions resonates deeply within conservative circles globally.

On the other hand, the contextual nuances of conservatism in different regions give rise to significant contrasts in policy approaches and ideological emphases. While economic conservatism may be paramount in certain countries, social conservatism could occupy a more prominent position in others.

Furthermore, the degree of emphasis on immigration, national security, environmental policies, and social welfare varies substantially, reflecting the distinct societal challenges and priorities that shape conservative agendas across the globe.

The comparative analysis of conservative movements worldwide reveals the resilience and adaptability of conservative ideologies in responding to the complex and dynamic challenges of the contemporary era. By discerning the commonalities and divergences, we gain valuable insights into the ways in which conservative agendas evolve and interact with the multifaceted realities of different societies. Furthermore, this analysis illuminates the potential for cross-national learning and collaboration, as conservative movements grapple with shared concerns, such as globalization, technological advancements, and sociocultural transformations.

The insights gained from this comparative exploration of conservative movements hold significant contemporary relevance, particularly in an era characterized by interconnected global dynamics and transnational issues. The ability of conservative entities to learn from each other's experiences, adapt successful strategies, and collaborate on common goals holds the promise of strengthening the collective impact of conservative movements on the international stage. Moreover, in addressing pressing global challenges, such as economic disparities, security threats, and cultural transformations, the collaboration and solidarity of conservative forces from diverse nations can yield innovative and effective solutions.

The Power of Conservative Ideas

AS AN ACCOMPLISHED political analyst with over two decades of dedicated research and scholarly contributions, I have delved deep into the intricate tapestry of conservative ideologies and policies, both at the national and international levels. My journey of expertise has been marked by a relentless pursuit of understanding the nuanced dynamics of conservatism, unraveling its complexities, and discerning its enduring impact on the political, cultural, and societal landscapes across different regions and nations.

My insightful analyses and incisive commentaries have been widely recognized and lauded, earning me a distinguished position in the realm of political thought leadership. With numerous publications in reputable academic journals and frequent appearances as a featured expert on major news outlets, I have consistently illuminated the tenets of conservative thought and policy, shaping critical discourse and fostering an informed understanding of conservative agendas in contemporary global affairs.

The accolades and honors that have adorned my career are not merely symbols of recognition; they serve as testaments to the depth of my contributions and the resonance of my ideas within academic and intellectual circles. My thought leadership in the domain of conservatism has been acknowledged through prestigious awards, fellowships, and invitations to address esteemed forums and symposia, underscoring the enduring impact of my pioneering research and intellectual stewardship in the field.

Yet, beyond the realm of academic rigor and scholarly acclaim, my personal investment in the subject of conservatism runs deep, rooted in a profound conviction that conservative ideas hold the key to addressing the challenges and opportunities of our contemporary world. Born out of formative experiences that shaped my worldview and kindled my intellectual curiosity, my journey of understanding conservatism has been a deeply personal odyssey, intertwined with the fabric of my beliefs, values, and aspirations for a better society.

This book, "The Conservative Agenda," serves as a gateway to empowerment, inviting readers to join me in an exclusive consortium of enlightenment, where the enduring power of conservative ideas is not merely expounded but embraced as a compelling force for positive change. It is a testament to my unwavering commitment to advancing the discourse on conservatism, offering a panoramic view of its multifaceted manifestations and its potential to shape the trajectory of global politics and governance.

In the preceding chapters, we embarked on a comparative analysis of conservative movements worldwide, unraveling the diverse manifestations of conservatism and discerning the underlying commonalities and disparities that define its global landscape. By scrutinizing the ideological foundations, policy priorities, electoral strategies, and sociocultural contexts within which conservative movements operate, we sought to provide a comprehensive understanding of the global future of conservatism and the possibilities for cross-border collaboration and solidarity among conservative entities.

As we delved into the comparative exploration of conservative movements, it became evident that despite the diversity of political systems and cultural backgrounds, certain fundamental principles and objectives underpin the conservative ethos. The emphasis on traditional values, individual freedoms, limited government intervention, and free-market economics often serves as a unifying thread across various conservative agendas. Moreover, the commitment to upholding national sovereignty and safeguarding traditional institutions resonates deeply within conservative circles globally.

However, the contextual nuances of conservatism in different regions give rise to significant contrasts in policy approaches and ideological emphases. While economic conservatism may occupy a prominent position in certain countries, social conservatism could be paramount in others. Furthermore, the degree of emphasis on immigration, national security, environmental policies, and social welfare varies substantially, reflecting the distinct societal challenges and priorities that shape conservative agendas across the globe.

The insights gained from this comparative exploration of conservative movements hold significant contemporary relevance, particularly in an era characterized by interconnected global dynamics and transnational issues. The ability of conservative entities to learn from each other's experiences, adapt successful strategies, and collaborate on common goals holds the promise of strengthening the collective impact of conservative movements on the international stage. Moreover, in addressing pressing global challenges, such as economic disparities, security threats, and cultural transformations, the collaboration and solidarity of conservative forces from diverse nations can yield innovative and effective solutions.

As we conclude this comprehensive analysis, it is imperative to underscore the enduring power of conservative ideas in shaping the future of governance, societal progress, and international cooperation. The depth and resilience of conservative ideologies in responding to the complex and dynamic challenges of the contemporary era are testament to their enduring relevance and adaptability. From the halls of government to the grassroots movements, conservative ideas have demonstrated an unwavering capacity to inspire change, foster resilience, and uphold the enduring values that form the bedrock of stable and prosperous societies.

The conservative agenda is not a relic of the past; it is a dynamic force that propels societies towards progress, underpinned by a commitment to individual liberties, economic opportunity, and the preservation of traditional values. As we navigate the complexities of the global landscape, it is imperative to recognize the enduring power of conservative ideas as a vital force for shaping a future that is anchored in stability, prosperity, and the preservation of fundamental freedoms.

This book stands as a testament to the enduring power of conservative ideas, offering a compelling narrative that transcends national boundaries and resonates with the aspirations of individuals and communities seeking a path to progress and prosperity. It is a call to action, a clarion call for embracing the enduring legacy of conservative thought and policy as a cornerstone of governance and societal advancement. As we chart the course for the future, let us heed the wisdom of conservative ideas, drawing upon their enduring power to forge a world that is grounded in enduring values, individual freedoms, and boundless opportunities for all.

Don't miss out!

Visit the website below and you can sign up to receive emails whenever Jack Donahue publishes a new book. There's no charge and no obligation.

https://books2read.com/r/B-A-WCSZ-IBFWC

BOOKS2READ

Connecting independent readers to independent writers.